TEACHINGS OF PRESIDENTS OF THE CHURCH
EZRA TAFT BENSON

Published by
The Church of Jesus Christ of Latter-day Saints
Salt Lake City, Utah

Books in the *Teachings of Presidents of the Church* Series

To obtain copies of these books, go to your local distribution center or visit store.lds.org. The books are also available at LDS.org and on the Gospel Library mobile application.

Your comments and suggestions about this book would be appreciated. Please submit them to Curriculum Development, 50 East North Temple Street, Salt Lake City, UT 84150-0024 USA.

Email: cur-development@ldschurch.org

Please give your name, address, ward, and stake. Be sure to include the title of the book. Then offer your comments and suggestions about the book's strengths and areas of potential improvement.

Contents

Introduction

The First Presidency and the Quorum of the Twelve Apostles have established the *Teachings of Presidents of the Church* series to help you draw closer to your Heavenly Father and deepen your understanding of the restored gospel of Jesus Christ. As the Church adds volumes to this series, you will build a collection of gospel reference books for your home. The volumes in this series are designed to be used for personal study and for Sunday instruction. They can also help you prepare other lessons or talks and answer questions about Church doctrine.

This book features the teachings of President Ezra Taft Benson, who served as President of The Church of Jesus Christ of Latter-day Saints from November 10, 1985, to May 30, 1994.

Personal Study

As you study the teachings of President Ezra Taft Benson, prayerfully seek the inspiration of the Holy Ghost. The questions at the end of each chapter will help you ponder, understand, and apply President Benson's teachings. The following ideas may also help you:

- Write thoughts and feelings that come to you from the Holy Ghost as you study.

- Underline passages you want to remember. Consider memorizing these passages or noting them in your scriptures next to related verses.

- Read a chapter or passage more than once so you can understand it more deeply.

- Ask yourself questions such as the following: How do President Benson's teachings increase my understanding of gospel principles? What does the Lord want me to learn from these teachings?

- Share what you learn with family members and friends.

- Ask yourself how the teachings in this book can help you with personal challenges and concerns.

Teaching from This Book

This book has been designed for use at home and at church. The following guidelines may help you teach from the book.

Prepare to Teach

Seek the guidance of the Holy Ghost as you prepare to teach. Prayerfully study the assigned chapter to become confident in your understanding of President Benson's teachings. You will teach with greater sincerity and power when his words have influenced you personally (see D&C 11:21).

If you are teaching a Melchizedek Priesthood or Relief Society lesson, you should not set this book aside or prepare a lesson from other materials. Prayerfully select from the chapter those teachings that you feel will be most helpful to those you teach. Some chapters contain more material than you will be able to discuss during class time.

Encourage participants to study the chapter before the lesson and to bring the book with them. When they do so, they will be better prepared to participate in discussions and edify one another.

In your preparation to teach, give special attention to the "Suggestions for Study and Teaching" at the end of each chapter. Under this heading, you will find questions, related scriptures, and a study help or teaching help. The questions and related scriptures correlate specifically with the chapter in which they are found. The study helps and teaching helps can guide you in all your efforts to learn and live the gospel and to help others do the same.

Introduce the Chapter

As you introduce the chapter, and throughout the lesson, work to establish an atmosphere in which the Spirit can touch the hearts and minds of those you teach. To start the lesson, help those you teach focus on the teachings in the chapter. You may want to use one or more of the following ideas:

- Read and discuss the section titled "From the Life of Ezra Taft Benson" at the beginning of the chapter.

- Discuss a picture or scripture from the chapter.

- Sing a related hymn together.

- Briefly share a personal experience about the topic.

Encourage Discussion about President Benson's Teachings

As you teach from this book, invite others to share their thoughts, ask questions, and teach one another. When they actively participate, they will be more prepared to learn and to receive personal revelation. Allow good discussions to continue rather than trying to cover all the teachings. To encourage discussion, use the questions at the end of each chapter. You may also develop your own questions especially for those you are teaching.

The following options may give you additional ideas:

- Ask participants to share what they have learned from their personal study of the chapter. It may be helpful to contact a few participants during the week and ask them to come prepared to share what they have learned.

- Assign participants to read selected questions at the end of the chapter (either individually or in small groups). Ask them to look for teachings in the chapter that relate to the questions. Then invite them to share their thoughts and insights.

- Read together some of President Benson's teachings in the chapter. Ask participants to share examples from the scriptures and from their own experience that illustrate those teachings.

- Ask participants to choose one section and read it silently. Invite them to gather in groups of two or three people who chose the same section and discuss what they have learned.

Encourage Sharing and Application

President Benson's teachings will be most meaningful for participants who share them with others and apply them in their lives. You may want to use one or more of the following ideas:

- Ask participants how they can apply President Benson's teachings in their responsibilities at home and in the Church. For example, you might help them ponder and discuss how they can apply his teachings as husbands, wives, parents, sons, daughters, home teachers, or visiting teachers.

- Encourage participants to share some of President Benson's teachings with family members and friends.

- Invite participants to apply what they have learned and share their experiences at the beginning of the next class.

Conclude the Discussion

Briefly summarize the lesson or ask one or two participants to do so. Testify of the teachings you have discussed. You may also want to invite others to share their testimonies.

Information about the Sources Quoted in This Book

The teachings in this book are direct quotations from President Ezra Taft Benson's sermons, articles, books, and journals. Quotations from published sources have retained the punctuation, spelling, capitalization, and paragraphing of the original sources unless editorial or typographic changes have been necessary to improve readability. For this reason, you may notice minor inconsistencies in the text. For example, pronouns referring to Deity are lowercased in some quotations and capitalized in others.

Also, President Benson often used terms such as *men, man,* or *mankind* to refer to all people, both male and female. He frequently used the pronouns *he, his,* and *him* to refer to both genders. This was common in the language of his era. Despite the differences between these language conventions and current usage, President Benson's teachings apply to both women and men.

Historical Summary

The following chronology provides a brief historical framework for the teachings of President Ezra Taft Benson in this book.

August 4, 1899	Born near Whitney, Idaho, to George Taft Benson Jr. and Sara Dunkley Benson.
1912 to 1913	Assumes many responsibilities at home while his father serves a mission in the northern United States.
1914 to 1919	Attends and graduates from Oneida Stake Academy in Preston, Idaho.
1918	Called to serve as an assistant Scoutmaster (a leader of young men) in his ward in Whitney.
1920	Meets Flora Smith Amussen, his future wife.
1921	Attends Utah Agricultural College (now Utah State University) in Logan, Utah.
July 13, 1921	Ordained an elder by his father.
July 15, 1921, to November 2, 1923	Serves as a full-time missionary in the British Mission.
August 25, 1924, to June 1926	Flora serves a full-time mission in the Hawaiian Islands.
Fall 1924	Joins his brother Orval in purchasing the family farm in Whitney.
Spring 1926	Graduates from Brigham Young University.
September 10, 1926	Marries Flora in the Salt Lake Temple.

September 1926 to June 1927	Attends the Iowa State College of Agriculture and Mechanical Arts (now the Iowa State University of Science and Technology), graduating with a master's degree in agricultural economics.
June 1927	Moves back to the family farm in Whitney.
1929	Accepts employment as the county agricultural agent for Franklin County, Idaho. Leaves the farm and moves to nearby Preston, Idaho.
1930 to 1939	Employed as an agricultural economist and specialist with the University of Idaho Extension Division.
January 1935 to November 1938	Serves as first counselor in the stake presidency of the Boise Stake.
November 1938 to March 1939	Serves as president of the Boise Stake.
1939 to 1943	Works as executive secretary for the National Council of Farmer Cooperatives in Washington, D.C. Lives with his family in Bethesda, Maryland.
June 1940	Called to serve as president of the Washington Stake in Washington, D.C.
July 26, 1943	Called to serve as a member of the Quorum of the Twelve Apostles.
October 7, 1943	Ordained an Apostle and set apart as a member of the Quorum of the Twelve Apostles by President Heber J. Grant.
January 1946 to December 1946	Serves as president of the European Mission, helping to bring temporal and spiritual relief to Latter-day Saints after the devastation of World War II.
July 16, 1946	Dedicates Finland for the preaching of the gospel.

January 1953 to January 1961	Serves as the United States secretary of agriculture under the leadership of President Dwight D. Eisenhower.
January 1964 to September 1965	Serves again as president of the European Mission.
November 10, 1966	Rededicates Italy for the preaching of the gospel.
April 14, 1969	Dedicates Singapore for the preaching of the gospel.
October 26, 1969	Dedicates Indonesia for the preaching of the gospel.
December 30, 1973	Set apart as President of the Quorum of the Twelve Apostles.
November 10, 1985	Set apart as President of The Church of Jesus Christ of Latter-day Saints.
October 24, 1986	Dedicates the Denver Colorado Temple.
August 28, 1987	Dedicates the Frankfurt Germany Temple. (Nine temples were dedicated during his service as President of the Church.)
October 2, 1988	Delivers his final general conference address in person. (After October 1988, his frail physical health prevented him from speaking at general conference. His counselors in the First Presidency read sermons on his behalf or quoted messages he had given in past addresses.)
August 14, 1992	Mourns the death of his wife, Flora.
May 30, 1994	Dies at his home in Salt Lake City, Utah, about two months before his 95th birthday.

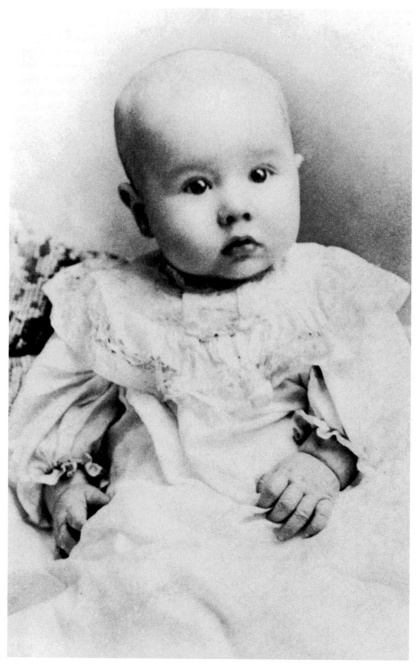

Ezra Taft Benson as a baby, 1900

The Life and Ministry of Ezra Taft Benson

Travelers on the highway between Logan, Utah, and Whitney, Idaho, witnessed something unusual on June 4, 1994. They saw people standing along portions of that 24-mile (39-kilometer) stretch of road. The next day, Elder Robert D. Hales of the Quorum of the Twelve Apostles explained why people had gathered there. They had been waiting for a funeral cortege, transporting the body of President Ezra Taft Benson to the cemetery in his hometown after funeral services in Salt Lake City, Utah. Elder Hales described the scene:

"The drive by the cortege to Whitney, Idaho, was a touching tribute to a prophet of God.

"There was a tribute by members of the Church as they lined the highway and stood on the overpasses along the road. Some were dressed in their Sunday best on a Saturday afternoon. Others paused in respect, stopping their cars and standing reverently, waiting for the prophet to pass. Farmers stood in their fields with their hats over their hearts. Probably more significant were the young boys taking their baseball hats off and putting them over their hearts. Flags waved good-bye as the prophet went by as well. There were signs that read, 'We love President Benson.' Others said, 'Read the Book of Mormon.'"[1]

This outpouring of affection was indeed a tribute, but it was more than that. It was visible evidence that people's lives had changed because they had followed the counsel of a prophet. And the people who gathered along the highway represented many more. Between the time Ezra Taft Benson was born near Whitney, Idaho, and the time his mortal remains were buried there, he served as an instrument in the Lord's hands, traveling throughout the world and helping millions come unto Christ.

Lessons Learned on the Family Farm

On August 4, 1899, Sarah Dunkley Benson and George Taft Benson Jr. welcomed their firstborn child to their family. They named him Ezra Taft Benson, after his great-grandfather, Elder Ezra T. Benson, who had served as a member of the Quorum of the Twelve Apostles.

Ezra was born in the two-room farmhouse that his father had built the previous year. The delivery was long and difficult, and the attending doctor thought the 11¾-pound (5.3-kg) baby would not survive. But the baby's grandmothers had a different idea. They filled two pans with water—one warm, the other cold—and dipped their grandson alternately in each pan until he started to cry.

Young Ezra Taft Benson, often called "T" by family members and friends, enjoyed a fulfilling childhood on the farm that surrounded the house where he was born. President Gordon B. Hinckley, who served with President Benson for almost 33 years in the Quorum of the Twelve Apostles and the First Presidency, told of the lessons young Ezra learned:

"He was a farm boy, literally and truly, an overall-clad, sunburned boy who at a very early age came to know the law of the harvest: 'Whatsoever a man soweth, that shall he also reap' (Gal. 6:7).

"He came to know in those lean days that without hard work, nothing grows but weeds. There must be labor, incessant and constant, if there is to be a harvest. And so there was plowing in the fall and plowing in the spring—the sweaty work of walking in a furrow all day long behind a team of strong horses. In those days a hand plow was used, and it was necessary to hold constantly the handles that twisted and shook as the sharp plow point cut the earth and neatly rolled it over. After a day of that, a boy was exhausted and slept well. But morning came very soon.

"The field needed the harrow, again horse-drawn, to break the clods and prepare a seed bed. Planting was an arduous, back-breaking task. And then there was irrigation. The Benson farm was in dry country, redeemed by the magic of irrigation. The water had to be watched, not only during the day but all through the night. There were no electric flashlights or propane lanterns. There were only kerosene lanterns which cast a feeble and sickly yellow glow. It was imperative that the water get to the end of the row. That was a lesson never to be forgotten.

"I can see in my mind's eye the little boy, shovel on his shoulder, walking the ditches and the fields to bring life-growing moisture to the parched soil.

"Soon came the time to cut hay, acres and acres of it. The team was hitched to the mower, the boy climbed up into the old steel seat, and the sickle bar flew back and forth, cutting a five-foot swath as the team walked forward. With flies and mosquitos, with dust and scorching heat, it was hard work. The hay then had to be raked, then pitched with a hand fork into cocks to dry. Timing was important. When it reached the right stage it was pitched onto a hayrack, a wagon with a big, flat bed. At the stack yard, a horse-driven derrick lifted it from the wagon to form a huge stack of hay. There was no baling in those days, nor were there mechanical loaders. There were only pitchforks and muscles.

". . . Small wonder that his frame grew large and his body strong. Those of us who knew him in his later life frequently commented on the size of his wrists. Robust health, the foundation for which was laid in his boyhood, was one of the great blessings of his life. Until the last few years, he was a man of tremendous energy.

"Throughout the years of his mature life, when he walked with presidents and kings, he never lost the touch of his boyhood farm days. He never lost his capacity for work. He never lost the will to rise at dawn and work into the night.

"But there was more than a tremendous habit of work that came out of that boyhood home. There was a certain strength that comes from the soil. There was a constant reminder of the dictum given Adam and Eve when they were driven from the garden: 'In the sweat of thy face shalt thou eat bread, till thou return unto the ground' (Gen. 3:19). A spirit of self-reliance was built into those who worked the soil. There were no government farm programs then, no subsidies of any kind. The vagaries of the seasons had to be accepted. Killing frosts, unseasonal storms, wind, and drought were all accepted as the risks of life against which there was no available insurance. Storage against a day of want was a necessity, else there would be hunger. The one constant resource against the risks of life was prayer, prayer to our eternal, loving Father, the Almighty God of the universe.

"There was much of prayer in that little home in Whitney, Idaho. There was family prayer, night and morning, in which thanks was expressed for life with its challenges and opportunities, and in which pleas were made for strength to do the work of the day. Those in need were remembered, and when the family arose from their knees, the mother, who was the ward Relief Society president, would have the buggy loaded to share food with those in need, her eldest son as her driver. Those lessons were never lost."[2]

Lessons Learned from Faithful Parents

These lessons of hard work, family unity, service, and gospel living began to be magnified one day when 12-year-old Ezra's parents came home from a Church meeting with unexpected news. President Benson later recalled:

"As Father drove the horse homeward, Mother opened the mail, and, to their surprise, there was a letter from Box B in Salt Lake City—a call to go on a mission. No one asked if one were ready, willing, or able. The bishop was supposed to know, and the bishop was Grandfather George T. Benson, my father's father.

"As Father and Mother drove into the yard, they were both crying—something we had never seen in our family. We gathered around the buggy—there were seven of us then—and asked them what was the matter.

"They said, 'Everything's fine.'

" 'Why are you crying then?' we asked.

" 'Come into the living room and we'll explain.'

"We gathered around the old sofa in the living room, and Father told us about his mission call. Then Mother said, 'We're proud to know that Father is considered worthy to go on a mission. We're crying a bit because it means two years of separation. You know, your father and I have never been separated more than two nights at a time since our marriage—and that's when Father was gone into the canyon to get logs, posts, and firewood.'"[3]

With his father on a mission, Ezra assumed much of the responsibility of running the family farm. He "did the work of a man, though he was only a boy," his sister Margaret later recalled. "He took the place of father for nearly two years."[4] Under Sarah's leadership, Ezra and his siblings worked together, prayed together, and read letters from their father together. Seventy-five years later, President Benson reflected on the blessings that came to his family because his father served a mission:

"I suppose some in the world might say that his acceptance of that call was proof he did not really love his family. To leave seven children and an expectant wife at home alone for two years, how could that be true love?

"But my father knew a greater vision of love. He knew that 'all things shall work together for good to them that love God' (Romans 8:28). He knew that the best thing he could do for his family was to obey God.

"While we missed him greatly during those years, and while his absence brought many challenges to our family, his acceptance proved to be a gift of charity. Father went on his mission, leaving Mother at home with seven children. (The eighth was born four months after he arrived in the field.) But there came into that home a spirit of missionary work that never left it. It was not without some sacrifice. Father had to sell our old dry farm in order to finance his mission. He had to move a married couple into part of our home to take care of the row crops, and he left his sons and wife the responsibility for the hay land, the pasture land, and a small herd of dairy cows.

"Father's letters were indeed a blessing to our family. To us children, they seemed to come from halfway around the world, but they were only from Springfield, Massachusetts; and Chicago, Illinois; and Cedar Rapids and Marshalltown, Iowa. Yes, there came into our home, as a result of Father's mission, a spirit of missionary work that never left it.

"Later the family grew to eleven children—seven sons and four daughters. All seven sons filled missions, some of them two or three missions. Later, two daughters and their husbands filled full-time missions. The two other sisters, both widows—one the mother of eight and the other the mother of ten—served as missionary companions in Birmingham, England.

"It is a legacy that still continues to bless the Benson family even into the third and fourth generations. Was not this truly a gift of love?"[5]

Church Service as a Young Man

Inspired by his parents' example and motivated by his own desire to help build the Lord's kingdom on the earth, Ezra Taft Benson enthusiastically accepted calls to serve. When he was 19 years old, his bishop, who was also his grandfather, asked him to serve as one of the adult leaders for 24 young men in the ward. The young men participated in Boy Scouts of America, and Ezra served as an assistant Scoutmaster.

In this calling, one of Ezra's many responsibilities was to help the young men sing in a choir. Under his leadership, the young men won a competition with choirs from other wards in their stake, thus qualifying for a regional competition. To help motivate them to practice and sing their best, Ezra promised them that if they won the regional competition, he would take them on a 35-mile (56-kilometer) hike over the mountains to a lake. The plan worked—the young men from Whitney won.

"We began planning our hike," President Benson recounted, "and during the meeting one little 12-year-old raised his hand and very formally said, '. . . I would like to make a motion.' . . . I said, 'All right, what?' He said, 'I'd like to make a motion, so we will not be bothered with combs and brushes on this trip, that we all clip our hair off.'"

Eventually all the young men agreed to get short haircuts in preparation for their hike. They became more enthusiastic about the idea when one of them suggested that the Scoutmasters cut their hair as well. President Benson continued:

"Two Scoutmasters took their places in the barber's chair while the barber very gleefully went over each head with the clippers. As he neared the end of the job, he said, 'Now, if you fellows would let me shave your heads, I would do it for nothing.' And so we started on that hike—24 boys with heads clipped and two Scoutmasters with heads shaven."

Reflecting on his experiences with the young men in his ward, President Benson said: "One of the joys of working with boys is the fact that you do get your pay as you go along. You have an opportunity to observe the results of your leadership daily as you work with them through the years and watch them grow into stalwart manhood, accepting eagerly its challenges and responsibilities. Such satisfaction cannot be purchased at any price; it must be earned through service and devotion. What a glorious thing it is to have even a small part in helping to build boys into men, real men."[6]

President Benson never forgot those young men, and he made efforts to keep in touch with them. Many years after that 35-mile hike, he visited the Whitney Ward as a member of the Quorum of the Twelve Apostles and spoke with a small group of them. They were able to tell him that 22 of the 24 had remained faithful in the Church. They had lost contact with the other two. President Benson eventually found those two men, helped them return to Church activity, and performed their temple sealings.[7]

Courting Flora

In the fall of 1920, Ezra went to Logan, Utah, about 25 miles (40 kilometers) from Whitney, to enroll at the Utah Agricultural College (now Utah State University). He was with some friends when a young woman caught his eye. He later recalled:

"We were out near the dairy barns when a young woman—very attractive and beautiful—drove by in her little car on her way to the dairy to get some milk. As the boys waved at her, she waved back. I said, 'Who is that girl?' They said 'That's Flora Amussen.'

"I told them, 'You know, I've just had the impression I'm going to marry her.'"

Flora Amussen, before she married Ezra Taft Benson

Ezra's friends laughed at his declaration, saying, "She's too popular for a farm boy." But he was undeterred. "That makes it all the more interesting," he replied.

Not long after this conversation, Flora and Ezra met for the first time in Whitney, where she had been invited to stay with one of Ezra's cousins. And soon after that, Ezra invited her to a dance. She accepted, and other dates led to what they later called a "wonderful courtship." But their courtship was interrupted—and, in many ways, enhanced—when Ezra received a call to serve as a full-time missionary in the British Mission.

In preparation for Ezra's mission, he and Flora talked about their relationship. They wanted their friendship to continue, but they also recognized the need for Ezra to be a devoted missionary. "Before I left, Flora and I had decided to write [letters] only once a month," he said. "We also decided that our letters would be of encouragement, confidence and news. We did just that."[8]

Two Missionaries

The British Mission, which had been such a fruitful field for early Latter-day Saint missionaries, was different for Elder Benson and his companions. Antagonists in the British Isles, including some clergy, had stirred up widespread hatred toward Latter-day Saints, publishing anti-Mormon articles, novels, plays, and movies. Elder Benson was no doubt saddened by people's bitter feelings about the restored gospel, but he did not allow such trials to weaken his faith. In fact, he wrote in his journal about local youth taunting him and his companions by yelling "Mormons!" His unspoken response was "Thank the Lord I'm one."[9]

In addition to sharing the gospel with people who were not members of the Church, Elder Benson served as a priesthood leader and a clerk among Latter-day Saints in Great Britain. These varied opportunities to serve led to sweet experiences, in bright contrast to the difficulties he often faced. Elder Benson baptized and confirmed a few people, and he helped many more draw nearer to the Lord. For example, he told of a time when, at a special meeting organized by faithful Church members, he was guided by the Spirit to speak in a way that helped the members' friends receive a witness that Joseph Smith was a prophet of God.[10] He recorded that he and a companion once gave a priesthood blessing to a severely sick woman who recovered about 10 minutes later.[11] He rejoiced when, as a clerk, he found Saints whose names were in the records of the Church but who had been lost to local leaders.[12] He received valuable leadership training, serving under the direction of two mission presidents who were also members of the Quorum of the Twelve Apostles: Elders Orson F. Whitney and David O. McKay.

Elder Benson was grateful for the protection of the Lord as he preached the gospel. One night he and his companion were surrounded by a mob of men who threatened to throw them in the river. He prayed silently for help. Then, as he later reported, "a big husky stranger pushed his way through to my side. He looked me straight in the eye and said in a strong, clear voice, 'Young man, I believe every word you said tonight.' As he spoke a little circle cleared around me. This to me was a direct answer to prayer. Then a British bobby [police officer] appeared."[13]

When Elder Benson was not actively serving others, he "kept himself going by 'devouring the Book of Mormon,' particularly the missionary experiences of the sons of Mosiah." [14] He also received comfort and support through letters from home, which he said he "read time and time again." Looking back on his mission, he commented: "Mother and father poured out their hearts to me in letters, and were a real strength to me as a young man. Flora's [letters] were full of spirit and encouragement, never any sentimental stuff. I think that increased my love and appreciation for her more than anything." [15]

Elder Benson received his release from full-time missionary service on November 2, 1923. He was hesitant to leave, saying that bidding farewell to the "dear good Saints" in Great Britain was "the hardest part of [his] mission." [16] Still, he was happy at the prospect of being reunited with his family, and he looked forward to seeing Flora.

Flora also looked forward to seeing Ezra. But she did more than anticipate the immediate prospect of spending time with him. She truly looked forward—to his future and his potential. From the time she was a teenager, she had maintained that she would "like to marry a farmer," [17] and she was happy with Ezra's apparent desire to settle on the family farm in Whitney, Idaho. However, she felt that he needed to finish his education first. She later said, "[I] prayed and fasted for the Lord to help me know how I could help him be of greatest service to his fellowmen. It came to me that if the Bishop thought I was worthy, [he would] call me on a mission. The Church came first with Ezra, so I knew he wouldn't say anything against it." [18]

Ezra was surprised when, after he and Flora had started courting again, she told him that she had accepted a call to serve a mission in the Hawaiian Islands. She was set apart on August 25, 1924, and she left the next day. Just after she departed, Ezra wrote in his journal: "We were both happy because we felt the future held much for us and that this separation would be made up to us later. It is difficult, though, to see one's hopes shattered. But though we sometimes had a cry about it, we received assurance from Him who told us it would all be for the best." [19]

It all was truly for the best. Flora was, in the words of her mission president, "a very good, energetic missionary" [20] who gave her "heart and soul, time, and talents to the work of the Lord."[21] She supervised the Primary organization in some areas of the mission, taught children at an elementary school, served in the temple, and participated in efforts to strengthen local Latter-day Saints. She even served for a time as a missionary companion to her widowed mother, Barbara Amussen, who was called on a short-term mission. Together, this mother-daughter companionship encountered a man who had joined the Church years earlier in the United States because of the efforts of Flora's father, Carl Amussen. The convert had since fallen away from Church activity, but Flora and her mother fellowshipped him and helped him return to the Church.[22]

While Flora was gone, Ezra stayed busy. He and his brother Orval purchased the family farm and continued their education. For a time, Ezra attended Brigham Young University in Provo, Utah, while Orval stayed in Whitney to take care of the farm. They agreed that after Ezra finished school, he would return to the farm while Orval served a mission and completed his schooling. Determined to finish quickly at BYU, Ezra pursued an ambitious class schedule. He also participated in social functions at the university, including dances, parties, and dramatic productions.

Although Ezra was voted "BYU's Most Popular Man" during his last year of school, no one was able to steal his attention from Flora. He later said that when she completed her mission in June 1926, he was "anxious" to see her, although he insisted that he had not been "waiting" for her to come back.[23] He graduated with honors just a few months before she returned.

Beginning Life Together

One month after Flora returned from her mission, she and Ezra announced their engagement. Some people continued to question Flora's judgment. They did not understand why someone so accomplished, wealthy, and popular would settle for a farm boy. But she continued to say that she had "always wanted to marry a farmer."[24] Ezra "was practical, sensible and solid," she said. And, she observed, "He was sweet to his parents, and I knew if he respected them, he'd respect me."[25] She recognized that he was "a diamond in the rough," and she said, "I am going to do all within my power to help him be known and felt for good, not only in this little community but for the entire world to know him."[26]

Flora and Ezra were sealed on September 10, 1926, in the Salt Lake Temple by Elder Orson F. Whitney of the Quorum of the Twelve Apostles. The only festivity after the wedding was a breakfast for family and friends. After the breakfast, the new couple left immediately in their Model T Ford pick-up truck for Ames, Iowa, where Ezra had been accepted into a master of science program in agricultural economics at the Iowa State College of Agriculture and Mechanical Arts (now the Iowa State University of Science and Technology).

Much of their trip was over dirt roads and through sparsely inhabited country. Along the way, they spent eight nights in a leaky tent. When they arrived in Ames, they rented an apartment one block from the college campus. The apartment was small, and the Bensons shared the space with a large family of cockroaches, but Ezra said that "it soon looked like the coziest little cottage one could ever imagine."[27] Ezra again dedicated himself to his education. Less than a year later, after countless hours of study, lectures, and writing, he graduated with a master's degree. The couple, now expecting their first baby, returned to the Benson farm in Whitney.

Balancing Professional Opportunities and Church Callings

When the Bensons returned to Whitney, Ezra engaged himself fully in the day-to-day operations of the farm, which included milking cows, raising hogs and chickens, and growing sugar beets, grain, alfalfa, and other crops. Orval was called to serve a full-time mission in Denmark.

Less than two years later, local government leaders offered Ezra a job as the county agricultural agent. With Flora's encouragement, Ezra accepted the position, even though it meant leaving the farm and moving to the nearby city of Preston. He hired a local farmer to run the farm until Orval returned.

Ezra's new responsibilities included counseling local farmers on issues affecting their productivity. More than anything, he felt that

Ezra Taft Benson when he graduated from
Brigham Young University in 1926

the farmers needed better marketing skills—something that became increasingly important after the onset of the Great Depression, and something that he, with his education in agricultural economics, was positioned to provide. He encouraged farmers to participate in farmers' cooperative associations, which would help them cut costs and get the best prices for labor.[28]

Ezra's abilities as an agricultural leader generated other employment opportunities. From 1930 to 1939, he worked as an agricultural economist and specialist with the University of Idaho Extension Division in Boise, the Idaho state capital. Those responsibilities were interrupted between August 1936 and June 1937, when the Bensons moved to California so Ezra could study agricultural economics at the University of California at Berkeley.

Even with pressing responsibilities at work and at home, Ezra and Flora Benson made time to serve in the Church. In Whitney, Preston, and Boise, they were called to teach and lead youth.[29]

They embraced these callings with enthusiasm, believing that "the youth are our future."[30] Ezra also received an opportunity to help with local missionary work.[31] In Boise, Ezra was called to serve as a counselor in a stake presidency. He even continued in that position during the time he and his family lived in California. The Boise Stake grew rapidly, and in November 1938, Elder Melvin J. Ballard of the Quorum of the Twelve Apostles divided the stake into three stakes. Ezra Taft Benson was called to serve as one of the stake presidents.

In January 1939, Ezra was surprised to be offered the position of executive secretary for the National Council of Farmer Cooperatives in Washington, D.C. He counseled with Flora about this opportunity. Because he had been set apart as a stake president only two months earlier, he also contacted the First Presidency to ask for their counsel. They encouraged him to accept the position, so he and his family said farewell to their friends in Boise in March 1939 and moved to Bethesda, Maryland, close to Washington, D.C. In June 1940 he was called to serve as stake president again, this time in the newly organized Washington Stake in Washington, D.C.

A Loving, Unified Family

Ezra and Flora Benson always remembered the eternal importance of their relationship with one another and their relationships with their children, their aging parents, and their siblings. Their emphasis on maintaining a unified family was more than a sense of duty; they genuinely loved each other, and they wanted to be together—in this life and throughout the eternities.

Ezra's many responsibilities in Church callings and professional assignments often took him away from home. Sometimes the expressions of the young children emphasized this fact. For example, as he left for a Church meeting one Sunday, daughter Barbara said, "Good-bye, daddy. And come back again and visit us sometime."[32] It was a challenge for Flora to raise their six children with her husband gone so frequently, and she occasionally admitted to feeling "lonesome and just a bit discouraged."[33] Still, through it all, she cherished her roles as a wife and mother, and she was pleased with her husband's dedication to the Lord and the family. In a letter to Ezra, she wrote: "As usual the days seem like months since you left. . . . [But] if all men . . . loved and lived their religion as you do, there would be very little sorrow [and] suffering. . . . You're always so devoted to your family and ready at all times to give help to others in need."[34]

Ezra showed this devotion whenever he was home. He took time to laugh and play with his six children, to listen to them, to ask for their opinions about important issues, to teach the gospel, to help with household chores, and to spend time with each of them individually. The children found comfort and strength in their parents' unified love for them. (Because family was so important to Ezra Taft Benson, this book contains two chapters of his teachings on the subject. Those chapters, titled "Marriage and Family—Ordained of God" and "The Sacred Callings of Fathers and Mothers," include reminiscences from the Benson children about the loving home of their childhood.)

The Call to the Apostleship

In the summer of 1943, Ezra left Maryland with his son Reed to tour several farming cooperatives in California as part of his responsibilities with the National Council of Farmer Cooperatives. He also planned to meet with Church leaders in Salt Lake City and visit family members in Idaho.

On July 26, after having accomplished the objectives of their trip, they returned to Salt Lake City before departing for home. They learned that President David O. McKay, with whom Ezra had met less than two weeks earlier, had been searching for him. Ezra called President McKay, who told him that President Heber J. Grant, then President of the Church, wanted to meet with him. Ezra and Reed were driven to President Grant's summer home a few minutes away from downtown Salt Lake City. When they arrived, "Ezra was immediately shown into President Grant's bedroom, where the aged prophet was resting. At the President's bidding, Ezra closed the door and approached him, sitting down on a chair next to the bed. President Grant took Ezra's right hand in both of his and, with tears filling his eyes, said simply, 'Brother Benson, with all my heart I congratulate you and pray God's blessing to attend you. You have been chosen as the youngest member of the Council of the Twelve Apostles.'"[35]

In his journal, Ezra recounted the experience:

"The announcement seemed unbelievable and overwhelming. . . . For several minutes [I] could say only, 'Oh, President Grant, that can't be!' which I must have repeated several times before I was able to collect my thoughts enough to realize what had happened. . . . He held my hand for a long time as we both shed tears. . . . For over an hour we were alone together, much of the time with our hands clasped warmly together. Though [he was] feeble, his mind was clear and alert, and I was deeply impressed with his sweet, kindly, humble spirit as he seemed to look into my soul.

"I felt so utterly weak and unworthy that his words of comfort and reassurance which followed were doubly appreciated. Among other things he stated, 'The Lord has a way of magnifying men who are called to positions of leadership.' When in my weakness I was able to state that I loved the Church he said, 'We know that, and the Lord wants men who will give everything for His work.'"[36]

After this interview, Ezra and Reed were driven to President McKay's home. On the way, Ezra did not share anything about his experience with President Grant, and Reed did not ask. When they arrived at the McKay home, President McKay told Reed what had transpired. Then Ezra and Reed embraced.

Ezra was restless that night as he and Reed began their train trip home. The next day, he called Flora and told her about his call to the Apostleship. "She said how wonderful she felt it was and expressed her complete confidence I could measure up," he recalled. "It was reassuring to talk to her. She has always shown more faith in me than I have myself."[37]

Over the next several weeks, Ezra and Flora made arrangements to move to Utah, and Ezra did all he could to provide a smooth transition for his successor at the National Council of Farmer Cooperatives. He and Spencer W. Kimball were sustained as members of the Quorum of the Twelve Apostles on October 1, 1943, and they were ordained Apostles on October 7, with Elder Kimball being ordained first.

The Quorum of the Twelve Apostles, sometime between October 1950 and April 1951. Standing, left to right: Delbert L. Stapley; Henry D. Moyle; Matthew Cowley; Mark E. Petersen; Harold B. Lee; Ezra Taft Benson; Spencer W. Kimball. Seated, left to right: John A. Widtsoe; Stephen L Richards; David O. McKay, President of the Quorum of the Twelve; Joseph Fielding Smith, Acting President; Joseph F. Merrill; Albert E. Bowen.

Thus began Elder Ezra Taft Benson's ministry as one of the "special witnesses of the name of Christ in all the world" (D&C 107:23).

Providing Food, Clothing, and Hope in Post-War Europe

On December 22, 1945, President George Albert Smith, then the President of the Church, called a special meeting for the First Presidency and Quorum of the Twelve Apostles. He announced that the First Presidency had felt inspired to send an Apostle to preside over the European Mission and supervise the Church's efforts there. World War II had ended earlier that year, and many European nations were just starting to recover from the widespread, overwhelming destruction of the war. Elder Ezra Taft Benson, the First Presidency felt, was the right man to do the job.

17

This news came as a "great shock" to Elder Benson, who was the newest and youngest member of the quorum. Like his father's mission call 34 years before, this assignment would require him to be separated from his young family. The First Presidency could not say how long he would be gone. However, he assured them that his wife and children would support him, and he expressed his complete willingness to serve.[38] He later described the assignment he had accepted:

"The magnitude of it seemed overwhelming. They [the First Presidency] gave us a four-point charge: First, to attend to the spiritual affairs of the Church in Europe; second, to work to make available food, clothing, and bedding to our suffering Saints in all parts of Europe; third, to direct the reorganization of the various missions of Europe; and, fourth, to prepare for the return of missionaries to those countries."[39] But President Smith gave him this comforting promise: "I am not at all concerned about you. You will be just as safe there as anywhere else in the world if you take care of yourself, and you will be able to accomplish a great work."[40]

Elder Benson described the experience when he shared the news with his wife and family: "In a sweet and impressive talk with my wife, sanctified by tears, Flora expressed loving gratitude and assured me of her wholehearted support. At dinner I told the children, who were surprised, interested, and fully loyal."[41]

When Elder Benson and his companion, Frederick W. Babbel, arrived in Europe, they were saddened by the sickness, poverty, and devastation they saw all around them. For example, in a letter to Flora, Elder Benson told of mothers who were grateful to receive a gift of soap, needles and thread, and an orange. They had not seen such things for years. Elder Benson could see that, with the meager rations they had been given in the past, they had "starved themselves to try and give more to their children in true mother spirit."[42] He told of Church meetings in "bombed-out building[s]" and in "almost total darkness."[43] He told of refugees—"poor, unwanted souls, . . . driven from their once happy homes to destinations unknown."[44] He also told of miracles amid the grim results of war.

One miracle was evident in the lives of Latter-day Saints throughout Europe. On the way there, Elder Benson wondered how the

Saints would receive him. "Would their hearts be filled with bitterness? Would there be hatred there? Would they have soured on the Church?" He was inspired by what he found:

"As I looked into their upturned faces, pale, thin, many of these Saints dressed in rags, some of them barefooted, I could see the light of faith in their eyes as they bore testimony to the divinity of this great latter-day work, and expressed their gratitude for the blessings of the Lord. . . .

"We found that our members had carried on in a marvelous way. Their faith was strong, their devotion greater, and their loyalty unsurpassed. We found very little, if any, bitterness or despair. There was a spirit of fellowship and brotherhood which had extended from one mission to the other, and as we traveled, the Saints asked us to take their greetings to their brothers and sisters in other countries although their nations had been at war only a few months before." Even the refugees "sang the songs of Zion with . . . fervor" and "knelt together in prayer night and morning and bore testimony . . . regarding the blessings of the gospel."[45]

Another miracle was the strength of the Church's welfare program. This effort, which had begun 10 years earlier, saved the lives of many Latter-day Saints in Europe. The Saints were blessed because they had embraced the principle of welfare themselves. They helped one another in their need, sharing food, clothing, and other supplies, and they even planted gardens in bombed-out buildings. They were also blessed because Latter-day Saints from other parts of the world donated goods to help them—approximately 2,000 tons of supplies. Elder Benson told of Church leaders weeping at the sight of basic food that they could distribute to local members, and he said that he stood before congregations in which it was estimated that 80 percent of all the clothing worn had been sent through the welfare program.[46] In a general conference address he delivered soon after returning home, he said: "My brethren and sisters, do you need any further evidence of the need for this program and the inspiration back of it? . . . I tell you God is directing this program. It is inspired!"[47]

Elder Benson and Brother Babbel experienced another recurring miracle as the Lord opened the way for them to travel among the

Elder Benson, right, inspecting welfare supplies in Bergen, Norway

war-torn nations in Europe. Time and time again, Elder Benson asked military officers for permission to enter certain regions to meet with the Saints and distribute goods. Time and time again, he received basically the same response from those leaders and others: "Don't you realize there has been a war here? No civilian travelers are permitted to enter." And time and time again, after he looked those leaders in the eyes and calmly explained his mission, he and Brother Babbel were permitted to travel about and accomplish what the Lord had sent them to do.[48]

After about 11 months, Elder Benson was replaced by Elder Alma Sonne, an Assistant to the Twelve, who served in Europe with his wife, Leona. Brother Babbel remained to assist the Sonnes. From the time Elder Benson left Salt Lake City on January 29, 1946, to the time he returned on December 13, 1946, he traveled a total of 61,236 miles (98,550 kilometers). Elder Benson felt the mission had been a success, but he was quick to say: "I know the source of the success which attended our labors. Never at any time have I felt it would be possible for me or my associates to accomplish the mission to which we were assigned without the directing power of the Almighty."[49] The success of the mission could be seen in the strength of the Church in European nations, newly organized and growing. Success could also be seen in the lives of individual Saints—individuals like a man who once approached President Thomas S. Monson many years later at a meeting in Zwickau, Germany. He asked President Monson to extend greetings to Ezra Taft Benson. Then he exclaimed: "He saved my life. He gave me food to eat and clothing to wear. He gave me hope. God bless him!"[50]

Patriotism, Statesmanship, and Service in the United States Government

While Elder Benson was away from home, he was reminded of something he had cherished since his youth: his citizenship in the United States of America. From his father, George Taft Benson Jr., he had learned to love his native land and the principles on which it had been founded. He had learned that the Constitution of the United States of America—the document that governed laws in the nation—had been prepared by inspired men. He cherished the right to vote, and he always remembered a conversation he had with his father after an election. George had publicly supported a certain candidate, and he had even prayed for this man in family prayers. After George learned that his candidate had lost the election, Ezra heard him pray for the man who had won. Ezra asked his father why he would pray for a candidate who wasn't his choice. "Son," George replied, "I think he'll need our prayers even more than my candidate would have."[51]

In April 1948, Elder Benson gave his first of many general conference addresses focusing on "the prophetic mission" of the United States of America and the importance of freedom. He testified that the Lord had prepared the United States "as the cradle of liberty" so the gospel could be restored there.[52] "We are followers of the Prince of Peace," he taught near the end of the discourse, "and we should rededicate our lives to the spread of truth and righteousness and the preservation of . . . liberty and freedom."[53] In subsequent discourses, he spoke of the United States of America as "the Lord's base of operations in these latter days."[54]

21

Elder Benson warned of threats to freedom in the United States and throughout the world. He often spoke forcefully against "coercive man-made systems" of government, "which are contrary to eternal principles."[55] He also warned of other influences that threatened freedom, including immoral entertainment, lack of respect for the Sabbath day, complacency, and false teachings.[56] He encouraged Latter-day Saints all over the world to use their influence to help ensure that wise and good people would be elected to public office.[57] He declared: "The effective preaching of the gospel can only thrive in an atmosphere of liberty. Yes, we all say, we love liberty. But that is not enough. We must protect and safeguard that which we love. We must save liberty."[58]

On November 24, 1952, Elder Benson's strong words of patriotism were tested as he received an invitation to serve his country. He had traveled to New York City at the invitation of Dwight D. Eisenhower, who had just been elected president of the United States. President-Elect Eisenhower was considering Elder Benson to serve on his cabinet—in other words, to be one of his top advisers—in the position of secretary of agriculture for the entire nation. Elder Benson was honored by the attention. "But," he later said, "I didn't want the job. . . . Nobody in his right mind, I told myself, would seek to be Secretary of Agriculture in times like these. . . . I knew something of what the post entailed: the splintering cross fires, the intense pressures, the tangled problems. . . .

"But it wasn't only the problems and pressures that concerned me. We all have those. Like many Americans, I was reluctant to get into politics actively. Sure, I wanted to see men of high ideals and good character elected and appointed to run the government, but that was vastly different from plunging in myself. . . .

"Most of all, however, I was more than satisfied with the work I was already doing as one of the Council of the Twelve. . . . I neither desired nor intended to make a change."[59]

Before going to meet President-Elect Eisenhower, Elder Benson had sought counsel from President David O. McKay, the President of the Church at the time. President McKay had told him: "Brother Benson, my mind is clear in the matter. If the opportunity comes in the proper spirit I think you should accept."[60] This direct counsel, combined with Elder Benson's foundational desire to "fight effectively for [his] beliefs as an American," caused what he called an "internal debate."[61]

When Mr. Eisenhower and Elder Benson met for the first time, it did not take long for the president-elect to offer Elder Benson the position of secretary of agriculture. Elder Benson immediately listed reasons why he might not be the right man for the job, but President-Elect Eisenhower did not back down. He said: "We've got a job to do. I didn't want to be President, frankly, when the pressure started. *But you can't refuse to serve America.* I want you on my team, and you can't say no."[62]

"That did it," recalled Elder Benson. "The conditions of President McKay's counsel had been met. Even though I felt I had already received from my Church what in my eyes was a greater honor than government could bestow, and I told him so, I accepted the responsibility of becoming Secretary of Agriculture to serve for not less than two years—if he wanted me that long."[63]

Immediately after accepting the position, Elder Benson accompanied President-Elect Eisenhower to a news conference, where his appointment was announced to the nation. As soon as the conference was over, he returned to his hotel. He called Flora and told her that President-Elect Eisenhower had asked him to serve and that he had accepted the invitation.

She replied: "I knew he would. And I knew you'd accept."

He explained: "It will mean a terrible responsibility—and a great many problems for both of us."

"I know," she said, "but it seems to be God's will."[64]

As Elder Benson had expected, his administration as secretary of agriculture was a tumultuous experience for him and his family. But he insisted that he was not trying "to win a popularity contest"—that he simply wanted "to serve agriculture and serve America"[65]—and he followed this personal pledge: "It is good strategy to stand up for the right, even when it is unpopular. Perhaps I should say, especially when it is unpopular."[66] It was fortunate for him that he was not concerned with popularity; while he remained steady and true to his convictions, his popularity among politicians and citizens fluctuated drastically. At times, people wanted him ousted from his position as secretary of agriculture.[67] At other times, people suggested that he would be a good choice for vice president of the United States.[68]

Even in his role as a government leader, Elder Benson was open about his Christian ideals, his testimony of the restored gospel, and his devotion to The Church of Jesus Christ of Latter-day Saints. Whenever he conducted a meeting with his associates in the Department of Agriculture, the meeting began with a prayer.[69] He sent President Eisenhower passages from the Book of Mormon that prophesied of the destiny of the United States of America, and the president later said that he had read them "with the greatest of interest."[70] He gave copies of the Book of Mormon to many other world leaders as well.[71] In 1954, Edward R. Murrow, a prominent television news reporter in the United States, asked Elder Benson for permission to feature the Benson family on a Friday night program called "Person to Person." Elder and Sister Benson declined at first, but they later consented after listening to their son Reed, who saw the invitation as a great missionary opportunity. On September 24, 1954, people all over the nation watched a live, unrehearsed family home evening in the Benson home. Mr. Murrow received more fan mail as a result of that program than he had received for any other. People from all over the country and from varied religious backgrounds wrote to thank the Bensons for their shining example.[72]

Elder Benson served as secretary of agriculture for eight years, the entire time President Eisenhower led the United States. President McKay said that Elder Benson's work would "stand for all time as a credit to the Church and the nation."[73] Elder Benson looked back on those years in the national spotlight and said: "I love this great land. It has been an honor to serve."[74] He also commented, "If I had it to do over again, I would follow very much the same course."[75] Looking ahead to his continuing ministry as an Apostle, he said, "Now [I] devote my time to the only thing I love better than agriculture."[76]

Although Elder Benson's government service came to an end in 1961, his love for his country and the principle of freedom continued. In many of his general conference addresses, he focused on these topics. He referred to the United States of America as "a land

Elder Benson being sworn in as United States secretary of agriculture by Chief Justice Fred M. Vinson, with President Dwight D. Eisenhower looking on

I love with all my heart."[77] He also said, "I cherish patriotism and love of country in all lands."[78] As he counseled all Latter-day Saints to love their countries, he taught: "Patriotism is more than flag-waving and brave words. It is how we respond to public issues. Let us rededicate ourselves as patriots in the truest sense."[79] "Unlike the political opportunist, the true statesman values principle above popularity and works to create popularity for those political principles which are wise and just."[80]

A Special Witness of the Name of Christ

As an Apostle of the Lord Jesus Christ, Elder Ezra Taft Benson obeyed the command to "go . . . into all the world, and preach the gospel to every creature" (Mark 16:15) and to "open the door by the proclamation of the gospel of Jesus Christ" (D&C 107:35). He served in many parts of the world, touring missions and teaching the people.

He cherished the privilege of meeting with Latter-day Saints. In a general conference address, he commented: "I have sometimes said to my wife, as I returned from visiting in the stakes, that I do not know exactly what heaven is going to be like, but I could ask nothing finer over there than to have the pleasure and joy of associating with the type of men and women I meet in the leadership of the stakes and wards of Zion and the missions of the earth. Truly we are richly blessed."[81] In another discourse he said: "There is a real spirit of brotherhood and fellowship in the Church. It's a very powerful thing, somewhat intangible, but very real. I feel it, as do my associates, as we travel throughout the stakes and wards of Zion and throughout the missions of the earth. . . . There is always that feeling of fellowship and brotherhood. It is one of the sweet things in connection with membership in the Church and kingdom of God."[82]

Elder Benson also loved sharing his witness of the Savior with people of other faiths. For example, in 1959 he went with Sister Benson and four members of the United States Department of Agriculture to tour seven countries, including the Soviet Union. Although he was there by virtue of his position as secretary of agriculture, his apostolic testimony touched the hearts of many. He recounted:

"On the way to the airport [our] last night in Moscow, I mentioned . . . to one of our guides my disappointment that we had had no opportunity to visit a church in Russia. He said a few words to the chauffeur, the car swung around in the middle of the avenue and we eventually pulled up before an old stucco building on a dark, narrow, cobblestone side street not far from Red Square. This was the Central Baptist Church.

"It was a rainy, disagreeable October night with a distinct chill in the air. But when we entered the church, we found it filled; people were standing in the hall, in the entry, even in the street. Every Sunday, Tuesday, and Thursday, we learned, similar crowds turn out.

"I looked at the faces of the people. Many were middle-aged and older but a surprising number were young. About four out of every five were women, most of them with scarves about their heads. We were ushered into a place beside the pulpit. . . .

"The minister spoke a few words, and then the organ struck a chord or two and began a hymn in which the entire congregation joined as one. Hearing a thousand to 1500 voices raised there became one of the most affecting experiences of my entire life. In our common faith as Christians, they reached out to us with a message of welcome that bridged all differences of language, of government, of history. And as I was trying to recover balance under this emotional impact, the minister asked me, through an interpreter who stood there, to address the congregation.

"It took me a moment of hard struggle to master my feelings sufficiently to agree. Then I said, in part, 'It was very kind of you to ask me to greet you.

"'I bring you greetings from the millions and millions of church people in America and around the world.' And suddenly it was the most natural thing in the world to be talking to these fellow Christians about the most sacred truths known to man.

"'Our Heavenly Father is not far away. He can be very close to us. God lives, I know that He lives. He is our Father. Jesus Christ, the Redeemer of the World, watches over this earth. He will direct all things. Be unafraid, keep His commandments, love one another, pray for peace and all will be well.'

"As each sentence was translated for the congregation, I saw the women take their handkerchiefs and as one observer put it begin to 'wave them like a mother bidding permanent goodby to her only son.' Their heads nodded vigorously as they moaned *ja, ja, ja!* (yes, yes, yes!). Then I noticed for the first time that even the gallery was filled and many persons were standing against the walls. I looked down on one old woman before me, head covered by a plain old scarf, a shawl about her shoulders, her aged, wrinkled face serene with faith. I spoke directly to her.

"'This life is only a part of eternity. We lived before we came here as spiritual children of God. We will live again after we leave this life. Christ broke the bonds of death and was resurrected. We will all be resurrected.

"'I believe very firmly in prayer. I know it is possible to reach out and tap that Unseen Power which gives us strength and such an anchor in time of need.' With each sentence I uttered, the old head nodded assent. And old, feeble, wrinkled as she was, that woman was beautiful in her devotion.

"I don't remember all that I said, but I recall feeling lifted up, inspired by the rapt faces of these men and women who were so steadfastly proving their faith in the God they served and loved.

"In closing I said, 'I leave you my witness as a Church servant for many years that the truth will endure. Time is on the side of truth. God bless you and keep you all the days of your life, I pray in the name of Jesus Christ, Amen.'

"With that I brought this broken little talk to an end, because I could say no more, and sat down. The whole congregation then broke into a favorite hymn of my childhood, 'God Be with You Till We Meet Again.' We left the church as they sang and as we walked down the aisle, they waved handkerchiefs in farewell—it seemed all 1500 were waving at us as we left.

"It has been my privilege to speak before many church bodies in all parts of the world, but the impact of that experience is almost indescribable. I shall never forget that evening as long as I live.

"Seldom, if ever, have I felt the oneness of mankind and the un-quenchable yearning of the human heart for freedom so keenly as at that moment. . . .

"I came [home] resolved to tell this story often—because it shows how the spirit of freedom, the spirit of brotherhood, and the spirit of religion live on and on despite all efforts to destroy them."[83]

President of the Quorum of the Twelve Apostles

On December 26, 1973, Elder Benson received the unexpected news that the President of the Church, President Harold B. Lee, had died suddenly. With President Lee's passing, the counselors in the First Presidency took their places in the Quorum of the Twelve. Four days later, Spencer W. Kimball was set apart as President of the Church, and Ezra Taft Benson was set apart as President of the Quorum of the Twelve Apostles. With this responsibility, President Benson assumed additional administrative duties. He presided at weekly quorum meetings and coordinated the work of his brethren, including their assignments to preside at stake conferences and mission tours and to call stake patriarchs. He also had some supervisory responsibilities over other General Authorities. An administrative staff took care of clerical tasks to help him and his brethren organize the work.[84]

In a meeting with the Quorum of the Twelve, President Benson shared his thoughts about serving as their President: "I have had a very anxious concern about this great responsibility—not a fearful feeling, because I know we cannot fail in this work . . . if we do our best. I know the Lord will sustain us, but it gives me great concern to be called to leadership over a body of men such as you—special witnesses of the Lord Jesus Christ."[85]

President Benson combined this humility with characteristic boldness and insistence on hard work. He often delegated responsibilities to others so they would have opportunities to serve. He expected the best from those he led, just as he expected the best from himself. But although he was demanding, he was kind. He listened to the views of his brethren, promoting open discussion in quorum meetings. Elders Boyd K. Packer, Russell M. Nelson, and Dallin H. Oaks, who were junior members of the Quorum of the Twelve under his leadership, said that he always encouraged them to share their viewpoints, even if their ideas were different from his.[86]

Members of the Quorum of the Twelve learned that President Benson's leadership was based on unchanging principles. For example, he repeatedly said, "Remember, Brethren, in this work it is the Spirit that counts."[87] And he had one standard by which he measured all the quorum's decisions: he asked, "What is best for the Kingdom?" Elder Mark E. Petersen, who served with him in the Quorum of the Twelve, said, "The answer to that question has been the deciding factor in every important matter that has come before President Ezra Taft Benson throughout his life."[88]

President of the Church

President Spencer W. Kimball died on November 5, 1985, after an extended illness. The leadership of the Church now rested on the Quorum of the Twelve Apostles, with President Ezra Taft Benson as their President and senior member. Five days later, in a solemn and reverent meeting of the Quorum of the Twelve in the Salt Lake Temple, President Benson was set apart as President of the Church. He was inspired to ask President Gordon B. Hinckley to serve as his First Counselor in the First Presidency and to ask President Thomas S. Monson to serve as his Second Counselor.

President Benson had known of President Kimball's precarious health, and he had hoped that his friend's physical strength would be renewed. "This is a day I have not anticipated," President Benson told a press conference shortly after he had been set apart as President of the Church. "My wife, Flora, and I have prayed continually that President Kimball's days would be prolonged on this earth, and another miracle performed on his behalf. Now that the Lord has spoken, we will do our best, under His guiding direction, to move the work forward in the earth."[89]

In his first general conference as President of the Church, President Benson shared what would be his primary emphasis for moving the Lord's work forward. "In our day," he declared, "the Lord has revealed the need to reemphasize the Book of Mormon."[90]

As a member of the Quorum of the Twelve, President Benson had repeatedly preached about the importance of the Book of Mormon.[91] As President of the Church, he gave the subject even greater attention. He declared that "the whole Church [was] under condemnation" because Latter-day Saints were not studying the Book of Mormon enough or giving enough heed to its teachings. He said: "The Book of Mormon has not been, nor is it yet, the center of our personal study, family teaching, preaching, and missionary work. Of this we must repent."[92] He frequently quoted the Prophet Joseph Smith's declaration that people "would get nearer to God by abiding by its precepts, than by any other book,"[93] and he expounded on that promise. "There is a power in the book," he said, "which will begin to flow into your lives the moment you begin a serious study of the book."[94] He urged Latter-day Saints to "flood the earth and [their] lives with the Book of Mormon."[95]

Throughout the world, Latter-day Saints heeded this counsel from their prophet. As a result, they were strengthened, individually and collectively.[96] President Howard W. Hunter said: "Will any

*President Benson with his counselors in the First Presidency: President
Gordon B. Hinckley (left) and President Thomas S. Monson (right)*

generation, including those yet unborn, look back on the administration of President Ezra Taft Benson and not immediately think of his love for the Book of Mormon? Perhaps no President of the Church since the Prophet Joseph Smith himself has done more to teach the truths of the Book of Mormon, to make it a daily course of study for the entire membership of the Church, and to 'flood the earth' with its distribution."[97]

Closely tied to President Benson's testimony of the Book of Mormon was his testimony of Jesus Christ. At a time when many people rejected "the divinity of the Savior," he asserted that "this divinely inspired book is a keystone in bearing witness to the world that Jesus is the Christ."[98] Since his ordination to the Apostleship in 1943, President Benson had served diligently as a witness of the Savior's living reality. As President of the Church, he testified of Jesus Christ and His Atonement with renewed vigor and urgency. He exhorted the Saints to be "captained by Christ" and "consumed in Christ,"[99] to "live a Christ-centered life."[100] Speaking of the Savior, he said, "With all my soul, I love Him."[101]

President Benson also taught other topics with urgency and power. He warned of the dangers of pride. He testified of the eternal importance of the family. He taught the principles of faith and repentance and emphasized the need for dedicated missionary work.

Although he did not speak about the United States of America as often as he had earlier in his ministry, he observed the 200th anniversary of the signing of the Constitution of the United States by speaking on the subject in the October 1987 general conference of the Church. And he continued to love freedom and true patriotism throughout the world. In the late 1980s and early 1990s, he rejoiced at the news that the Berlin Wall had fallen and that people in Russia and eastern Europe were receiving greater freedom, with governments that were more open to religious worship.[102]

President Benson gave a series of talks to specific groups of Church members. Starting in April 1986, he prepared sermons directed to young men, young women, mothers, home teachers, fathers, single adult men, single adult women, children, and the elderly. As President Howard W. Hunter said: "He spoke to everyone and had concern for all. He spoke to the women of the Church and to the men. He spoke to the elderly. He spoke to those who were single, to those in their youth, and he loved speaking to the children in the Church. He gave wonderful, personalized counsel to the entire membership, whatever their personal circumstances were. Those sermons will continue to sustain us and guide us as we reflect on them for many years to come."[103]

President Benson wept when he received a letter from a family that had been influenced by one of these talks. In the letter, a young father explained that he and his wife had been watching general conference on television. Their three-year-old son was playing in a nearby room, where conference was playing on the radio. After hearing President Benson's message to the children, the mother and father walked into the room where their son was playing. The little boy "reported excitedly, 'That man on the radio said that even when we make mistakes, our Heavenly Father still loves us.' That simple statement," said the father, "has left a lasting and meaningful impression on our young son. I can still ask him today what President

Benson said and receive the same enthusiastic reply. It is a comfort to him to know that he has a kind and loving Father in Heaven." [104]

Soon after the October 1988 general conference, President Benson suffered a stroke that made it impossible for him to speak in public. He attended general conferences and other public gatherings for a time. In the 1989 conferences, his counselors read sermons he had prepared. Beginning in 1990, his counselors conveyed his love for the Saints and quoted from his past sermons. The April 1991 conference was the last he attended. From that time on, he was physically unable to do more than watch the proceedings on television. [105]

President Gordon B. Hinckley recalled: "As might well be expected, his body began to fail with age. He could not walk as he once walked. He could not speak as he once spoke. There was a gradual decline, but he was still the chosen prophet of the Lord for so long as he lived." [106] President Hinckley and President Thomas S. Monson guided the Church with the authority President Benson delegated to them, but the Church never went forward with new initiatives without President Benson's knowledge and approval. [107]

As President Benson became weaker physically, Flora's health faltered as well, and she died on August 14, 1992. Less than two years later, on May 30, 1994, he joined her, and his mortal remains were buried next to hers in their beloved Whitney. At President Benson's funeral, President Monson recalled: "He said to me on one occasion, 'Brother Monson, remember, regardless of what anyone else may suggest, I desire to be buried in Whitney, Idaho.' President Benson, we are fulfilling that wish today. His body will go home to Whitney, but his eternal spirit has gone home to God. He no doubt is rejoicing with his family, his friends, and his own beloved Flora. . . .

"The plowboy who became God's prophet has gone home. God bless his memory." [108]

Notes

1. Robert D. Hales, "A Testimony of Prophets," June 5, 1994, speeches.byu.edu; see also Twila Van Leer, "Church Leader Buried beside Wife, Cache Pays Tribute as Cortege Passes," *Deseret News,* June 5, 1994.

2. Gordon B. Hinckley, "Farewell to a Prophet," *Ensign,* July 1994, 37–38.

3. Ezra Taft Benson, "Godly Characteristics of the Master," *Ensign,* Nov. 1986, 46.

4. Margaret Benson Keller, in Sheri L. Dew, *Ezra Taft Benson: A Biography* (1987), 34.

5. Ezra Taft Benson, "Godly Characteristics of the Master," 47–48.

6. Ezra Taft Benson, "Scouting Builds Men," *New Era*, Feb. 1975, 15–16.

7. See *Ezra Taft Benson: A Biography*, 44.

8. See "After 60 Years 'Still in Love,'" *Church News*, Sept. 14, 1986, 4, 10.

9. Ezra Taft Benson, in *Ezra Taft Benson: A Biography*, 58.

10. See *Ezra Taft Benson: A Biography*, 55; see also chapter 7 in this book.

11. See *Ezra Taft Benson: A Biography*, 59.

12. See *Ezra Taft Benson: A Biography*, 59.

13. Ezra Taft Benson, in *Ezra Taft Benson: A Biography*, 62.

14. Sheri L. Dew, *Ezra Taft Benson: A Biography*, 59.

15. Ezra Taft Benson, in *Ezra Taft Benson: A Biography*, 53.

16. Ezra Taft Benson, in *Ezra Taft Benson: A Biography*, 63.

17. Flora Amussen Benson, in *Ezra Taft Benson: A Biography*, 75.

18. Flora Amussen Benson, in *Ezra Taft Benson: A Biography*, 79.

19. Ezra Taft Benson, in *Ezra Taft Benson: A Biography*, 79.

20. Eugene J. Neff, in *Ezra Taft Benson: A Biography*, 84.

21. Eugene J. Neff, in *Ezra Taft Benson: A Biography*, 87.

22. See *Ezra Taft Benson: A Biography*, 87.

23. See *Ezra Taft Benson: A Biography*, 87.

24. Flora Amussen Benson, in *Ezra Taft Benson: A Biography*, 96.

25. Flora Amussen Benson, in *Ezra Taft Benson: A Biography*, 88.

26. Flora Amussen Benson, in *Ezra Taft Benson: A Biography*, 89.

27. Ezra Taft Benson, in *Ezra Taft Benson: A Biography*, 92.

28. Francis M. Gibbons, *Ezra Taft Benson: Statesman, Patriot, Prophet of God* (1996), 85–89.

29. See *Ezra Taft Benson: A Biography*, 99–100, 101, 115.

30. Ezra Taft Benson, in *Ezra Taft Benson: A Biography*, 115.

31. See *Ezra Taft Benson: A Biography*, 100.

32. Barbara Benson Walker, in *Ezra Taft Benson: A Biography*, 130.

33. Flora Amussen Benson, in *Ezra Taft Benson: A Biography*, 121.

34. Flora Amussen Benson, in *Ezra Taft Benson: A Biography*, 121.

35. Sheri L. Dew, *Ezra Taft Benson: A Biography*, 174; including quotations from Ezra Taft Benson, personal journal, July 26, 1943.

36. Ezra Taft Benson, personal journal, July 26, 1943; quoted in *Ezra Taft Benson: A Biography*, 174–75; spelling standardized.

37. Ezra Taft Benson, in *Ezra Taft Benson: A Biography*, 176.

38. See Ezra Taft Benson, *A Labor of Love: The 1946 European Mission of Ezra Taft Benson* (1989), 7.

39. Ezra Taft Benson, in Conference Report, Apr. 1947, 152–53.

40. George Albert Smith, in *A Labor of Love*, 7.

41. Ezra Taft Benson, *A Labor of Love*, 7–8.

42. Ezra Taft Benson, *A Labor of Love*, 120.

43. Ezra Taft Benson, in Conference Report, Apr. 1947, 154.

44. Ezra Taft Benson, in Conference Report, Apr. 1947, 155.

45. Ezra Taft Benson, in Conference Report, Apr. 1947, 153–55.

46. See Ezra Taft Benson, in Conference Report, Apr. 1947, 155–56.

47. Ezra Taft Benson, in Conference Report, Apr. 1947, 156.

48. See Frederick W. Babbel, *On Wings of Faith* (1972), 28–33, 46–47, 106–8, 111–12, 122, 131–34, 136, 154.

49. Ezra Taft Benson, in Conference Report, Apr. 1947, 152.

50. Thomas S. Monson, "President Ezra Taft Benson—A Giant among Men," *Ensign*, July 1994, 36.

51. See *Ezra Taft Benson: A Biography*, 37.

52. See Ezra Taft Benson, in Conference Report, Apr. 1948, 83.

53. Ezra Taft Benson, in Conference Report, Apr. 1948, 86.

54. Ezra Taft Benson, in Conference Report, Apr. 1962, 104.

55. See Ezra Taft Benson, in Conference Report, Apr. 1948, 85.

56. See Ezra Taft Benson, in Conference Report, Apr. 1962, 104–5.

57. See Ezra Taft Benson, in Conference Report, Oct. 1954, 121.

58. Ezra Taft Benson, in Conference Report, Oct. 1962, 19.

59. Ezra Taft Benson, *Cross Fire: The Eight Years with Eisenhower* (1962), 3–4.

60. David O. McKay, in *Cross Fire*, 5.

61. Ezra Taft Benson, *Cross Fire*, 10.

62. Dwight D. Eisenhower, in *Cross Fire*, 12.

63. Ezra Taft Benson, *Cross Fire*, 12.

64. Ezra Taft Benson, *Cross Fire*, 13.

65. Ezra Taft Benson, in *Ezra Taft Benson: A Biography*, 355.

66. Ezra Taft Benson, in Sheri Dew, "President Ezra Taft Benson: Confidence in the Lord," *New Era*, Aug. 1989, 36.

67. See *Ezra Taft Benson: A Biography*, 313, 345.

68. See *Ezra Taft Benson: A Biography*, 331.

69. See chapter 2 in this book.

70. Dwight D. Eisenhower, in *Ezra Taft Benson: A Biography*, 292.

71. See *Ezra Taft Benson: A Biography*, 292.

72. See *Ezra Taft Benson: A Biography*, 297–99.

73. David O. McKay, in *Cross Fire*, 519.

74. Ezra Taft Benson, in Conference Report, Apr. 1961, 113.

75. Ezra Taft Benson, in *Ezra Taft Benson: A Biography*, 358.

76. Ezra Taft Benson, in *Ezra Taft Benson: A Biography*, 355.

77. Ezra Taft Benson, "A Witness and a Warning," *Ensign*, Nov. 1979, 31.

78. Ezra Taft Benson, "The Constitution—A Glorious Standard, *Ensign*, May 1976, 91.

79. Ezra Taft Benson, in Conference Report, Apr. 1960, 99.

80. Ezra Taft Benson, in Conference Report, Oct. 1968, 17.

81. Ezra Taft Benson, in Conference Report, Oct. 1948, 98.

82. Ezra Taft Benson, in Conference Report, Oct. 1950, 143–44.

83. Ezra Taft Benson, *Cross Fire*, 485–88.

84. See Francis M. Gibbons, *Statesman, Patriot, Prophet of God*, 270–71.

85. Ezra Taft Benson, in *Ezra Taft Benson: A Biography*, 430–31.

86. See *Ezra Taft Benson: A Biography*, 429–30.

87. Ezra Taft Benson, in Thomas S. Monson, "A Provident Plan—A Precious Promise," *Ensign*, May 1986, 63.

88. Mark E. Petersen, "President Ezra Taft Benson," *Ensign*, Jan. 1986, 2–3.

89. Ezra Taft Benson, in *Church News*, Nov. 17, 1985, 3.

90. Ezra Taft Benson, "A Sacred Responsibility," *Ensign*, May 1986, 78.

91. See, for example, "The Book of Mormon Is the Word of God," *Ensign*, May 1975, 63–65; "A New Witness for Christ," *Ensign*, Nov. 1984, 6–8; see also *Ezra Taft Benson: A Biography*, 491–93.

92. Ezra Taft Benson, "Cleansing the Inner Vessel," *Ensign*, May 1986, 5–6.

93. Joseph Smith, quoted in the introduction to the Book of Mormon.

94. Ezra Taft Benson, "The Book of Mormon—Keystone of Our Religion," *Ensign*, Nov. 1986, 7.

95. Ezra Taft Benson, "Beware of Pride," *Ensign*, May 1989, 4.

96. See chapter 10 in this book.

97. Howard W. Hunter, "A Strong and Mighty Man," *Ensign*, July 1994, 42.

98. Ezra Taft Benson, "The Book of Mormon—Keystone of Our Religion," 4, 5.

99. Ezra Taft Benson, "Born of God," *Ensign*, July 1989, 4.

100. Ezra Taft Benson, "Come unto Christ," *Ensign*, Nov. 1987, 84.

101. Ezra Taft Benson, "Jesus Christ: Our Savior and Redeemer," *Ensign*, June 1990, 6.

102. See Russell M. Nelson, "Drama on the European Stage," *Ensign*, Dec. 1991, 16.

103. Howard W. Hunter, "A Strong and Mighty Man," 42.

104. Thomas S. Monson, "The Lord Bless You," *Ensign*, Nov. 1991, 87.

105. See Francis M. Gibbons, *Statesman, Patriot, Prophet of God*, 315.

106. Gordon B. Hinckley, "Farewell to a Prophet," 40.

107. See Francis M. Gibbons, *Statesman, Patriot, Prophet of God*, 317–18.

108. Thomas S. Monson, "President Ezra Taft Benson—A Giant among Men," *Ensign*, July 1994, 36.

As the Savior taught the rich young man, we show our love for the Lord when we help other people (see Matthew 19:16–21).

The Great Commandment— Love the Lord

"When we put God first, all other things fall into their proper place or drop out of our lives."

From the Life of Ezra Taft Benson

President Ezra Taft Benson's life reflected his love for the Lord and his steadfast commitment to living the gospel. An extended family member once said, "To Ezra and his family religion is a complete way of life—something to be lived seven days a week. It takes first place in his consideration when the time comes for making decisions."[1]

People outside the Benson family also noticed President Benson's love for the Lord. In 1939, when President Benson was serving as a stake president, he was invited to Washington, D.C., to meet with the directors of the National Council of Farmer Cooperatives. "After looking him over and questioning him, the board of trustees offered him the position of executive secretary of that organization. . . . Though he was thrilled by this unsolicited bid for his services, he did not wish to accept it. As he understood it, the job would entail lobbying by the use of cocktail parties, which would not be compatible with his religion.

"'Mr. Benson,' Judge John D. Miller, head of the group, replied, 'that is why we selected you. We know what your standards are.' With full assurance from the board that he would not be expected to seek an understanding of agricultural problems over cocktail glasses, he was delighted to accept the position, but only after consultation with the First Presidency and his wife."[2]

President Benson taught that we manifest our love for the Lord by our willingness to do the Lord's will. He said: "I wish that every

Latter-day Saint could say and mean it with all his heart: 'I'll go where you want me to go. I'll say what you want me to say. I'll be what you want me to be' [see *Hymns,* no. 270]. If we could all do that, we would be assured of the maximum of happiness here and exaltation in the celestial kingdom of God hereafter."[3]

In a sermon at the April 1988 general conference—the sermon upon which this chapter is based—President Benson focused on the first and great commandment: to love God. Regarding this sermon, Elder Francis M. Gibbons of the Seventy observed, "All that President Ezra Taft Benson worked for, all that he stood for, and all that he hoped for—for himself, for his family, and for the Church—is embodied in this sermon."[4]

Teachings of Ezra Taft Benson

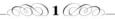

The first and great commandment is to love the Lord.

The great test of life is obedience to God. "We will prove them herewith," said the Lord, "to see if they will do all things whatsoever the Lord their God shall command them" (Abraham 3:25).

The great task of life is to learn the will of the Lord and then do it.

The great commandment of life is to love the Lord.

"Come unto Christ," exhorts Moroni in his closing testimony, ". . . and love God with all your might, mind and strength" (Moroni 10:32).

This, then, is the first and great commandment: "Thou shalt love the Lord thy God with all thy heart, and with all thy soul, and with all thy mind, and with all thy strength" (Mark 12:30; see also Matthew 22:37; Deuteronomy 6:5; Luke 10:27; Moroni 10:32; D&C 59:5).

It is the pure love of Christ, called charity, that the Book of Mormon testifies is the greatest of all—that never faileth, that endureth forever, that all men should have, and that without which they are nothing (see Moroni 7:44–47; 2 Nephi 26:30).

"Wherefore, my beloved brethren," pleads Moroni, "pray unto the Father with all the energy of [your] heart, that ye may be filled with this love, which he hath bestowed upon all who are true followers of his Son, Jesus Christ; that ye may become the sons of God; that when he shall appear we shall be like him" (Moroni 7:48).

In the closing accounts of both the Jaredites and the Nephites, Moroni records that except men shall have this pure love of Christ, called charity, they cannot inherit that place which Christ has prepared in the mansions of His Father nor can they be saved in the kingdom of God (see Ether 12:34; Moroni 10:21).

The fruit that Lehi partook of in his vision and that filled his soul with exceeding great joy and that was most desirable above all things was the love of God.[5]

When I think of charity, I . . . think of my father and that day he was called on his mission [see pages 4–6 in this book]. I suppose some in the world might say that his acceptance of that call was proof he did not really love his family. To leave seven children and an expectant wife at home alone for two years, how could that be true love? But my father knew a greater vision of love. He knew that "all things shall work together for good to them that love God" (Romans 8:28). He knew that the best thing he could do for his family was to obey God.[6]

To love God with all your heart, soul, mind, and strength is all-consuming and all-encompassing. It is no lukewarm endeavor. It is total commitment of our very being—physically, mentally, emotionally, and spiritually—to a love of the Lord.

The breadth, depth, and height of this love of God extend into every facet of one's life. Our desires, be they spiritual or temporal, should be rooted in a love of the Lord. Our thoughts and affections should be centered on the Lord. "Let all thy thoughts be directed unto the Lord," said Alma, "yea, let the affections of thy heart be placed upon the Lord forever" (Alma 37:36).[7]

 **2**

We show our love for God when we put Him first in our lives.

Why did God put the first commandment first? Because He knew that if we truly loved Him we would want to keep all of His other

Joseph of Egypt was willing to go to prison rather than deny his loyalty to God.

commandments. "For this is the love of God," says John, "that we keep his commandments" (1 John 5:3; see also 2 John 1:6).

We must put God in the forefront of everything else in our lives. He must come first, just as He declares in the first of His Ten Commandments: "Thou shalt have no other gods before me" (Exodus 20:3).

When we put God first, all other things fall into their proper place or drop out of our lives. Our love of the Lord will govern the claims for our affection, the demands on our time, the interests we pursue, and the order of our priorities.

We should put God ahead of *everyone else* in our lives.

When Joseph was in Egypt, what came first in his life—God, his job, or Potiphar's wife? When she tried to seduce him, he responded by saying, "How then can I do this great wickedness, and sin against God?" (Genesis 39:9).

Joseph was put in prison because he put God first. If we were faced with a similar choice, where would we place our first loyalty? Can we put God ahead of security, peace, passions, wealth, and the honors of men?

When Joseph was forced to choose, he was more anxious to please God than to please his employer's wife. When we are required to choose, are we more anxious to please God than our boss, our teacher, our neighbor, or our date?

The Lord said, "He that loveth father or mother more than me is not worthy of me: and he that loveth son or daughter more than me is not worthy of me" (Matthew 10:37). One of the most difficult tests of all is when you have to choose between pleasing God or pleasing someone you love or respect—particularly a family member.

Nephi faced that test and handled it well when his good father temporarily murmured against the Lord (see 1 Nephi 16:18–25). Job maintained his integrity with the Lord even though his wife told him to curse God and die (see Job 2:9–10).

The scripture says, "Honour thy father and thy mother" (Exodus 20:12; see also Mosiah 13:20). Sometimes one must choose to honor Heavenly Father over a mortal father.

We should give God, the Father of our spirits, an exclusive pre-eminence in our lives. He has a prior parental claim on our eternal welfare, ahead of all other ties that may bind us here or hereafter.

God, our Father; Jesus, our Elder Brother and our Redeemer; and the Holy Ghost, the Testator, are perfect. They know us best and love us most and will not leave one thing undone for our eternal welfare. Should we not love them for it and honor them first?

There are faithful members who joined the Church in spite of the objections of their mortal relatives. By putting God first, many later became the instruments to lead those loved ones into the kingdom of God.

Jesus said, "I do always those things that please [God]" (John 8:29).

What is the condition in our homes? Are we striving to put the Lord first and to please Him?

Fathers, would it please the Lord if there were daily family prayer and scripture reading in your home? And what about the holding of weekly home evenings and periodically having individual time with your wife and each child? And if your child went temporarily astray, do you think it would please the Lord and He would honor your efforts if you continued to live an exemplary life, consistently prayed and frequently fasted for that child, and kept the name of that son or daughter on the temple prayer roll?

You mothers, who are especially charged with the righteous rearing of the youth of Zion, are you not putting God first when you honor your divine calling? . . . Our mothers put God first when they fill their highest mission within the walls of their own homes.

Children, do you pray for your parents? Do you try to support them in their noble endeavors? They will make mistakes, like you, but they have a divine mission to accomplish in your life. Will you help them do so? Will you add honor to their name and bring comfort and support to them in their older years?

If someone wants to marry you outside the temple, whom will you strive to please—God or a mortal? If you insist on a temple marriage, you will be pleasing the Lord and blessing the other party. Why? Because that person will either become worthy to go to the temple—which would be a blessing—or will leave—which could also be a blessing—because neither of you should want to be unequally yoked (see 2 Corinthians 6:14).

You should qualify for the temple. Then you will know that there is no one good enough for you to marry outside the temple. If such individuals are that good, they will get themselves in a condition so that they too can be married in the temple.[8]

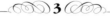

When we choose to put God first in our lives, His blessings come in abundance.

Men and women who turn their lives over to God will discover that He can make a lot more out of their lives than they can. He will deepen their joys, expand their vision, quicken their minds, strengthen their muscles, lift their spirits, multiply their blessings, increase their opportunities, comfort their souls, raise up friends, and pour out peace. Whoever will lose his life in the service of God will find eternal life.[9]

God asked Abraham to sacrifice Isaac. Had Abraham loved Isaac more than God, would he have consented? As the Lord indicates in the Doctrine and Covenants, both Abraham and Isaac now sit as gods (see D&C 132:37). They were willing to offer or to be offered up as God required. They have a deeper love and respect for each other because both were willing to put God first.

The Book of Mormon teaches that "it must needs be, that there is an opposition in all things" (2 Nephi 2:11)—and so there is. Opposition provides choices, and choices bring consequences—good or bad.

The Book of Mormon explains that men "are free to choose liberty and eternal life, through the great Mediator of all men, or to choose captivity and death, according to the captivity and power of the devil" (2 Nephi 2:27).

God loves us; the devil hates us. God wants us to have a fulness of joy as He has. The devil wants us to be miserable as he is. God gives us commandments to bless us. The devil would have us break these commandments to curse us.

Daily, constantly, we choose by our desires, our thoughts, and our actions whether we want to be blessed or cursed, happy or miserable. One of the trials of life is that we do not usually receive immediately the full blessing for righteousness or the full cursing for wickedness. That it will come is certain, but ofttimes there is a waiting period that occurs, as was the case with Job and Joseph.

In the meantime the wicked think they are getting away with something. The Book of Mormon teaches that the wicked "have joy in their works for a season, [but] by and by the end cometh, and they are hewn down and cast into the fire, from whence there is no return" (3 Nephi 27:11).

During this testing time the righteous must continue to love God, trust in His promises, be patient, and be assured, as the poet said, that "who does God's work will get God's pay." . . .

I testify to you that God's pay is the best pay that this world or any other world knows anything about. And it comes in full abundance only to those who love the Lord and put Him first.

The great test of life is obedience to God.

The great task of life is to learn the will of the Lord and then do it.

The great commandment of life is, "Thou shalt love the Lord thy God with all thy heart, and with all thy soul, and with all thy mind, and with all thy strength" (Mark 12:30).

May God bless us to put the first commandment first and, as a result, reap peace in this life and eternal life with a fulness of joy in the life to come.[10]

Suggestions for Study and Teaching

Questions
- In section 1, President Benson teaches about "the first and great commandment" (Matthew 22:38). Why do you think this commandment should come first for us? What insights do you gain from the way President Benson related charity to this commandment?

- What does it mean to you to "put God first"? (For some examples, see section 2.) When have you seen that "all other things fall into their proper place or drop out of our lives" when we put God first?

- Ponder President Benson's promises to those who "turn their lives over to God" (section 3). What examples have you seen of people turning their lives over to God? In what ways did God make those people better than they could have become on their own?

Related Scriptures
Joshua 24:14–15; Matthew 6:33; 7:21; John 14:15, 21–24; 17:3; 1 Corinthians 2:9; 1 Nephi 3:7; Moroni 10:32

Teaching Help
"Be sure you don't believe you are the 'true teacher.' That is a serious mistake. . . . Be careful you do not get in the way. The major role of a teacher is to prepare the way such that the people will

have a spiritual experience with the Lord" (Gene R. Cook, quoted in *Teaching, No Greater Call* [1999], 41).

Notes

1. *Descendants of the George T. Benson Jr. Family* (1968), n.p.

2. Merlo J. Pusey, "Ezra Taft Benson: A Living Witness for Christ," *Improvement Era,* Apr. 1956, 269.

3. *The Teachings of Ezra Taft Benson* (1988), 344.

4. Francis M. Gibbons, *Ezra Taft Benson: Statesman, Patriot, Prophet of God* (1996), 313.

5. In Conference Report, Apr. 1988, 3; see also *Ensign,* May 1988, 4.

6. "Godly Characteristics of the Master," *Ensign,* Nov. 1986, 47–48.

7. In Conference Report, Apr. 1988, 3; see also *Ensign,* May 1988, 4.

8. In Conference Report, Apr. 1988, 3–5; see also *Ensign,* May 1988, 4–6.

9. "Jesus Christ—Gifts and Expectations," *Ensign,* Dec. 1988, 4.

10. In Conference Report, Apr. 1988, 5–6; see also *Ensign,* May 1988, 6; line from poem by Denis A. McCarthy as quoted in Ralph S. Cushman, *The Message of Stewardship* (1922), 191.

"If we would advance in holiness—increase in favor
with God—nothing can take the place of prayer."

Pray Always

"I would humbly urge all . . . to keep in close touch with our Father in heaven through prayer."

From the Life of Ezra Taft Benson

"All through my life the counsel to depend on prayer has been prized above almost any other advice I have received," said President Ezra Taft Benson. "It has become an integral part of me, an anchor, a constant source of strength, and the basis for my knowledge of things divine.

"'Remember that whatever you do or wherever you are, you are never alone' was my father's familiar counsel to me as a boy. 'Our Heavenly Father is always near. You can reach out and receive His aid through prayer.' I have found this counsel to be true. Thank God we can reach out and tap that unseen power, without which no man can do his best."[1]

President Benson followed this counsel in every aspect of his life. When he was appointed to serve as the United States secretary of agriculture, he "prayerfully and carefully" selected a group of men to work with him, "asking God to give [him] a spirit of discernment."[2] At their first meeting, he asked "if anyone objected to opening their meetings with prayer. No one dissented. And so began a practice that [he] perpetuated for eight years. He invited each staff member to take turns offering the invocation."[3] His associates came to appreciate this practice, even though they may have been uncomfortable with it at first. One staff member later admitted that some of the men had not prayed aloud since they were children. "We stumbled and fumbled for words," he said. "But the Boss [President Benson] never let on that he noticed. And after a few trials everybody was at ease. Has it helped? Well, I'd say that when you start a meeting that way, people aren't stuck up with the pride of their opinions. You pretty quickly come to an agreement as to what *ought* to be done in any situation."[4]

President Benson's brethren in the First Presidency and Quorum of the Twelve Apostles also benefited from his prayerful nature. President Gordon B. Hinckley, who served as President Benson's First Counselor in the First Presidency, said:

"I have knelt with him and heard him pray.

"His prayers were always interesting. Almost without exception, they consisted for the most part of expressions of thanks. He asked for very little. He expressed gratitude for very much.

"He thanked the Lord for life, for family, for the gospel, for faith, for sunlight and rain, the bounties of nature, and the freedom-loving instincts of man. He thanked the Lord for friends and associates. He expressed love for the Savior and gratitude for His atoning sacrifice. He thanked the Lord for the opportunity to serve the people."[5]

President Benson and his wife, Flora, established a home where everyone prayed, individually and together. Their son Mark observed: "When Dad knelt down to pray, he didn't rush things. There was meaning behind his words. It came through loud and clear that he was communicating with our Father in heaven."[6] President and Sister Benson taught their children to pray for personal guidance and strength and also to pray for one another. A friend of the family once observed the influence of those teachings when she attended a session of general conference with the Bensons. She wrote:

"On an April day . . . , I discovered one source of a General Authority's strength.

"I was seated with the six children of Elder Ezra Taft Benson, one of whom was my college roommate. My interest heightened when President [David O.] McKay arose and announced the next speaker. I watched respectfully as Elder Benson, whom I had not yet met, walked toward the microphone. He was a big man, well over six feet tall. He was . . . a man internationally known as the United States Secretary of Agriculture and a special witness of the Lord, a man who seemed serene and sure, one who had addressed audiences throughout the world. Suddenly a hand touched my arm. A little girl leaned toward me and whispered urgently, 'Pray for Dad.'

"Somewhat startled, I thought, 'This message is being passed down the row, and I am to pass it on. Shall I say, "Pray for Elder Benson"? Shall I say, "You're supposed to say a prayer for your father"?' Sensing the immediate need to act, I leaned over and whispered simply, 'Pray for Dad.'

"I watched that whisper move along the row to where Sister Benson sat, her head already bowed. . . .

"As years have passed, general conferences have come and gone, and each time President Benson has stood to speak, I have thought, 'His children, who are scattered across the continent, are united now in prayer for their father.'" [7]

Teachings of Ezra Taft Benson

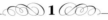
1

Jesus Christ has taught that we should pray always.

During His earthly ministry, Jesus taught us a pattern for prayer:

"After this manner therefore pray ye: Our Father which art in heaven, Hallowed be thy name.

"Thy kingdom come. Thy will be done in earth, as it is in heaven.

"Give us this day our daily bread.

"And forgive us our debts, as we forgive our debtors.

"And lead us not into temptation, but deliver us from evil: For thine is the kingdom, and the power, and the glory, for ever. Amen." (Matt. 6:9–13.)

He further instructed, "Men ought always to pray, and not to faint." (Luke 18:1.)

"Watch and pray," He said, "that ye enter not into temptation." (Matt. 26:41.)

In this dispensation He admonished, "Pray always lest that wicked one have power in you, and remove you out of your place." (D&C 93:49.)

The Savior declared to Joseph Smith, "In nothing doth man offend God, or against none is his wrath kindled, save those who confess not his hand in all things, and obey not his command-ments." (D&C 59:21.)

We have this instruction from our risen Lord as He ministered among the Nephite people on [the] Western Hemisphere: "Ye must watch and pray always, lest ye be tempted by the devil, and ye be led away captive by him. . . .

"Ye must watch and pray always lest ye enter into temptation; for Satan desireth to have you, that he may sift you as wheat.

"Therefore ye must always pray unto the Father in my name;

"And whatsoever ye shall ask the Father in my name, which is right, believing that ye shall receive, behold it shall be given unto you." (3 Ne. 18:15, 18–20.)[8]

If we would advance in holiness—increase in favor with God—nothing can take the place of prayer. And so I adjure you to give prayer—daily prayer—secret prayer—a foremost place in your lives. Let no day pass without it. Communion with the Almighty has been a source of strength, inspiration, and enlightenment to men and women through the world's history who have shaped the destinies of individuals and nations for good.[9]

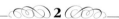

2

Families that pray together are blessed with stronger ties of love and the peace of heaven.

The Lord indicates that it is the responsibility of parents to teach their children to pray [see D&C 68:28]. This does not mean secret prayers only. I am sure it means to teach by example through family prayers. We need the sanctifying influence which comes from devotion in the home—prayer as a family.[10]

We need as families to kneel in family prayer, night and morning. Just a few words added to the blessing on the food, which is becoming the custom in some parts, is not enough. We need to get onto our knees in prayer and gratitude.[11]

Prayer has been and is the ever-present anchor for strength and a source of direction in our family activities. I remember kneeling at the bedside of our young children, helping them with prayers in their younger years, and later seeing the older brothers and sisters

"We need the sanctifying influence which comes from . . . prayer as a family."

helping the younger ones. We had family prayer night and morning, with children given the opportunity to lead, and had special prayers to meet particular problems. Mention was made in family prayer, for instance, of children with [Church] assignments. . . . We asked for help when one of the children faced a difficult examination in high school. Special mention was made of members of the family [who were] away. . . . This special mention of particular concerns in our family prayers gave confidence, assurance, and strength to members of the family facing difficult problems and assignments.[12]

The differences and irritations of the day melt away as families approach the throne of heaven together. Unity increases. The ties of love and affection are re-enforced and the peace of heaven enters.

In such homes secret prayers are said night and morning by members of the household. Individual and family problems are approached with confidence after invoking the favor of heaven.

Young people participating in such a family devotional have hearts freed from evil intent as they leave for an evening of entertainment. These [young people] will be the restraining influence in the group when gilded temptations arise. Parents who surround their children with the refining influence of daily devotion are making their contribution to the safeguarding of the . . . home.[13]

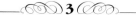

We can improve our communication with our Heavenly Father.

Here are five ways to improve our communication with our Heavenly Father:

1. *We should pray frequently.* We should be alone with our Heavenly Father at least two or three times each day—"morning, mid-day, and evening," as the scripture indicates. (Alma 34:21.) In addition, we are told to pray always. (See 2 Ne. 32:9; D&C 88:126.) This means that our hearts should be full, drawn out in prayer unto our Heavenly Father continually. (See Alma 34:27.)

2. *We should find an appropriate place where we can meditate and pray.* We are admonished that this should be "in [our] closets, and [our] secret places, and in [our] wilderness." (Alma 34:26.) That is, it should be free from distraction, in secret. (See 3 Ne. 13:5–6.)

3. *We should prepare ourselves for prayer.* If we do not feel like praying, then we should pray until we do feel like praying. We should be humble. (See D&C 112:10.) We should pray for forgiveness and mercy. (See Alma 34:17–18.) We must forgive anyone against whom we have bad feelings. (See Mark 11:25.) Yet the scriptures warn that our prayers will be vain if we "turn away the needy, and the naked, and visit not the sick and afflicted, and impart [not] of [our] substance." (Alma 34:28.)

4. *Our prayers should be meaningful and pertinent.* We should avoid using the same phrases in each prayer. Any of us would become offended if a friend said the same words to us each day, treated the conversation as a chore, and could hardly wait to finish in order to turn on the television set and forget us. . . .

For what should we pray? We should pray about our work, against the power of our enemies and the devil, for our welfare and the welfare of those around us. We should counsel with the Lord regarding all our decisions and activities. (See Alma 37:36–37.) We should be grateful enough to give thanks for all we have. (See D&C 59:21.) We should confess His hand in all things. Ingratitude is one of our great sins.

The Lord has declared in modern revelation: "And he who receiveth all things with thankfulness shall be made glorious; and the things of this earth shall be added unto him, even an hundred fold, yea, more." (D&C 78:19.)

We should ask for what we need, taking care that we not ask for things that would be to our detriment. (See James 4:3.) We should ask for strength to overcome our problems. (See Alma 31:31–33.) We should pray for the inspiration and well-being of the President of the Church, the General Authorities, our stake president, our bishop, our quorum president, our home teachers, family members, and our civic leaders. Other suggestions could be made, but with the help of the Holy Ghost we will know about what we should pray. (See Rom. 8:26–27.)

5. *After making a request through prayer, we have a responsibility to assist in its being granted.* We should listen. Perhaps while we are on our knees, the Lord wants to counsel us.[14]

God is mindful of us and ready to respond to our prayers when we place our trust in Him and do that which is right.

There is power in prayer. All things are possible through prayer. It was through prayer that the heavens were opened in this dispensation. The prayer of a boy fourteen years of age, in the Sacred Grove, opened a new gospel dispensation, and brought forth a vision of the Father and the Son, as they appeared as glorified heavenly beings before the boy, Joseph [see Joseph Smith—History 1:11–17].[15]

It is my testimony, my brothers and sisters and friends, that God does hear and answer prayers. I have never doubted that fact. From childhood, at my mother's knee where I first learned to pray; as a young man in my teens; as a missionary in foreign lands; as a father; as a Church leader; as a government official, I know without any question that it is possible for men and women to reach out in humility and prayer and tap that Unseen Power; to have prayers answered. Man does not stand alone, or at least, he need not stand alone. Prayer will open doors; prayer will remove barriers; prayer will ease pressures; prayer will give inner peace and comfort during times of strain and stress and difficulty. Thank God for prayer.[16]

Even during hours of trial and anxiety, it is possible to draw close to the Lord, to feel of his influence and of his sustaining power—that one is never alone, if he will only humble himself before the Almighty. I am grateful for that testimony, for that assurance.[17]

Out of personal experience, I know the efficacy and power of prayer. . . .

In 1946 I was assigned by President George Albert Smith to go to war-torn Europe and reestablish our missions from Norway to South Africa and to set up a program for the distribution of welfare supplies.

We established headquarters in London. We then made preliminary arrangements with the military on the continent. One of the first men I wished to see was the commander of the American forces in Europe. He was stationed in Frankfurt, Germany.

When we arrived in Frankfurt, my companion and I went in to seek an appointment with the general. The appointment officer said, "Gentlemen, there will be no opportunity for you to see the general for at least three days. He's very busy and his calendar is filled up with appointments."

I said, "It is very important that we see him, and we can't wait that long. We're due in Berlin tomorrow."

He said, "I'm sorry."

We left the building, went out to our car, removed our hats, and united in prayer. We then went back into the building and found a different officer at the appointment post. In less than fifteen minutes we were in the presence of the general. We had prayed that we would be able to see him and to touch his heart, knowing that all relief supplies contributed from any source were then required to be placed in the hands of the military for distribution. Our objective, as we explained it to the general, was to distribute our own supplies to our own people through our own channels, and also to make gifts for general child feeding.

We explained the welfare program and how it operated. Finally, he said, "Well, gentlemen, you go ahead and collect your supplies; and by the time you get them collected, the policy may be changed." We said, "General, our supplies are already collected; they're always collected. Within twenty-four hours from the time we wire the First Presidency of the Church in Salt Lake City, carloads of supplies will be rolling toward Germany. We have many storehouses filled with basic commodities."

He then said, "I've never heard of a people with such vision." His heart was touched as we had prayed it would be. Before we left his office, we had a written authorization to make our own distribution to our own people through our own channels.

It is soul-satisfying to know that God is mindful of us and ready to respond when we place our trust in Him and do that which is right. There is no place for fear among men and women who place their trust in the Almighty, who do not hesitate to humble themselves in seeking divine guidance through prayer. Though persecutions arise, though reverses come, in prayer we can find reassurance, for God will speak peace to the soul. That peace, that spirit of serenity, is life's greatest blessing.

As a boy in the Aaronic Priesthood, I learned this little poem about prayer. It has remained with me:

> *I know not by what methods rare,*
> *But this I know, God answers prayer.*
> *I know that He has given His Word,*
> *Which tells me prayer is always heard,*
> *And will be answered, soon or late.*
> *And so I pray and calmly wait.*
> *I know not if the blessing sought*
> *Will come in just the way I thought;*
> *But leave my prayers with Him alone,*

*Elder Ezra Taft Benson and his companions prayed for guidance
as they administered relief in Europe after World War II.*

Whose will is wiser than my own,
Assured that He will grant my quest,
Or send some answer far more blest.

. . . I bear witness to you, my beloved brethren and sisters, that
God lives. He is not dead. . . . I testify there is a God in heaven who
hears and answers prayer. I know this to be true. I would humbly urge all . . . to keep in close touch with our Father in heaven
through prayer. Never before in this gospel dispensation has there
been a greater need for prayer. That we will constantly depend
upon our Heavenly Father and conscientiously strive to improve
our communication with Him is my earnest plea.[18]

Suggestions for Study and Teaching

Questions
- President Benson said that we should "let no day pass" without
  personal prayer (section 1). How have you been blessed as a
  result of personal prayer?

- In section 2, President Benson mentions several blessings that come to families who pray together regularly. When have you seen family prayer lead to these blessings? What can we do to make family prayer a priority?

- Consider President Benson's five suggestions in section 3. How can each of these suggestions help us "improve our communication with our Heavenly Father"? Think about what you will do to follow this counsel.

- How might President Benson's words in section 4 help someone who doubts the power of prayer? What words of testimony can you add to President Benson's?

Related Scriptures

James 1:5–6; Enos 1:1–8; 3 Nephi 14:7–8; D&C 10:5; 19:38; 88:63

Study Help

A principle is a truth that guides decisions and actions. "As you read, ask yourself, 'What gospel principle is taught in this passage? How can I apply this in my life?'" (*Teaching, No Greater Call* [1999], 17).

Notes

1. "Prayer," *Ensign,* May 1977, 32.
2. *Cross Fire: The Eight Years with Eisenhower* (1962), 31.
3. Sheri L. Dew, *Ezra Taft Benson: A Biography* (1987), 268.
4. Quoted in *Ezra Taft Benson: A Biography,* 268.
5. Gordon B. Hinckley, "Farewell to a Prophet," *Ensign,* July 1994, 40.
6. Quoted in *Ezra Taft Benson: A Biography,* 140.
7. Elaine S. McKay, "Pray for Dad," *New Era,* June 1975, 33.
8. "Pray Always," *Ensign,* Feb. 1990, 2.
9. In Conference Report, Apr. 1966, 131.
10. In Conference Report, Oct. 1947, 24.
11. In Conference Report, Oct. 1950, 147.
12. "Family Joys," *New Era,* Jan. 1973, 4.
13. In Conference Report, Apr. 1949, 197–98.
14. "Pray Always," 2, 4.
15. In Conference Report, Oct. 1956, 108.
16. In Conference Report, Oct. 1956, 104.
17. In Conference Report, Apr. 1953, 39.
18. "Prayer," 33–34; poem titled "Prayer" by Eliza M. Hickok, as quoted from *Best Loved Religious Poems,* ed. James Gilchrist Lawson (1933), 160.

*The premortal Jesus Christ followed Heavenly Father's plan
of salvation, which preserved our freedom of choice.*

Freedom of Choice, an Eternal Principle

"Agency has been given to all of us to make important decisions that will have bearing on our salvation. Those decisions affect our happiness in eternity."

From the Life of Ezra Taft Benson

Living and working on a farm, Ezra Taft Benson learned about the consequences of good decisions. He recalled: "I grew up believing that the willingness and ability to work is the basic ingredient of successful farming. Hard, intelligent work is the key. Use it, and your chances for success are good."[1] At a young age, Ezra learned that he and his family would have more to eat if they chose to take care of their garden. He learned that if he wanted the family to be successful in their dairy business, he had to decide to get out of bed early every day to milk the cows.[2] He saw that when he made the choice to work hard, local farmers hired him to thin their beets and pitch their hay.[3] He saw that trials come even to the faithful, but he also saw that individuals and families could decide to respond to trials in a way that would help them be happy and successful.[4]

For young Ezra Taft Benson, some consequences of good decisions could be measured in buckets of milk, on trucks loaded with hay, and with generous pay for a day of hard work. Others were harder to measure but more lasting. For example, as he observed his parents, he saw the joy, peace, and strength that come when family members choose to be faithful to one another and the Lord.[5] He learned that the law of the harvest—"whatsoever a man soweth, that shall he also reap" (Galatians 6:7)—applies to spiritual pursuits as well as physical labor.

With this experience as a foundation, President Ezra Taft Benson frequently reminded Latter-day Saints and others of the importance of agency—the freedom "to choose the course they should follow."[6] His teachings about the principle of agency included more than just a reminder to "choose between right and wrong."[7] He spoke of agency as the ability to "make important decisions that will have bearing on our salvation" and that will "affect our happiness in eternity."[8] He encouraged Latter-day Saints and others to use their agency to "act on their own," without waiting to be commanded in all things.[9] The principle of agency, he said, "runs like a golden thread throughout the gospel plan of the Lord for the blessing of his children."[10]

Teachings of Ezra Taft Benson

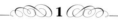 **1**

Agency—freedom of choice—is a God-given, eternal principle.

I testify that we are the spirit offspring of a loving God, our Heavenly Father (see Acts 17:29; 1 Ne. 17:36). He has a great plan of salvation whereby His children might be perfected as He is and might have a fulness of joy as He enjoys. (See 1 Ne. 10:18; 2 Ne. 2:25; Alma 24:14; 34:9; 3 Ne. 12:48; 28:10.)

I testify that in our premortal state our Elder Brother in the spirit, even Jesus Christ, became our foreordained Savior in the Father's plan of salvation. (See Mosiah 4:6–7; Alma 34:9.) He is the captain of our salvation and the only means through whom we can return to our Father in Heaven to gain that fulness of joy. (See Heb. 2:10; Mosiah 3:17; Alma 38:9.)

I testify that Lucifer was also in the council of heaven. He sought to destroy the agency of man. He rebelled. (See Moses 4:3.) There was a war in heaven, and a third of the hosts were cast to the earth and denied a body. (See Rev. 12:7–9; D&C 29:36–37.) Lucifer is the enemy of all righteousness and seeks the misery of all mankind. (See 2 Ne. 2:18, 27; Mosiah 4:14.)[11]

The central issue in that premortal council was: Shall the children of God have untrammeled agency to choose the course they should follow, whether good or evil, or shall they be coerced and forced to be obedient? Christ and all who followed Him stood for the former proposition—freedom of choice; Satan stood for the latter—coercion and force.[12]

The scriptures make clear that there was a great war in heaven, a struggle over the principle of freedom, the right of choice. (See Moses 4:1–4; D&C 29:36–38; 76:25–27; Rev. 12:7–9.)[13]

The war that began in heaven over this issue is not yet over. The conflict continues on the battlefield of mortality.[14]

Freedom of choice is a God-given eternal principle. The great plan of liberty is the plan of the gospel. There is no coercion about it; no force, no intimidation. A man is free to accept the gospel or reject it. He may accept it and then refuse to live it, or he may accept it and live it fully. But God will never force us to live the gospel. He will use persuasion through His servants. He will call us and He will direct us and He will persuade us and encourage us and He will bless us when we respond, but He will never force the human mind. (See *Hymns*, 1985, no. 240.)[15]

This life is a time of testing in which we are free to choose between good and evil.

Abraham was shown the spirit children of our Heavenly Father before they came to earth. He, too, was shown the creation of the earth, and the Lord said to him: "And we will prove them herewith, to see if they will do all things whatsoever the Lord their God shall command them." (Abraham 3:25.) In that divine statement is embodied also the right of choice.[16]

This life is a probation: a probation in which you and I prove our mettle, a probation that has eternal consequences for each of us. And now is our time and season—as every generation has had theirs—to learn our duties and to do them.[17]

That the Lord is displeased with wickedness is true. That He desires that it not occur is also true. That He will help those who oppose it is true. But that He allows wickedness to occur at all through His children here in mortality is proof of His having given them their freedom to choose, while reserving for Him a basis for their final judgment.[18]

There is no evil that [Jesus Christ] cannot arrest. All things are in His hands. This earth is His rightful dominion. Yet He permits evil so that we can make choices between good and evil.[19]

Life is a testing time in man's eternal existence, during which he is given . . . the right to choose between right and wrong. . . . On those choices hang great consequences, not only in this life, but, even more important, in the life to come. There are boundaries beyond which Satan cannot go. Within those bounds, he is presently being permitted to offer an unrighteous alternative to God's righteous principles, thus allowing men to choose between good and evil and thereby determine the station they shall occupy in the next life.[20]

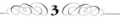

3

We use our agency to make decisions that determine our happiness now and throughout eternity.

God loves you as He loves each and every one of His children, and His desire and purpose and glory is to have you return to Him pure and undefiled, having proven yourselves worthy of an eternity of joy in His presence.

Your Father in heaven is mindful of you. He has given you commandments to guide you, to discipline you. He has also given you your agency—freedom of choice—"to see if [you] will do all things whatsoever [He] shall command." (Abr. 3:25.) His kingdom here on earth is well organized, and your leaders are dedicated to helping you. May you know that you have our constant love, our concern, and prayers.

Satan is also mindful of you. He is committed to your destruction. He does not discipline you with commandments, but offers instead a freedom to "do your own thing." . . . Satan's program is "play now and pay later." He seeks for all to be miserable like unto himself [see 2 Nephi 2:27]. The Lord's program is happiness now and joy forever through gospel living.[21]

We are free to choose, but we are not free to alter the consequences of those choices.[22]

Clearly, there would be little trial of faith if we received our full reward immediately for every goodly deed, or immediate retribution for every sin. But that there will be an eventual reckoning for each, there is no question.[23]

While a man may take some temporary pleasure in sin, the end result is unhappiness. "Wickedness never was happiness." (Alma 41:10.) Sin creates disharmony with God and is depressing to the spirit. Therefore, a man would do well to examine himself to see that he is in harmony with all of God's laws. Every law kept brings a particular blessing. Every law broken brings a particular blight. Those who are heavy-laden with despair should come unto the Lord, for his yoke is easy and his burden is light. (See Matt. 11:28–30.)[24]

The biggest business of any life is making decisions. While one of the greatest gifts of God to man is . . . the right of choice, he has also given man responsibility for these choices. . . . We put our own lives in the direction of success or failure. We may not only choose our ultimate goals, but we may also determine and decide for ourselves, in many cases, the means by which we will arrive at those goals, and by our industry or lack of it determine the speed by which they may be reached. This takes individual effort and energy and will not be without opposition or conflict.[25]

The fate of humanity and all civilization hinges on whether man will use his . . . agency to govern himself or ignore eternal laws at his own peril and reap the consequences. The real issues of today are, therefore, not economic or political. They are spiritual—meaning that man must learn to conform to the laws which God has given to mankind.[26]

Agency has been given to all of us to make important decisions that will have bearing on our salvation. Those decisions affect our happiness in eternity.[27]

Our decisions have made us what we are. Our eternal destiny will be determined by the decisions we yet will make.[28]

 4

Decisions of crucial importance
require our prayerful effort.

If we are to make proper, Christ-like decisions, we must first of all live so we can reach out and tap that unseen power without which no man can do his best in decision making.

One of the greatest decisions of this age was when the boy Joseph Smith decided that he would follow the admonition in James: "If any of you lack wisdom, let him ask of God, that giveth to all men liberally, and upbraideth not; and it shall be given him. But let him ask in faith, nothing wavering. For he that wavereth is like a wave of the sea driven with the wind and tossed." (James 1:5–6.)

The very salvation of millions of men and women in the dispensation of the fulness of times depends upon that decision! We must keep in mind that individuals do matter and that decisions they make may greatly affect the lives of others.[29]

The Lord said, "Knock and it shall be opened unto you" (3 Nephi 14:7; Matthew 7:7). In other words, it requires effort on our part.[30]

Wise decisions are usually arrived at following work, struggle, and prayerful effort. The Lord's response to Oliver Cowdery's ineffective effort makes this clear: "But, behold, I say unto you, that you must study it out in your mind; then you must ask me if it be right, and if it is right I will cause that your bosom shall burn within you; therefore, you shall feel that it is right." (D&C 9:8.)

Let us begin, therefore, by saying that earnestly seeking our Father in heaven, having faith that he will answer our prayers, is a comforting base on which to begin. . . . The Lord will not take water from a dry well, so we must do our part. Sometimes attempting to find a correct decision takes great amounts of energy, study, and long-suffering.[31]

In decisions of crucial importance, fasting combined with prayer can bring great spiritual insight.[32]

The Lord wants us to use our agency to be "anxiously engaged in a good cause" (D&C 58:27).

 **5**

We are agents unto ourselves, and the Lord expects us to do good things of our own free will.

In 1831 the Lord said this to his Church:

"For behold, it is not meet that I should command in all things; for he that is compelled in all things, the same is a slothful and not a wise servant; wherefore he receiveth no reward.

"Verily I say, men should be anxiously engaged in a good cause, and do many things of their own free will, and bring to pass much righteousness;

"For the power is in them, wherein they are agents unto themselves. And inasmuch as men do good they shall in nowise lose their reward.

"But he that doeth not anything until he is commanded, and receiveth a commandment with doubtful heart, and keepeth it with slothfulness, the same is damned." (D&C 58:26–29.)

The purposes of the Lord—the great objectives—continue the same: the salvation and exaltation of his children.

Usually the Lord gives us the overall objectives to be accomplished and some guidelines to follow, but he expects us to work out most of the details and methods. The methods and procedures are usually developed through study and prayer and by living so that we can obtain and follow the promptings of the Spirit. Less spiritually advanced people, such as those in the days of Moses, had to be commanded in many things. Today those spiritually alert look at the objectives, check the guidelines laid down by the Lord and his prophets, and then prayerfully act—without having to be commanded "in all things." This attitude prepares men for godhood. . . .

Sometimes the Lord hopefully waits on his children to act on their own, and when they do not, they lose the greater prize, and the Lord will either drop the entire matter and let them suffer the consequences or else he will have to spell it out in greater detail. Usually, I fear, the more he has to spell it out, the smaller is our reward.[33]

We should be "anxiously engaged" in good causes and leave the world a better place for having lived in it.[34]

Suggestions for Study and Teaching

Questions

- In what ways have you seen that "the war that began in heaven . . . is not yet over"? (See section 1.) What can we do to continue to stand for the principle of agency?

- People often wonder why God allows evil to exist in the world. How do President Benson's teachings in section 2 help to answer that question?

- What can we do to help children and youth understand the truths in section 3? What can we do to help children and youth understand the impact of the decisions they make?

- Ponder President Benson's counsel about making "proper, Christlike decisions" (section 4). What have you learned about combining prayer with diligent effort in making decisions?

• What does it mean to you to be "anxiously engaged in a good cause"? How does your life change when you do good things "of [your] own free will" rather than waiting to be commanded? (See section 5.)

Related Scriptures

Deuteronomy 11:26–28; Joshua 24:15; 2 Nephi 2:14–16; Alma 42:2–4; Helaman 14:30–31; D&C 29:39–45; 101:78

Teaching Help

Discussions in small groups "give a large number of people the opportunity to participate in a lesson. Individuals who are usually hesitant to participate might share ideas in small groups that they would not express in front of the entire group" (*Teaching, No Greater Call* [1999], 161).

Notes

1. Quoted in Gene Allred Sessions, *Latter-day Patriots* (1975), 77–78.

2. See Sheri L. Dew, *Ezra Taft Benson: A Biography* (1987), 18–19, 34.

3. See *Ezra Taft Benson: A Biography*, 40–41.

4. See *Ezra Taft Benson: A Biography*, 19–20.

5. See *Ezra Taft Benson: A Biography*, 17, 22, 25–26, 29–31, 34–37.

6. "The Constitution—A Glorious Standard," *Ensign*, Sept. 1987, 6.

7. *God, Family, Country: Our Three Great Loyalties* (1975), 402.

8. *The Teachings of Ezra Taft Benson* (1988), 24.

9. See Conference Report, Apr. 1965, 122.

10. In Conference Report, Oct. 1966, 121.

11. "I Testify," *Ensign*, Nov. 1988, 86.

12. "The Constitution—A Glorious Standard," 6.

13. In Conference Report, Oct. 1966, 121.

14. "The Constitution—A Glorious Standard," 6.

15. *The Teachings of Ezra Taft Benson*, 82.

16. *So Shall Ye Reap* (1960), 221.

17. In Conference Report, Apr. 1967, 59.

18. *Strength for the Battle: An Address Given by Ezra Taft Benson at the New England Rally for God, Family and Country* (1966), 14–15.

19. *Come unto Christ* (1983), 132.

20. *God, Family, Country*, 402.

21. "A Message to the Rising Generation," *Ensign*, Nov. 1977, 30.

22. *Come unto Christ*, 40.

23. *God, Family, Country*, 326.

24. "Do Not Despair," *Ensign*, Oct. 1986, 2.

25. *God, Family, Country*, 145.

26. *The Teachings of Ezra Taft Benson*, 83–84.

27. *The Teachings of Ezra Taft Benson*, 24.

28. *God, Family, Country*, 143.

29. *God, Family, Country*, 144.

30. *The Teachings of Ezra Taft Benson*, 451.

31. *God, Family, Country*, 149.

32. *God, Family, Country*, 152.

33. In Conference Report, Apr. 1965, 121–22.

34. *The Teachings of Ezra Taft Benson*, 676–77.

President Ezra Taft Benson set an example of joyful living.

Living Joyfully in Troubled Times

"Happiness here and now consists in freely, lovingly, joyfully acknowledging God's will for us—and doing it in all ways and all affairs big and small."

From the Life of Ezra Taft Benson

One of President Ezra Taft Benson's early assignments as an Apostle was to help bring relief to the Saints in Europe after World War II. While traveling in Germany, he met faithful people who were able to rise above the devastation all around them. He recorded in his journal:

"The worst destruction I have witnessed was seen today. . . . As I rode through the streets [of Berlin] and walked through some impassable by auto, I . . . saw half-starved women paying exorbitant prices anxiously for potato peelings. . . . I saw old men and women with small hatchets eagerly digging at tree stumps and roots in an effort to get scraps of fuel and then pulling those home for miles on anything that would roll—from two little wheels of a once baby carriage to small wagons—as beasts of burden.

"Later I faced in a cold half-wrecked third floor auditorium off a bombed street 480 cold half-starved but faithful Latter-day Saints in a conference meeting. It was an inspiration to see the light of faith. . . . There was no bitterness or anger but a sweet reciprocation and expression of faith in the gospel."[1]

"Not a single member registered any complaint about their circumstances in spite of the fact that some were in the last stages of starvation right before our very eyes.

". . . Our Saints . . . are full of hope, courage, and faith, and everywhere they look cheerfully forward with expressions of deepest faith for the gospel and for their membership in the Church. It was one of the greatest demonstrations we have ever seen of the real fruits of the gospel in the lives of men and women."[2]

President Benson also saw examples of hope and optimism close to home, where many of his fellow farmers remained cheerful even when they faced severe difficulties. He said:

"I remember attending a meeting near Bancroft, Idaho. . . . We'd had a wonderful meeting, and after it was over, I was greeting some of the wonderful farmers who were there, and among them was a man by the name of Brother Yost, and I said, 'Brother Yost, how are things out on the farm?' Brother Yost said, 'Oh, things are fine, Brother Benson, but I'm about 20 thousand dollars worse off than I was three days ago.' I said, 'What's the matter—another frost?' He said, 'Yes, it hit the wheat just in the dough stage, and you know what that means.' He said, 'We're starting the mowing machines in the morning, but everything's all right. We've still got a little wheat in the bin, and we've got at least part of our year's supply laid away. We're not going to starve, and there'll be another crop.' As we left him, I said to my wife, 'What a wonderful spirit.'

"We drove on down to Logan [a city in Utah, about 80 miles, or 130 kilometers, from Bancroft]. We had our children with us, and we stopped on Main Street to go into a grocery store to pick up a few cookies for the kiddies. And who should I meet on the sidewalk but Brother Yost. I said, 'Well, what are you doing way down here?' He said, 'Brother Benson, it's our day to go to the temple.' And I said, 'Well, reverses don't dampen your spirits any, do they?' Then he taught me a lesson. He said, 'Brother Benson, when reverses come we need the temple all the more.'"[3]

President Benson's own responses to adversity lifted those who knew him, just as the example of other Saints strengthened him. Elder Neal A. Maxwell of the Quorum of the Twelve Apostles described President Benson as a "careful watcher of events, [who] maintains a certain buoyancy and cheerfulness we would do well to watch. Such buoyancy," Elder Maxwell said, "comes not from ignoring enveloping events, but from noticing these and yet looking beyond them to promises having to do with how the kingdom will finally prevail."[4]

Teachings of Ezra Taft Benson

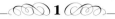 1

With faith in our Heavenly Father, we can have hope for the future, optimism in our present tasks, and inner peace.

We will all have disappointments and discouragements—that is part of life. But if we will have faith, our setbacks will be but a moment and success will come out of our seeming failures. Our Heavenly Father can accomplish miracles through each of us if we will but place our confidence and trust in Him.[5]

It is a great blessing to have an inner peace, to have an assurance, to have a spirit of serenity and inward calm during times of strife and struggle, during times of sorrow and reverses. It is soul-satisfying to know that God is at the helm, that He is mindful of His children, and that we can with full confidence place our trust in Him.[6]

Prayer—persistent prayer—can put us in touch with God, our greatest source of comfort and counsel. "Pray always, that you may come off conqueror." (D&C 10:5.) "Exerting all my powers to call upon God to deliver me" is how the young Joseph Smith describes the method that he used in the Sacred Grove to keep the adversary from destroying him. (JS—H 1:16.)[7]

Without faith in our Heavenly Father, we cannot be successful. Faith gives us vision of what may happen, hope for the future, and optimism in our present tasks. Where faith is, we do not doubt the ultimate success of the work.[8]

Of all people, we as Latter-day Saints should be the most optimistic and the least pessimistic. For while we know that "peace shall be taken from the earth, and the devil shall have power over his own dominion," we are also assured that "the Lord shall have power over his saints, and shall reign in their midst." (D&C 1:35–36.)

With the assurance that the Church shall remain intact with God directing it through the troubled times ahead, it then becomes our individual responsibility to see that each of us remains faithful to the Church and its teachings. "He that remaineth steadfast and is not overcome, the same shall be saved." (JS—M 1:11.)[9]

Happiness must be earned from day to day, but it is worth the effort.

We have no cause to really worry. Live the gospel, keep the commandments. Attend to your prayers night and morning in your home. Maintain the standards of the Church. Try and live calmly and cheerfully. . . . Happiness must be earned from day to day. But it is worth the effort.[10]

When George A. Smith was very ill, he was visited by his cousin, the Prophet Joseph Smith. The afflicted man reported: "He [the Prophet] told me I should never get discouraged, whatever difficulties might surround me. If I were sunk into the lowest pit of Nova Scotia and all the Rocky Mountains piled on top of me, I ought not to be discouraged, but hang on, exercise faith, and keep up good courage, and I should come out on the top of the heap." . . .

There are times when you simply have to righteously hang on and outlast the devil until his depressive spirit leaves you. As the Lord told the Prophet Joseph Smith: "Thine adversity and thine afflictions shall be but a small moment;

"And then, if thou endure it well, God shall exalt thee on high." (D&C 121:7–8.)

Pressing on in noble endeavors, even while surrounded by a cloud of depression, will eventually bring you out on top into the sunshine. Even our master Jesus the Christ, while facing that supreme test of being temporarily left alone by our Father during the crucifixion, continued performing his labors for the children of men, and then shortly thereafter he was glorified and received a fulness of joy. While you are going through your trial, you can recall your past victories and count the blessings that you do have with a sure hope of greater ones to follow if you are faithful. And you can have that certain knowledge that in due time God will wipe away all tears and that "eye hath not seen, nor ear heard, neither have entered into the heart of man, the things which God hath prepared for them that love him." (1 Cor. 2:9.)[11]

"To live happily is to grow in spiritual strength toward perfection."

Be cheerful in all that you do. Live joyfully. Live happily. Live enthusiastically, knowing that God does not dwell in gloom and melancholy, but in light and love.[12]

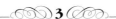

3

Heavenly Father wants us to be happy, and He will bless us as we follow His will for us.

"Men are that they might have joy" (2 Nephi 2:25). Our Heavenly Father wants us to be happy. He expects us to be happy. But there is no happiness in a letting down of standards. There is no happiness when you fail to live according to your convictions, according to that which you know to be right. It is so easy to form the habit of taking it just a little easy on certain things. It is so easy to form the habit of faultfinding, or criticizing, of carrying in our hearts reservations regarding certain things in the Church. It is so easy for us to become a bit bitter, and then dwell on that, to become sad and carry a sad face with us. A sad face never won a battle in war or love.[13]

Do we realize that happiness here and now consists in freely, lovingly, joyfully acknowledging God's will for us—and doing it in all ways and all affairs big and small? To live perfectly is to live happily. To live happily is to grow in spiritual strength toward perfection. Every action performed in accord with God's will is part of that growth. Let us not partition our lives. Let us unify our lives, being contemptuous of fictitious honors and glories that do not come with God's approval. Let us remember that the real source of our strength and happiness is beyond the reach of men and circumstances.[14]

We must learn and learn again that only through accepting and living the gospel of love as taught by the Master and only through doing His will can we break the bonds of ignorance and doubt that bind us. We must learn this simple, glorious truth so that we can experience the sweet joys of the Spirit now and eternally. We must lose ourselves in doing His will. We must place Him first in our lives. Yes, our blessings multiply as we share His love with our neighbor.[15]

"Brethren," said Paul, "but this one thing I do, forgetting those things which are behind, and reaching forth unto those things which are before,

"I press toward the mark for the prize of the high calling of God in Christ Jesus." (Philip. 3:13–14.)

Let your minds be filled with the goal of being like the Lord, and you will crowd out depressing thoughts as you anxiously seek to know him and do his will. "Let this mind be in you," said Paul. (Philip. 2:5.) "Look unto me in every thought," said Jesus. (D&C 6:36.) And what will follow if we do? "Thou wilt keep him in perfect peace, whose mind is stayed on thee." (Isa. 26:3.)[16]

We will never be alone if we live as we should, because our Father will always be with us to bless us. He wants us to be successful. He wants us to be happy. He wants us to achieve the good goals we set. He will do His part if we do our part.[17]

Suggestions for Study and Teaching

Questions

- Why do you think faith in God gives us "hope for the future, and optimism in our present tasks"? Which words of counsel from section 1 might you share with someone who yearns for inner peace? Why would you choose those words?

- As you review section 2, reflect on a time when you needed to "righteously hang on" during adversity. Consider what you have gained from that experience. In what ways does the Lord help us when we are willing to endure trials faithfully?

- What are some experiences that have helped you know that Heavenly Father wants you to be happy and successful? Why do you think "happiness here and now consists in . . . acknowledging God's will for us"? (See section 3.)

Related Scriptures

Matthew 11:28–30; John 14:27; 16:33; Galatians 5:22; Mosiah 2:41; Moroni 9:25–26; D&C 101:11–16

Study Help

"Get an overview, either by reading the book, chapter, or passage quickly or by reviewing headings. Seek to understand the context and background" (*Preach My Gospel* [2004], 23). Consider reading a chapter or passage more than once so you can understand it more deeply. As you do so, you may uncover profound insights.

Notes

1. *A Labor of Love: The 1946 European Mission of Ezra Taft Benson* (1989), 64, 65.
2. *A Labor of Love,* 65.
3. "Receive All Things with Thankfulness," *New Era,* Nov. 1976, 7–8.
4. Neal A. Maxwell, *Wherefore, Ye Must Press Forward* (1977), 69.
5. *The Teachings of Ezra Taft Benson* (1988), 68.
6. *The Teachings of Ezra Taft Benson,* 68.
7. "Do Not Despair," *Ensign,* Oct. 1986, 2.
8. *The Teachings of Ezra Taft Benson,* 67.
9. "Do Not Despair," 2.
10. *The Teachings of Ezra Taft Benson,* 342.
11. "Do Not Despair," 4–5; the statement by Joseph Smith is found in *Teachings of Presidents of the Church: Joseph Smith* (2007), 235.
12. *The Teachings of Ezra Taft Benson,* 339.
13. *The Teachings of Ezra Taft Benson,* 361.
14. *The Teachings of Ezra Taft Benson,* 339.
15. *The Teachings of Ezra Taft Benson,* 360.
16. "Do Not Despair," 5.
17. *The Teachings of Ezra Taft Benson,* 385.

*The Lord said, "My grace is sufficient for all men
that humble themselves before me" (Ether 12:27).*

Principles of True Repentance

"For those who pay the price required by true repentance, the promise is sure. You can be clean again. The despair can be lifted. The sweet peace of forgiveness will flow into your lives."

From the Life of Ezra Taft Benson

In his first general conference address as President of the Church, President Ezra Taft Benson stated: "As I have sought direction from the Lord, I have had reaffirmed in my mind and heart the declaration of the Lord to 'say nothing but repentance unto this generation.' (D&C 6:9; 11:9.) This has been a theme of every latter-day prophet."[1]

Even before his call as President of the Church, President Benson made repentance an important theme of his ministry. He had been counseled to do so by George Albert Smith, President of the Quorum of the Twelve Apostles at the time. In a letter written not long after President Benson's call to the apostleship, President Smith said, "Your mission from now on is to find ways and means to disseminate the truth and warn the people that you come in contact with in as kind a way as possible that repentance will be the only panacea for the ills of this world."[2]

President Benson was faithful to this charge as he taught the gospel throughout the world. He taught that "it is better to prepare and prevent than it is to repair and repent."[3] But he also observed that "we all have need to repent."[4] He emphasized the "mighty change" of heart associated with repentance (see Alma 5:12–14) and explained the Savior's role in bringing about such change:

"The Lord works from the inside out. The world works from the outside in. The world would take people out of the slums. Christ takes the slums out of people, and then they take themselves out of the slums. The world would mold men by changing their environment. Christ changes men, who then change their environment. The world would shape human behavior, but Christ can change human nature. . . .

"Yes, Christ changes men, and changed men can change the world."[5]

Teachings of Ezra Taft Benson

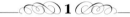 **1**

To truly repent, we must first realize that the gospel plan is the plan of happiness.

In the usual sense of the term, *Church membership* means that a person has his or her name officially recorded on the membership records of the Church. . . .

But the Lord defines a member of His kingdom in quite a different way. In 1828, through the Prophet Joseph Smith, He said, "Behold, this is my doctrine—whosoever repenteth and cometh unto me, *the same is my church.*" (D&C 10:67; italics added.) To Him whose Church this is, membership involves far more than simply being a member of record.

I would therefore like to set forth important concepts that we must understand and apply if we are to truly repent and come unto the Lord.

One of Satan's most frequently used deceptions is the notion that the commandments of God are meant to restrict freedom and limit happiness. Young people especially sometimes feel that the standards of the Lord are like fences and chains, blocking them from those activities that seem most enjoyable in life. But exactly the opposite is true. The gospel plan is *the* plan by which men are brought to a fulness of joy. This is the first concept I wish to stress. The gospel principles are the steps and guidelines that will help us find true happiness and joy.

The understanding of this concept caused the Psalmist to exclaim, "O how love I thy law! . . . Thou through thy commandments hast made me wiser than mine enemies. . . . Thy word is a lamp unto my feet, and a light unto my path. . . . Thy testimonies have I taken as an heritage for ever: for they are the rejoicing of my heart." (Ps. 119:97–98, 105, 111.)

If we wish to truly repent and come unto Him so that we can be called members of His Church, we must first and foremost come to realize this eternal truth—the gospel plan is *the* plan of happiness. *Wickedness never did, never does, never will* bring us happiness [see Alma 41:10]. Violation of the laws of God brings only misery, bondage, and darkness.[6]

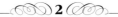

2

Faith in Jesus Christ precedes true repentance.

A second concept that is important to our understanding is the relationship of repentance to the principle of faith. Repentance is the second fundamental principle of the gospel. The first is that we must have faith in the Lord Jesus Christ. Why is this so? Why must faith in the Lord precede true repentance?

To answer this question, we must understand something about the atoning sacrifice of the Master. Lehi taught that "no flesh . . . can dwell in the presence of God, save it be through the merits, and mercy, and grace of the Holy Messiah." (2 Ne. 2:8.) Even the most just and upright man cannot save himself solely on his own merits, for, as the Apostle Paul tells us, "all have sinned, and come short of the glory of God." (Rom. 3:23.)

If it were not for the perfect, sinless life of the Savior, which He willingly laid down for us, there could be no remission of sins.

Therefore, repentance means more than simply a reformation of behavior. Many men and women in the world demonstrate great willpower and self-discipline in overcoming bad habits and the weaknesses of the flesh. Yet at the same time they give no thought to the Master, sometimes even openly rejecting Him. Such changes of behavior, even if in a positive direction, do not constitute true repentance.

Faith in the Lord Jesus Christ is the foundation upon which sincere and meaningful repentance must be built. If we truly seek to put away sin, we must first look to Him who is the Author of our salvation.[7]

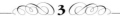

Repentance involves a mighty change of heart.

The third important principle for us to understand if we would be true members of the Church is that repentance involves not just a change of actions, but a change of heart.

When King Benjamin finished his remarkable address in the land of Zarahemla, the people all cried with one voice that they believed his words. They knew of a surety that his promises of redemption were true, because, said they, "the Spirit of the Lord Omnipotent . . . has wrought a mighty change in us, or in our hearts, [and note this] that we have no more disposition to do evil, but to do good continually." (Mosiah 5:2.)[8]

Can human hearts be changed? Why, of course! It happens every day in the great missionary work of the Church. It is one of the most widespread of Christ's modern miracles. If it hasn't happened to you—it should.

Our Lord told Nicodemus that "except a man be born again, he cannot see the kingdom of God." (John 3:3.) . . .

Alma states: "And the Lord said unto me: Marvel not that all mankind, yea, men and women, all nations, kindreds, tongues and people, must be born again; yea, born of God, changed from their carnal and fallen state, to a state of righteousness, being redeemed of God, becoming his sons and daughters;

"And thus they become new creatures; and unless they do this, they can in nowise inherit the kingdom of God." (Mosiah 27:25–26.) . . .

The fourth chapter of Alma describes a period in Nephite history when "the church began to fail in its progress." (Alma 4:10.) Alma met this challenge by resigning his seat as chief judge in government "and confined himself wholly to the high priesthood" responsibility which was his. (Alma 4:20.)

He bore down "in pure testimony" against the people (Alma 4:19), and in the fifth chapter of Alma he asks over forty crucial questions. Speaking frankly to the members of the Church, he declared, "I ask of you, my brethren of the church, have ye spiritually

*Through repentance, Alma the Younger experienced
a miraculous change of heart.*

been born of God? Have ye received his image in your countenances? Have ye experienced this mighty change in your hearts?" (Alma 5:14.)

He continued, "If ye have experienced a change of heart, and if ye have felt to sing the song of redeeming love, I would ask, can ye feel so now?" (Alma 5:26.)

Would not the progress of the Church increase dramatically today with an increasing number of those who are spiritually reborn? Can you imagine what would happen in our homes? Can you imagine what would happen with an increasing number of copies of the Book of Mormon in the hands of an increasing number of missionaries who know how to use it and who have been born of God? When this happens, we will get the bounteous harvest of souls that the Lord promised. It was the "born of God" Alma who as a missionary was so able to impart the word that many others were also born of God. (See Alma 36:23–26.)[9]

When we have undergone this mighty change, which is brought about only through faith in Jesus Christ and through the operation of the Spirit upon us, it is as though we have become a new person. Thus, the change is likened to a new birth. Thousands of you have experienced this change. You have forsaken lives of sin, sometimes deep and offensive sin, and through applying the blood of Christ in your lives, have become clean. You have no more disposition to return to your old ways. You are in reality a new person. This is what is meant by a change of heart.[10]

 **4**

Godly sorrow leads to true repentance.

The fourth concept I would like to stress is what the scriptures term "godly sorrow" for our sins. It is not uncommon to find men and women in the world who feel remorse for the things they do wrong. Sometimes this is because their actions cause them or loved ones great sorrow and misery. Sometimes their sorrow is caused because they are caught and punished for their actions. Such worldly feelings do not constitute "godly sorrow."

. . . In the final days of the Nephite nation, Mormon said of his people: "their sorrowing was not unto repentance, because of the goodness of God; but it was rather the sorrowing of the damned, because the Lord would not always suffer them to take happiness in sin.

"And they did not come unto Jesus with broken hearts and contrite spirits, but they did curse God, and wish to die." (Morm. 2:13–14.)

In the Eastern Hemisphere, the Apostle Paul labored among the people of Corinth. After reports came of serious problems among the Saints, including immorality (see 1 Cor. 5:1), Paul wrote a sharp letter of rebuke. The people responded in the proper spirit, and evidently the problems were corrected, for in his second epistle to them, Paul wrote: "Now I rejoice, not that ye were made sorry, but that ye sorrowed to repentance: for ye were made sorry after a godly manner. . . .

"For godly sorrow worketh repentance to salvation not to be repented of: but the sorrow of the world worketh death." (2 Cor. 7:9–10.)

In both of these scriptures, godly sorrow is defined as a sorrow that leads us to repentance.

Godly sorrow is a gift of the Spirit. It is a deep realization that our actions have offended our Father and our God. It is the sharp and keen awareness that our behavior caused the Savior, He who knew no sin, even the greatest of all, to endure agony and suffering. Our sins caused Him to bleed at every pore. This very real mental and spiritual anguish is what the scriptures refer to as having "a broken heart and a contrite spirit." (See 3 Ne. 9:20; Moro. 6:2; D&C 20:37; 59:8; Ps. 34:18; 51:17; Isa. 57:15.) Such a spirit is the absolute prerequisite for true repentance.[11]

5

Heavenly Father and Jesus Christ are anxious to see us change our lives, and They will help us.

The next principle I would like to discuss is this: No one is more anxious to see us change our lives than the Father and the Savior. In the book of Revelation is a powerful and profound invitation from the Savior. He says, "I stand at the door, and knock: if any man hear my voice, and open the door, I will come in to him." (Rev. 3:20.) Note that He does not say, "I stand at the door and wait for you to knock." He is calling, beckoning, asking that we simply open our hearts and let Him in.

In Moroni's great sermon on faith, the principle is even more clearly taught. He was told by the Lord, "If men come unto me I will show unto them their weakness. I give unto men weakness that they may be humble; and my grace is sufficient for all men." It matters not what is our lack or our weakness or our insufficiency. His gifts and powers are sufficient to overcome them all.

Moroni continues with the words of the Lord: "My grace is sufficient for all men that humble themselves before me; for if they humble themselves before me, and have faith in me, *then will I make weak things become strong unto them.*" (Ether 12:27; italics added.)

What a promise from the Lord! The very source of our troubles can be changed, molded, and formed into a strength and a source of power. This promise is repeated in one form or another in many other scriptures. Isaiah said, "He giveth power to the faint; and to them that have no might he increaseth strength." (Isa. 40:29.) Paul was told by the Lord, "My grace is sufficient for thee: for my strength is made perfect in weakness." (2 Cor. 12:9.) In the Doctrine and Covenants we read, "He that trembleth under my power shall be made strong, and shall bring forth fruits of praise and wisdom." (D&C 52:17; see also 1 Ne. 17:3; 2 Ne. 3:13; D&C 1:28; 133:58–59.)[12]

One of Satan's most effective strategies with those whom he has lured into sin is to whisper in their ears that they are not worthy to pray. He will tell you that Heavenly Father is so displeased with you that He will never hear your prayers. This is a lie, and he says it to deceive us. The power of sin is great. If we are to extricate ourselves from it, especially serious sin, we must have a power greater than ourselves.

No one is more anxious to help you flee from sin than your Heavenly Father. Go to Him. Acknowledge your sin, confess your shame and your guilt, and then plead with Him for help. He has the power to help you triumph.[13]

Brothers and sisters, we must take our sins to the Lord in humble and sorrowful repentance. We must plead with Him for power to overcome them. The promises are sure. He will come to our aid. We will find the power to change our lives.[14]

_____ 6 _____

We must not lose hope as we seek to become Christlike.

The sixth and final point I wish to make about the process of repentance is that we must be careful, as we seek to become more and more godlike, that we do not become discouraged and lose hope. Becoming Christlike is a lifetime pursuit and very often involves growth and change that is slow, almost imperceptible. The scriptures record remarkable accounts of men whose lives changed dramatically, in an instant, as it were: Alma the Younger, Paul on the road to Damascus, Enos praying far into the night, King Lamoni. Such astonishing examples of the power to change even those

*"True repentance is based on and flows from faith
in the Lord Jesus Christ. There is no other way."*

steeped in sin give confidence that the Atonement can reach even
those deepest in despair.

But we must be cautious as we discuss these remarkable examples. Though they are real and powerful, they are the exception
more than the rule. For every Paul, for every Enos, and for every
King Lamoni, there are hundreds and thousands of people who find
the process of repentance much more subtle, much more imperceptible. Day by day they move closer to the Lord, little realizing they
are building a godlike life. They live quiet lives of goodness, service,
and commitment. They are like the Lamanites, who the Lord said
"were baptized with fire and with the Holy Ghost, *and they knew
it not.*" (3 Ne. 9:20; italics added.)

We must not lose hope. Hope is an anchor to the souls of men.
Satan would have us cast away that anchor. In this way he can bring
discouragement and surrender. But we must not lose hope. The
Lord is pleased with every effort, even the tiny, daily ones in which

we strive to be more like Him. Though we may see that we have far to go on the road to perfection, we must not give up hope.[15]

For those who pay the price required by true repentance, the promise is sure. You can be clean again. The despair can be lifted. The sweet peace of forgiveness will flow into your lives.

The words of the Lord through Isaiah are sure: "Come now, and let us reason together, saith the Lord: though your sins be as scarlet, they shall be as white as snow; though they be red like crimson, they shall be as wool" (Isa. 1:18).

And in this dispensation the Lord spoke with equal clarity when He said, "Behold, he who has repented of his sins, the same is forgiven, and I, the Lord, remember them no more" (D&C 58:42).[16]

I hope we will not live in the past. People who live in the past don't have very much future. There is a great tendency for us to lament about our losses, about decisions that we have made that we think in retrospect were probably wrong decisions. There is a great tendency for us to feel badly about the circumstances with which we are surrounded, thinking they might have been better had we made different decisions. We can profit by the experience of the past. But let us not spend our time worrying about decisions that have been made, mistakes that have been made. Let us live in the present and in the future.[17]

My beloved brothers and sisters, as we seek to qualify to be members of Christ's Church—members in the sense in which He uses the term, members who have repented and come unto Him—let us remember these six principles. First, the gospel is the Lord's plan of happiness, and repentance is designed to bring us joy. Second, true repentance is based on and flows from faith in the Lord Jesus Christ. There is no other way. Third, true repentance involves a change of heart and not just a change of behavior. Fourth, part of this mighty change of heart is to feel godly sorrow for our sins. This is what is meant by a broken heart and a contrite spirit. Fifth, God's gifts are sufficient to help us overcome every sin and weakness if we will but turn to Him for help. Finally, we must remember that most repentance does not involve sensational or dramatic changes, but rather is a step-by-step, steady, and consistent movement toward godliness.

If we will strive to incorporate these principles into our lives and implement them on a daily basis, we shall then qualify to be more than members of record in the Church of Jesus Christ. As true members, we have claim to His promise: "Whosoever is of my church, and endureth of my church to the end, him will I establish upon my rock, and the gates of hell shall not prevail against them." (D&C 10:69.)

My prayer is that we may all win that promise for ourselves.[18]

Suggestions for Study and Teaching

Questions

- President Benson said that to truly repent, we must first realize that "the gospel plan is *the* plan of happiness" and that wickedness "*never will* bring us happiness" (section 1). Why do you think this understanding is essential in the repentance process?

- In our efforts to repent, why is a change of behavior not enough? (See section 2.) Why do you think we need to look to Jesus Christ in order to truly repent?

- In what ways have you experienced a "mighty change of heart," as explained in section 3? What can we do to help others experience this change?

- In what ways is "godly sorrow" different from the regret some people feel when they have done something wrong? (See section 4.) How might a parent or bishop use the teachings in section 4 to help someone who needs to repent?

- As you review section 5, what teachings do you find particularly comforting? Why are these teachings comforting for you?

- Testifying of the power of the Savior's Atonement, President Benson said, "We must not lose hope" (section 6). As you review section 6, what truths about the Atonement do you find that offer you hope?

Related Scriptures

Luke 15:11–32; Mosiah 4:10–12; 26:30–31; Alma 34:17–18; 3 Nephi 27:19–20; D&C 18:10–16; 19:15–19

Teaching Help

"Your main concern should be helping others learn the gospel, not making an impressive presentation. This includes providing opportunities for learners to teach one another" (*Teaching, No Greater Call* [1999], 64).

Notes

1. "Cleansing the Inner Vessel," *Ensign,* May 1986, 4.
2. In Sheri L. Dew, *Ezra Taft Benson: A Biography* (1987), 184.
3. "The Law of Chastity," *New Era,* Jan. 1988, 6.
4. In Conference Report, Apr. 1955, 47.
5. "Born of God," *Ensign,* July 1989, 4.
6. "A Mighty Change of Heart," *Ensign,* Oct. 1989, 2.
7. "A Mighty Change of Heart," 2.
8. "A Mighty Change of Heart," 2, 4.
9. "Born of God," 2, 4.
10. "A Mighty Change of Heart," 4.
11. "A Mighty Change of Heart," 4.
12. "A Mighty Change of Heart," 4–5.
13. "The Law of Chastity," 7.
14. "A Mighty Change of Heart," 5.
15. "A Mighty Change of Heart," 5.
16. "The Law of Chastity," 7.
17. *The Teachings of Ezra Taft Benson* (1988), 387.
18. "A Mighty Change of Heart," 5.

Jesus Christ, Our Savior and Redeemer

"We declare the divinity of Jesus Christ. We look to Him as the only source of our salvation."

From the Life of Ezra Taft Benson

"I cannot recall a time that I did not believe in Jesus Christ," President Ezra Taft Benson said. "It seems that the reality of His life, death, and resurrection has always been a part of me. I was reared in a home by faithful parents who earnestly believed in and testified of Christ, for which I am most grateful." [1]

This testimony of Jesus Christ was the foundation of President Benson's life. It shaped his priorities, guided his decisions, and helped him through trials. It provided perspective on the purpose of mortality and confidence in the promises and blessings of eternal life.

During his apostolic ministry as a special witness of Jesus Christ, President Benson frequently bore testimony of the Savior. Acknowledging that "the question is sometimes asked, 'Are Mormons Christians?'" he testified:

"We declare the divinity of Jesus Christ. We look to Him as the only source of our salvation. We strive to live His teachings, and we look forward to the time that He shall come again on this earth to rule and reign as King of Kings and Lord of Lords. In the words of a Book of Mormon prophet, we say . . . , 'There [is] no other name given nor any other way nor means whereby salvation can come unto the children of men, only in and through the name of Christ, the Lord Omnipotent' (Mosiah 3:17)." [2]

President Benson's declarations of the divinity of Jesus Christ were often linked to the Book of Mormon. [3] "Through the Book of

"No event could be more important to individuals
or nations than the resurrection of the Master."

Mormon God has provided for our day tangible evidence that Jesus is the Christ," he said.[4] He taught that the Book of Mormon's "major mission" is to convince people of this truth.[5] "Over one-half of all the verses in the Book of Mormon refer to our Lord," he noted. "He is given over one hundred different names in the Book of Mormon. Those names have a particular significance in describing His divine nature."[6]

President Benson's testimony of the Savior revealed the personal closeness he felt with Him:

"With all my soul, I love Him.

"I humbly testify that He is the same loving, compassionate Lord today as when He walked the dusty roads of Palestine. He is close to His servants on this earth. He cares about and loves each of us today. Of that you can be assured.

"He lives today as our Lord, our Master, our Savior, our Redeemer, and our God.

"God bless us all to believe in Him, to accept Him, to worship Him, to fully trust in Him, and to follow Him."[7]

Teachings of Ezra Taft Benson

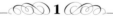 1

Because of His infinite love for us, Jesus Christ redeemed us from physical and spiritual death.

No other single influence has had so great an impact on this earth as the life of Jesus the Christ. We cannot conceive of our lives without His teachings. Without Him we would be lost in a mirage of beliefs and worships born in fear and darkness where the sensual and materialistic hold sway. We are far short of the goal He set for us, but we must never lose sight of it, nor must we forget that our great climb toward the light, toward perfection, would not be possible except for His teaching, His life, His death, and His resurrection.[8]

To have any measure of appreciation and gratitude for what [Jesus Christ] accomplished in our behalf, we must remember these vital truths:

Jesus came to earth to do our Father's will.

He came with a foreknowledge that He would bear the burden of the sins of us all.

He knew he would be lifted up on the cross.

He was born to be the Savior and Redeemer of all mankind.

He was *able* to accomplish His mission because He was the Son of God and He possessed the power of God.

He was *willing* to accomplish His mission because He loves us.

No mortal being had the power or capability to redeem all other mortals from their lost and fallen condition, nor could any other voluntarily forfeit his life and thereby bring to pass a universal resurrection for all other mortals.

Only Jesus Christ was able and willing to accomplish such a redeeming act of love.[9]

Jesus Christ . . . came to this earth at a fore-appointed time through a royal birthright that preserved His godhood. Combined in His nature were the human attributes of His mortal mother and the divine attributes and powers of His Eternal Father.

His unique heredity made Him heir to the honored title—The Only Begotten Son of God in the flesh. As the Son of God, He inherited powers and intelligence which no human ever had before or since. He was literally Immanuel, which means "God with us." (See Isa. 7:14; Matt. 1:23.)

Even though He was God's Son sent to earth, the divine plan of the Father required that Jesus be subjected to all the difficulties and tribulations of mortality. Thus He became subject to "temptations, . . . hunger, thirst, and fatigue." (Mosiah 3:7.)

To qualify as the *Redeemer* of all our Father's children, Jesus had to be perfectly obedient to all the laws of God. Because He subjected Himself to the will of the Father, He grew "from grace to grace, until he received a fulness" of the Father's power. Thus He had "all power, both in heaven and on earth." (D&C 93:13, 17.)[10]

Because [Jesus] was God—even the Son of God—He could carry the weight and burden of other men's sins on Himself. Isaiah

*"No other single influence has had so great an impact
on this earth as the life of Jesus the Christ."*

prophesied [of] our Savior's willingness to do this in these words:
"Surely he hath borne our griefs, and carried our sorrows: . . . he
was wounded for our transgressions, he was bruised for our iniquities: the chastisement of our peace was upon him; and with his
stripes we are healed." (Isa. 53:4–5.)

That holy, unselfish act of voluntarily taking on Himself the sins
of all other men is the Atonement. How *One* could bear the sins for
all is beyond the comprehension of mortal man. But this I know:
He did take on Himself the sins of all and did so out of His infinite
love for each of us. He has said: "For behold, I, God, have suffered
these things for all, that they might not suffer if they would repent;
. . . which suffering caused myself, even God, the greatest of all, to
tremble because of pain, and to bleed at every pore, and to suffer
both body and spirit—and would that I might not drink the bitter
cup, and shrink." (D&C 19:16, 18.)

In spite of that excruciating ordeal, He took the cup and drank.
He suffered the pains of all men so we would not have to suffer.

He endured the humiliation and insults of His persecutors without complaint or retaliation. He bore the flogging and then the ignominy of the brutal execution—the cross.[11]

In Gethsemane and on Calvary, [Jesus] worked out the infinite and eternal atonement. It was the greatest single act of love in recorded history. Then followed His death and resurrection.

Thus He became our Redeemer—redeeming all of us from physical death, and redeeming those of us from spiritual death who will obey the laws and ordinances of the gospel.[12]

We may never understand nor comprehend in mortality *how* He accomplished what He did, but we must not fail to understand *why* He did what He did.

Everything He did was prompted by His unselfish, infinite love for us.[13]

Jesus Christ came forth from the tomb, and He lives today as a resurrected being.

The greatest events of history are those that affect the greatest number of people for the longest periods. By this standard, no event could be more important to individuals or nations than the resurrection of the Master.

The literal resurrection of every soul who has lived and died on earth is a certainty, and surely one should make careful preparation for this event. A glorious resurrection should be the goal of every man and woman, for resurrection will be a reality.

Nothing is more absolutely universal than the resurrection. Every living being will be resurrected. "As in Adam all die, even so in Christ shall all be made alive." (1 Cor. 15:22.)

The scriptural record tells us that on the third day following Jesus' crucifixion, there was a great earthquake. The stone was rolled back from the door of the tomb. Some of the women, among the most devoted of His followers, came to the place with spices "and found not the body of the Lord Jesus."

Angels appeared and said simply, "Why seek ye the living among the dead? He is not here, but is risen." (Luke 24:3–6.) Nothing in history equals that dramatic announcement: "He is not here, but is risen."

The fact of our Lord's resurrection is based on the testimonies of *many* credible witnesses. The risen Lord appeared to several women, to the two disciples on the road to Emmaus, to Peter, to the Apostles; and "after that," as Paul reported, "he was seen of above five hundred brethren at once. . . . And last of all he was seen of [Paul] also." (1 Cor. 15:6, 8.) . . .

As one of His latter-day witnesses, I testify that He lives today. He is a resurrected Being. He is our Savior, our Lord, the very Son of God. I testify that He will come again as our glorified, resurrected Lord. That day is not far distant. To all who accept Him as Savior and Lord, His literal resurrection means that life does not end at death, for He promised: "Because I live, ye shall live also." (John 14:19.)[14]

He alone had the power of resurrection. And so on the third day following His burial, He came forth from the tomb alive and showed Himself to many. . . . As one of [His] special witnesses so called in this day, I testify to you that He lives. He lives with a resurrected body. There is no truth or fact of which I am more assured or more confident than the truth of the literal resurrection of our Lord.[15]

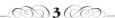

3

We must be valiant in our testimony of Jesus Christ.

A most priceless blessing available to every member of the Church is a testimony of the divinity of Jesus Christ and His church. A testimony is one of the few possessions we may take with us when we leave this life.

To have a testimony of Jesus is to possess knowledge through the Holy Ghost of the divine mission of Jesus Christ.

A testimony of Jesus is to know the divine nature of our Lord's birth—that He is indeed the *Only* Begotten Son in the flesh.

A testimony of Jesus is to know that He was the promised Messiah and that while He sojourned among men He accomplished many mighty miracles.

A testimony of Jesus is to know that the laws which He prescribed as His doctrine are true and then to abide by these laws and ordinances.

To possess a testimony of Jesus is to know that He voluntarily took upon Himself the sins of all mankind in the Garden of Gethsemane, which caused Him to suffer in both body and spirit and to bleed from every pore. All this He did so that we would not have to suffer if we would repent. (See D&C 19:16, 18.)

To possess a testimony of Jesus is to know that He came forth triumphantly from the grave with a physical, resurrected body. And because He lives, so shall all mankind.

To possess a testimony of Jesus is to know that God the Father and Jesus Christ did indeed appear to the Prophet Joseph Smith to establish a new dispensation of His gospel so that salvation may be preached to all nations before He comes.

To possess a testimony of Jesus is to know that the Church, which He established in the meridian of time and restored in modern times is, as the Lord has declared, "the only true and living church upon the face of the whole earth." (D&C 1:30.)

Having such a testimony is vital. But of even greater importance is being valiant in our testimony.

A testimony of Jesus means that we accept the divine mission of Jesus Christ, embrace His gospel, and do His works. It also means we accept the prophetic mission of Joseph Smith and his successors and follow their counsel. As Jesus said, "Whether by mine own voice or by the voice of my servants, it is the same." (D&C 1:38.)

Speaking of those who will eventually receive the blessings of the celestial kingdom, the Lord said to Joseph Smith:

"They are they who received the testimony of Jesus, and believed on his name and were baptized after the manner of his burial, being buried in the water in his name, and this according to the commandment which he has given." (D&C 76:51.)

These are they who are valiant in their testimony of Jesus, who, as the Lord has declared, "overcome by faith, and are sealed by the

Holy Spirit of promise, which the Father sheds forth upon all those who are just and true." (D&C 76:53.)[16]

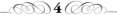

Faith in Jesus Christ consists of relying completely on Him and following His teachings.

The fundamental principle of our religion is faith in the Lord Jesus Christ. Why is it expedient that we center our confidence, our hope, and our trust in one solitary figure? Why is faith in Him so necessary to peace of mind in this life and hope in the world to come?

Our answers to these questions determine whether we face the future with courage, hope, and optimism or with apprehension, anxiety, and pessimism.

My message and testimony is this: Only Jesus Christ is uniquely qualified to provide that hope, that confidence, and that strength we need to overcome the world and rise above our human failings. To do so, we must place our faith in Him and live by His laws and teachings. . . .

Faith in Him is more than mere acknowledgment that He lives. It is more than professing belief.

Faith in Jesus Christ consists of complete reliance on Him. As God, He has infinite power, intelligence, and love. There is no human problem beyond His capacity to solve. Because He descended below all things (see D&C 122:8), He knows how to help us rise above our daily difficulties.

Faith in Him means believing that even though we do not understand all things, He does. We, therefore, must look to Him "in every thought; doubt not, fear not." (D&C 6:36.)

Faith in Him means trusting that He has all power over all men and all nations. There is no evil which He cannot arrest. All things are in His hands. This earth is His rightful dominion. Yet He permits evil so that we can make choices between good and evil.

His gospel is the perfect prescription for all human problems and social ills.

"Come ye after me" (Mark 1:17).

But His gospel is only effective as it is applied in our lives. Therefore, we must "feast upon the words of Christ; for behold, the words of Christ will tell you all things what ye should do." (2 Ne. 32:3.)

Unless we *do* His teachings, we do not demonstrate faith in Him.

Think what a different world this would be if all mankind would do as He said: "Love the Lord thy God with all thy heart, and with all thy soul, and with all thy mind. . . . Thou shalt love thy neighbour as thyself." (Matt. 22:37, 39.)

What then is the answer to the question "What is to be done concerning the problems and dilemmas that individuals, communities, and nations face today?" Here is His simple prescription:

"Believe in God; believe that he is, and that he created all things, both in heaven and in earth; believe that he has *all* wisdom, and *all* power, both in heaven and in earth; believe that man doth not comprehend all the things which the Lord can comprehend. . . .

"Believe that ye must repent of your sins and forsake them, and humble yourselves before God; and ask in sincerity of heart that he would forgive you; and now, if you believe all these things, *see that ye do them.*" (Mosiah 4:9–10; italics added.)[17]

We are most blessed and joyful when we strive to be like Jesus Christ.

One of the purposes of this life is for us to be tested to see whether we "will do all things whatsoever the Lord" our God shall command us. (Abr. 3:25.) In short, we are to learn the will of the Lord and do it. We are to follow the model of Jesus Christ and be like Him.

The essential question of life should be the same one posed by Paul: "Lord, what wilt thou have me to do?" (Acts 9:6.) . . .

We need more men and women of Christ who will always remember Him, who will keep His commandments which He has given them. The greatest yardstick of success is to see how closely we can walk each moment in His steps.[18]

Some . . . are willing to die for their faith, but they are not willing to fully live for it. Christ both lived and died for us. Through His atonement and by walking in His steps, we can gain the greatest gift of all—eternal life, which is that kind of life of the great Eternal One—our Father in Heaven.

Christ asked the question, "What manner of men ought [we] to be?" He then answered by saying we ought to be even as He is. (3 Ne. 27:27.)

That [person] is greatest and most blessed and joyful whose life most closely approaches the pattern of the Christ. This has nothing to do with earthly wealth, power, or prestige. The only true test of greatness, blessedness, joyfulness is how close a life can come to being like the Master, Jesus Christ. He is the right way, the full truth, and the abundant life.

The constant and most recurring question in our minds, touching every thought and deed of our lives, should be, "Lord, what wilt thou have me to do?" (Acts 9:6.) The answer to that question comes only through the Light of Christ and the Holy Ghost. Fortunate are those who so live that their being is filled with both. . . .

Considering all that [Jesus Christ] has done and is doing for us, there is something that we might give Him in return.

Christ's great gift to us was His life and sacrifice. Should that not then be our small gift to Him—our lives and sacrifices, not only now but in the future?[19]

[Those who are] captained by Christ will be consumed in Christ. . . . Their will is swallowed up in His will. (See John 5:30.) They do always those things that please the Lord. (See John 8:29.) Not only would they die for the Lord, but, more important, they want to live for Him.

Enter their homes, and the pictures on their walls, the books on their shelves, the music in the air, their words and acts reveal them as Christians. They stand as witnesses of God at all times, and in all things, and in all places. (See Mosiah 18:9.) They have Christ on their minds, as they look unto Him in every thought. (See D&C 6:36.) They have Christ in their hearts as their affections are placed on Him forever. (See Alma 37:36.)

Almost every week they partake of the sacrament and witness anew to their Eternal Father that they are willing to take upon them the name of His Son, always remember Him, and keep His commandments. (See Moro. 4:3.)

In Book of Mormon language, they "feast upon the words of Christ" (2 Ne. 32:3), "talk of Christ" (2 Ne. 25:26), "rejoice in Christ" (2 Ne. 25:26), "are made alive in Christ" (2 Ne. 25:25), and "glory in [their] Jesus" (see 2 Ne. 33:6). In short, they lose themselves in the Lord and find eternal life. (See Luke 17:33.)[20]

Suggestions for Study and Teaching

Questions
- President Benson taught that while we cannot completely understand *how* the Savior carried out the Atonement, we can understand *why* He did it (see section 1). In what ways does this understanding influence your life?

- As you study section 2, think about the impact of the Savior's Resurrection. How does His Resurrection influence your life?

- Why do you think a testimony of Jesus Christ is "a most priceless blessing"? (See section 3.) What does it mean to you to be valiant in your testimony of the Savior?

- Ponder President Benson's words about faith in Jesus Christ (see section 4). In what ways does this description of faith in Christ go beyond "mere acknowledgment that He lives"?

- President Benson said that people who are "captained by Christ" are willing to "die for the Lord, but, more important, they want to live for Him" (section 5). What does it mean to you to live for the Savior?

Related Scriptures

John 10:17–18; 2 Nephi 9:20–24; 31:20–21; Mosiah 16:6–11; 3 Nephi 27:20–22; Moroni 7:33; D&C 19:1–3, 16–19; 76:22–24; Articles of Faith 1:3

Study Help

"As you feel the joy that comes from understanding the gospel, you will want to apply what you learn. Strive to live in harmony with your understanding. Doing so will strengthen your faith, knowledge, and testimony" (*Preach My Gospel* [2004], 19).

Notes

1. "The Meaning of Easter," *Ensign,* Apr. 1992, 2.

2. *The Teachings of Ezra Taft Benson* (1988), 10.

3. See "Come unto Christ," *Ensign,* Nov. 1987, 83–85; "I Testify," *Ensign,* Nov. 1988, 86–87.

4. "I Testify," 86.

5. "Come unto Christ," 83; see also "Born of God," *Ensign,* July 1989, 2.

6. "Come unto Christ," 83.

7. "Jesus Christ: Our Savior and Redeemer," *Ensign,* June 1990, 6.

8. "Life Is Eternal," *Ensign,* Aug. 1991, 4.

9. "Jesus Christ: Our Savior and Redeemer," 4.

10. "Jesus Christ: Our Savior and Redeemer," 2.

11. "Jesus Christ: Our Savior, Our God," *Ensign,* Apr. 1991, 2, 4.

12. "Keeping Christ in Christmas," *Ensign,* Dec. 1993, 4.

13. "Jesus Christ: Our Savior and Redeemer," 4.

14. "The Meaning of Easter," 2, 4.

15. "Jesus Christ: Our Savior, Our God," 4.

16. "Valiant in the Testimony of Jesus," *Ensign,* Feb. 1987, 2.

17. "Jesus Christ: Our Savior and Redeemer," 2, 6.

18. "In His Steps," *Ensign,* Sept. 1988, 5, 6.

19. "Jesus Christ—Gifts and Expectations," *Ensign,* Dec. 1988, 2, 4.

20. "Born of God," 4–5.

*The message of the First Vision was "intended for all of
our Father's children living upon the face of the earth."*

Joseph Smith, an Instrument in the Hands of the Lord

"Joseph Smith, the latter-day Prophet, was an instrument in the hands of the Lord in opening a new gospel dispensation, the last and greatest of all gospel dispensations."

From the Life of Ezra Taft Benson

When Elder Ezra Taft Benson served as a full-time missionary in England in the early 1920s, he and his companions experienced what he called "great opposition to the Church." He later recounted:

"The newspapers, the magazines, even anti-Mormon moving pictures [movies] were all over Great Britain." Because the opposition was so great, some forms of missionary work, such as holding street meetings and handing out pamphlets, were discontinued. "But up in northern England where we were laboring," he said, "we had a group of people out at South Shields Branch who were very faithful and very devoted and very loyal, and they had invited my companion and me to come over and speak in their sacrament meeting. They said, 'Many of our neighbors don't believe the lies that are being printed. If you will come, we will fill the little chapel.'

"And so we accepted the invitation and we started preparing and I started studying about the apostasy. It was a subject I liked, and I thought they needed it; and I worked and I studied, and I thought I could talk fifteen minutes on the subject.

"We went over to the little chapel and it was filled. Everyone was happy. And after the opening exercises my companion spoke, then I spoke with a freedom I had never enjoyed in all my life. And when I sat down and looked at my watch, I had talked twenty-five minutes, and I hadn't mentioned the apostasy, I hadn't even thought of the apostasy. I had talked about Joseph Smith, and I had borne witness that he was a prophet of God and I knew it. I told about the coming forth of the Book of Mormon as a new witness for Christ, and I had borne testimony. When I realized what had happened, I couldn't hold back the tears.

"At the end of the meeting, many of the Saints came forward and expressed their gratitude that something had been said about Joseph Smith. They said, 'Several of our neighbors have said, "We can accept everything about the Church except Joseph Smith."' And then some of those same neighbors came up and said, 'We are now ready. We are ready tonight. We have received the witness that Joseph Smith is a prophet of God.'" [1]

President Benson continued to find opportunities throughout his life to share his witness of Joseph Smith's calling. For example, when he was serving as United States secretary of agriculture, a radio station invited him to choose a favorite scripture passage to be read over the air, and he chose a portion of Joseph Smith—History in the Pearl of Great Price. [2]

Above all, he regularly bore a firm and powerful testimony to his fellow Saints. "Joseph Smith was a prophet of the Living God," he declared, "one of the greatest prophets that has ever lived upon the earth. He was the instrument in God's hand in ushering in a great gospel dispensation, the greatest ever, and the last of all in preparation for the second coming of the Master." [3]

Teachings of Ezra Taft Benson

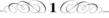

Joseph Smith's First Vision was the greatest event in this world since the Resurrection of Jesus Christ.

As a young man, Joseph Smith was a seeker after truth. Confusion among existing churches led him to inquire of God which of them was true. In answer to that prayer, he asserted that a pillar of brilliant light appeared. These are his words:

"When the light rested upon me I saw two Personages, whose brightness and glory defy all description, standing above me in the air. One of them spake unto me, calling me by name and said, pointing to the other—*This is My Beloved Son. Hear Him!*" (JS—H 1:17.)

Joseph asked the second personage, who was Jesus Christ, which one of the Christian sects was correct. He was told that he must not join any of them, that none were correct.[4]

When God the Father and his Son Jesus Christ come to earth, as they did in 1820 when they appeared to the young boy prophet, Joseph Smith, it is not something that concerns only a handful of people. It is a message and a revelation intended for all of our Father's children living upon the face of the earth. It was the greatest event that has ever happened in this world since the resurrection of the Master. Sometimes I think we are so close to it that we don't fully appreciate its significance and importance and the magnitude of it.[5]

The first vision of the Prophet Joseph Smith is bedrock theology to the Church.[6]

The most evident truth that emerged from the Prophet's experience in 1820 was the reality of God's existence and the fact that Jesus Christ was indeed resurrected. He saw them as separate, distinct, glorified Personages who spoke to him as one man speaks to another.[7]

I am humbly grateful for the knowledge that I have that God the Father and his Son, Jesus Christ, as glorified beings have again come to this earth in our day, in this dispensation; that they did in very deed appear unto the boy prophet. . . . This was the most glorious manifestation of God the Father and the Son of which we have record.[8]

2

Consistent with New Testament prophecy, Joseph Smith received new revelation and angelic visitations.

It is generally understood that the faith of members of The Church of Jesus Christ of Latter-day Saints rests on the claim that Joseph Smith is a prophet of God, and also that he declared the coming forth of the Book of Mormon was the result of angelic visitations to him between the years 1823 and 1827.

Upon learning of this claim, some people contend that it seems preposterous that angels would visit the earth in this modern era.

The Bible contains testimony that God directed the affairs of His church on earth for over four thousand years by revelation and, when necessary, by heavenly ministrations.

In describing conditions of the last days incident to the second coming of Jesus Christ, John prophesied in the New Testament that before the Savior's return, the world would receive a warning that the hour of God's judgment was near. That warning would come by an angel from heaven declaring an "everlasting gospel." Hear his words:

"I saw another angel fly in the midst of heaven, having the everlasting gospel to preach unto them that dwell on the earth, and to every nation, and kindred, and tongue, and people,

"Saying with a loud voice, Fear God, and give glory to him; for the hour of his judgment is come: and worship him that made heaven, and earth, and the sea, and the fountains of waters." (Rev. 14:6–7.)

If one accepts the testimony of John the Revelator, new revelation and a visitation by a heavenly messenger to earth should be expected.

Our solemn testimony is that this angelic messenger appeared to the Prophet Joseph Smith in the early nineteenth century. This announcement that an angel from God appeared to a prophet in our times is entirely consistent with the prophecies of the New Testament and should therefore command the interest of every earnest seeker after truth.[9]

On the evening of 21 September 1823, an angel appeared to the Prophet Joseph Smith. The angel's name was Moroni. He was the last of a long line of ancient prophets of two great civilizations who lived . . . on the American Continent centuries ago.[10]

Moroni came to Joseph Smith in fulfillment of prophecy.

The Book of Mormon is the most singular evidence of Joseph Smith's calling as a prophet.

The most singular evidence in support of Joseph Smith's claim to being a spokesman for Almighty God was the publication of a scriptural record, the Book of Mormon.

The Book of Mormon is a record of the ancient inhabitants of the American continent and records the visit and ministry of Jesus Christ to the people on this continent following His ascension at Jerusalem. The major purpose of the record is to convince a later generation that Jesus is the Christ, the Son of God. The Book of Mormon, therefore, constitutes an additional witness, along with the Bible, to the divinity of Jesus Christ.

Joseph Smith obtained this ancient record from a heavenly messenger, just as John prophesied. This angel appeared to him and revealed the location of ancient records which were inscribed on metallic plates and buried in a stone vault. In due time, the young prophet was given the plates and the means by which they were translated. The book was then published to the world as canonized scripture.

Also, in harmony with the testimony of John, the book contains "the everlasting gospel." It is now preached by our missionaries to the world.

We invite you to test the validity of our witness about the origin of the Book of Mormon. You can do this by reading it and asking our Heavenly Father if these things are true. I promise you, if you are sincere, you will receive a confirmation of the truthfulness by the Holy Ghost. Millions, with soberness and sincerity, testify they know it is from God.[11]

If the Book of Mormon is true, then Jesus is the Christ, Joseph Smith was His prophet, The Church of Jesus Christ of Latter-day Saints is true, and it is being led today by a prophet receiving revelation.[12]

4

God reestablished His kingdom on the earth through the Prophet Joseph Smith.

Christian denominations the world over have prayed for centuries for the kingdom of God to come [see Matthew 6:10]. We earnestly and publicly declare: that day is now here![13]

The prayer of a boy fourteen years of age, in the Sacred Grove, opened a new gospel dispensation.[14]

God has again established his kingdom on the earth in fulfillment of prophecy. . . .

. . . Joseph Smith was called of God to reestablish that kingdom—The Church of Jesus Christ of Latter-day Saints. I testify that he accomplished this work, that he laid the foundations and that he committed to the Church the keys and powers to continue the great Latter-day work, which he began under the direction of Almighty God.[15]

To Joseph Smith appeared other beings, including John the Baptist and Peter, James, and John, who ordained him with authority to act in the name of God (see JS—H 1:68–72; D&C 27:5–13). The church and kingdom of God was restored in these latter days, even The Church of Jesus Christ of Latter-day Saints, with all the gifts, rights, powers, doctrines, officers, and blessings of the former-day Church. (See D&C 65; 115:3–4.)[16]

The Prophet Joseph was commanded to go forth as an instrument in the hands of God and organize the Church, to publish to the world as an added testimony to the divinity of Jesus Christ, the Book of Mormon which was taken from the sacred records. . . .

This restoration of the gospel, the bringing back of light and truth, is intended for the benefit and blessing of all God's children. And so, humbly and gratefully, our missionaries go out into the world to proclaim that there has been an apostasy from the truth, but that through the goodness of God the heavens have again been opened and the gospel revealed unto man through Joseph Smith, the Prophet.[17]

5

Joseph Smith was loyal and true even unto death.

Simultaneous with the early development of the Church was a spirit of opposition and persecution. Wherever the tiny "mustard seed" was planted, attempts were made to frustrate its growth.[18]

The fourteen-year-old boy stood true against the world. God knew his son when he was chosen. He knew he would be loyal and true even to death.[19]

Some treated [Joseph Smith's] testimony with great contempt and began to incite false stories and persecution against him. The young prophet, like the Apostle Paul of old, would not recant his testimony, but defended his claim in these words:

"I had seen a vision; I knew it, and I knew that God knew it, and I could not deny it, neither dared I do it; at least I knew that by so doing I would offend God, and come under condemnation." (JS—H 1:25.)[20]

Joseph Smith the Prophet went willingly to his death. He sealed his testimony with his life—his own blood. On that fateful day in Nauvoo, Illinois, as he looked back upon his city and people whom he loved, on his way to Carthage Jail and his martyrdom, he declared: "This is the loveliest place and the best people under the heavens; little do they know the trials that await them" [*History of the Church*, 6:554].

Later the Prophet said feelingly, but calmly and courageously, "I am going like a lamb to the slaughter, but I am as calm as a summer's morning. I have a conscience void of offense toward God and toward all men. If they take my life I shall die an innocent man, and my blood shall cry from the ground for vengeance, and it shall be said of me, 'He was murdered in cold blood'" [*History of the Church*, 6:555].[21]

Thus did the Prophet Joseph Smith climax his earth life and fulfill the mortal part of his divinely appointed mission. This mortal mission, he made clear, was not to end until fully completed. Like the mission of the Savior, "a lamb slain before the foundation of the world" [see Revelation 13:8], Joseph was truly foreordained to his great mission.[22]

6

Joseph Smith stands today as the head of this last and greatest of all gospel dispensations.

I know that Joseph Smith, although slain as a martyr to the truth, still lives and that as head of this dispensation—the greatest of all gospel dispensations—he will continue so to stand throughout the eternities to come.[23]

The message of Joseph Smith—the message of The Church of Jesus Christ of Latter-day Saints, the message of Mormonism—is the most important message in this world. And Joseph Smith the Prophet, who lives today, continues to have an important part in its direction here on earth.[24]

To get a vision of the magnitude of the Prophet's earthly mission we must view it in the light of eternity. He was among "the noble and great ones" whom Abraham described as follows:

"Now the Lord had shown unto me, Abraham, the intelligences that were organized before the world was; and among all these there were many of the noble and great ones;

"And God saw these souls that they were good, and he stood in the midst of them, and he said: These I will make my rulers; for he stood among those that were spirits, and he saw that they were good; and he said unto me: Abraham, thou art one of them; thou wast chosen before thou wast born." (Abraham 3:22–23.)

So it was with Joseph Smith. He too was there. He too sat in council with the noble and great ones. Occupying a prominent place of honor and distinction, he unquestionably helped in the planning and execution of the great work of the Lord to "bring to pass the immortality and eternal life of man," the salvation of all our Father's children [see Moses 1:39]. His mission had had, and was to have, impact on all who had come to earth, all who then dwelt on earth, and the millions yet unborn.

The Prophet Joseph Smith made this eternal fact clear in these words: "Every man who has a calling to minister to the inhabitants of the world was ordained to that very purpose in the grand council of heaven before this world was. I suppose that I was ordained to this very office in that grand council. It is the testimony that I want that I am God's servant, and this people His people" [see *History of the Church,* 6:364]. . . .

The greatest activity in this world or in the world to come is directly related to the work and mission of Joseph Smith—man of destiny, prophet of God. That work is the salvation and eternal life of man. For that great purpose this earth was created, prophets of God are called, heavenly messengers are sent forth, and on sacred and important occasions even God, the Father of us all, condescends to come to earth and to introduce his beloved Son.

The Prophet Joseph Smith was not only "one of the noble and great ones," but he gave and continues to give attention to important matters here on the earth even today from the realms above. For in the eyes of the Lord, the God of this world under the Father, it is all one great eternal program in which the Prophet Joseph plays an important role, all through the eternal priesthood and authority of God.[25]

I testify to you that Joseph Smith was and is a prophet of God, one of the truly great prophets of all time, a man of destiny, a man of character, a man of courage, a man of deep spirituality, a God-like prophet of the Lord, a truly noble and great one of all time.[26]

Yes, Joseph Smith, the latter-day Prophet, was an instrument in the hands of the Lord in opening a new gospel dispensation, the last and greatest of all gospel dispensations.[27]

Suggestions for Study and Teaching

Questions
- Why do you think Joseph Smith's First Vision was "the greatest event . . . since the resurrection of the Master"? (See section 1.) In what ways has this event influenced your life?

- How does it help you to know that John the Revelator prophesied of Moroni's visits to Joseph Smith? (See section 2.)

- President Benson said that the Book of Mormon is "the most singular evidence" that Joseph Smith is a prophet (see section 3). How has your study of the Book of Mormon influenced your testimony of Joseph Smith's mission?

- Ponder President Benson's words of testimony in section 4. What are some blessings that have come to you and your family because of the Restoration of the gospel?

- What do you learn from section 5 about facing persecution? What can we learn from Joseph Smith's example that will help us when people challenge our testimonies?

- Referring to Joseph Smith's foreordination, President Benson said, "His mission had had, and was to have, impact on all who had come to earth, all who then dwelt on earth, and the millions yet unborn" (section 6). How has the mission of Joseph Smith impacted all who have lived on the earth? How has it impacted you personally?

Related Scriptures
Isaiah 29:13–14; 2 Nephi 3:3–15; 3 Nephi 21:9–11; D&C 5:9–10; 135; Joseph Smith—History

Teaching Help
"Ask participants to share what they have learned from their personal study of the chapter. It may be helpful to contact a few

participants during the week and ask them to come prepared to share what they have learned" (page vii in this book).

Notes

1. *The Teachings of Ezra Taft Benson* (1988), 206, 207.

2. See Sheri L. Dew, *Ezra Taft Benson: A Biography* (1987), 292.

3. In Conference Report, Apr. 1961, 114.

4. "Joseph Smith: Prophet to Our Generation," *Ensign,* Nov. 1981, 61–62.

5. *God, Family, Country: Our Three Great Loyalties* (1974), 57.

6. *The Teachings of Ezra Taft Benson,* 101.

7. *Come unto Christ* (1983), 74.

8. In Conference Report, Apr. 1958, 60.

9. "Joseph Smith: Prophet to Our Generation," 61.

10. *The Teachings of Ezra Taft Benson,* 46.

11. "Joseph Smith: Prophet to Our Generation," 61.

12. "The Book of Mormon Is the Word of God," *Ensign,* Jan. 1988, 4.

13. "May the Kingdom of God Go Forth," *Ensign,* May 1978, 34.

14. In Conference Report, Oct. 1956, 108.

15. "A Message to the World," *Ensign,* Nov. 1975, 34.

16. "I Testify," *Ensign,* Nov. 1988, 86.

17. In Conference Report, Oct. 1949, 27, 28.

18. *Come unto Christ,* 81.

19. *God, Family, Country,* 38.

20. "Joseph Smith: Prophet to Our Generation," 62.

21. *God, Family, Country,* 37–38.

22. *God, Family, Country,* 29.

23. "A Message to the World," 34.

24. *God, Family, Country,* 40–41.

25. *God, Family, Country,* 30–31.

26. *God, Family, Country,* 37.

27. *God, Family, Country,* 39.

President Ezra Taft Benson frequently testified of the power of God's word.

The Power of the Word

"The word of God, as found in the scriptures,
in the words of living prophets, and in personal
revelation, has the power to fortify the Saints and
arm them with the Spirit so they can resist evil,
hold fast to the good, and find joy in this life."

From the Life of Ezra Taft Benson

When President Thomas S. Monson was serving as President Ezra Taft Benson's Second Counselor in the First Presidency, he observed: "President Benson grasps quickly matters which come to his attention. He doesn't need to consider an item at great length before he finds the inspiration of the Lord directing him in a decision. With the expansive nature of the Church today, throughout the world, and with the multitude of matters that come before the First Presidency, this ability to cut through detail and get to the heart of the issue is vital to carrying out the administrative work of the Church."[1]

On April 4, 1986, in connection with his first general conference as President of the Church, President Benson presided over a special meeting for priesthood leaders. The brethren in attendance saw his ability to "cut through detail and get to the heart of the issue." When he addressed the congregation, he mentioned many of the challenges that Latter-day Saints faced—such as temptation, family struggles, and difficulties with keeping the commandments and fulfilling Church duties—and he shared what he saw as the solution to these challenges.

President Benson gave only a portion of his talk in that priesthood leadership meeting, so he requested that the entire sermon be included in the conference issue of the Church magazines. This chapter contains that talk in its entirety. Although President Benson directed his remarks to priesthood leaders, he taught principles that apply to all members of the Church.

Teachings of Ezra Taft Benson

 1

As we face the great challenges of our time, we need to hold fast to the word of God.

My dear brethren, what a thrilling sight it is to look out over this body of priesthood leadership and to know how many thousands of Saints you serve and how much dedication and faithfulness you collectively represent! There is no other body anywhere in the world today that meets for the same righteous purpose as does this group, nor is there any other group—political, religious or military—that holds the power that you do here tonight.

We live in a day of great challenge. We live in that time of which the Lord spoke when he said, "Peace shall be taken from the earth, and the devil shall have power over his own dominion." (D&C 1:35.) We live in that day which John the Revelator foresaw when "the dragon was wroth with the woman, and went to make war with the remnant of her seed, which keep the commandments of God, and have the testimony of Jesus Christ." (Rev. 12:17.) The dragon is Satan; the woman represents the Church of Jesus Christ. Satan is waging war against the members of the Church who have testimonies and are trying to keep the commandments. And while many of our members are remaining faithful and strong, some are wavering. Some are falling. Some are fulfilling John's prophecy that in the war with Satan, some Saints would be overcome. (See Rev. 13:7.)

The prophet Lehi also saw our day in his great visionary dream of the tree of life. He saw that many people would wander blindly in the mists of darkness, which symbolized the temptations of the devil. (See 1 Ne. 12:17.) He saw some fall away "in forbidden paths," others drown in rivers of filthiness, and still others wander in "strange roads." (1 Ne. 8:28, 32.) When we read of the spreading curse of drugs, or read of the pernicious flood of pornography and immorality, do any of us doubt that these are the forbidden paths and rivers of filthiness Lehi described?

Not all of those Lehi saw perishing were of the world. Some had come to the tree and partaken of the fruit. In other words, some members of the Church today are among those souls Lehi saw which were lost.

The Apostle Paul also saw our day. He described it as a time when such things as blasphemy, dishonesty, cruelty, unnatural affection, pride, and pleasure seeking would abound. (See 2 Tim. 3:1–7.) He also warned that "evil men and seducers shall wax worse and worse, deceiving, and being deceived." (2 Tim. 3:13.)

Such grim predictions by prophets of old would be cause for great fear and discouragement if those same prophets had not, at the same time, offered the solution. In their inspired counsel we can find the answer to the spiritual crises of our age.

In his dream, Lehi saw an iron rod which led through the mists of darkness. He saw that if people would hold fast to that rod, they could avoid the rivers of filthiness, stay away from the forbidden paths, stop from wandering in the strange roads that lead to destruction. Later his son Nephi clearly explained the symbolism of the iron rod. When Laman and Lemuel asked, "What meaneth the rod of iron?" Nephi answered, "It was the word of God; and [note this promise] *whoso would hearken unto the word of God, and would hold fast unto it, they would never perish; neither could the temptations and the fiery darts of the adversary overpower them unto blindness, to lead them away to destruction.*" (1 Ne. 15:23–24; italics added.) Not only will the word of God lead us to the fruit which is desirable above all others, but in the word of God and through it we can find the power to resist temptation, the power to thwart the work of Satan and his emissaries.

Paul's message is the same as Lehi's. After portraying the terrible wickedness of future times—future to him, but present to us!—he said this to Timothy: "But continue thou in the things which thou hast learned. . . .

"From a child thou hast known the holy scriptures, *which are able to make thee wise unto salvation.*" (2 Tim. 3:14–15; italics added.)

My dear brethren, this is an answer to the great challenge of our time. The word of God, as found in the scriptures, in the words of living prophets, and in personal revelation, has the power to fortify the Saints and arm them with the Spirit so they can resist evil, hold fast to the good, and find joy in this life.[2]

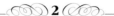

2

When individual members and families immerse themselves in the scriptures, other aspects of Church activity automatically come.

Now to you priesthood leaders we say, look to the prophetic counsel of Lehi and Paul and others like them. In that counsel you will find the solution to the challenges you face in keeping your flocks safe from the "ravening wolves" that surround them. (See Matt. 7:15; Acts 20:29.) We know that you too have great anxiety for the members of your wards and stakes and expend great time and effort in their behalf. There is much that we ask of you who have been chosen for leadership. We place many loads upon your shoulders. You are asked to run the programs of the Church, interview and counsel with the members, see that the financial affairs of the stakes and wards are properly handled, manage welfare projects, build buildings, and engage in a host of other time-consuming activities.

While none of those activities can be ignored and laid aside, they are not the most important thing you can do for those you serve. In recent years, time and again we have counseled you that certain activities bring greater spiritual returns than others. As early as 1970, President Harold B. Lee told the regional representatives:

"We are convinced that our members are hungry for the gospel, undiluted, with its abundant truths and insights. . . . There are those who have seemed to forget that the most powerful weapons the Lord has given us against all that is evil are His own declarations, the plain simple doctrines of salvation as found in the scriptures." (In Regional Representatives' Seminar, 1 Oct. 1970, p. 6.)

*Great blessings come "when individual members
and families immerse themselves in the scriptures."*

In a First Presidency message in 1976, President [Spencer W.] Kimball said:

"I am convinced that each of us, at least some time in our lives, must discover the scriptures for ourselves—and not just discover them once, but rediscover them again and again. . . .

"The Lord is not trifling with us when he gives us these things, for 'unto whomsoever much is given, of him shall be much required.' (Luke 12:48.) Access to these things means responsibility for them. We must study the scriptures according to the Lord's commandment (see 3 Ne. 23:1–5); and we must let them govern our lives." (*Ensign,* Sept. 1976, pp. 4–5.)

In April 1982, Elder Bruce R. McConkie spoke to the regional representatives about the priority the scriptures should take in our labors. He said: "We are so wound up in programs and statistics and trends, in properties, lands and mammon, and in achieving goals that will highlight the excellence of our work, that we have 'omitted the weightier matters of the law.' . . . However talented men may be in administrative matters; however eloquent they may be in expressing their views; however learned they may be in the worldly things—they will be denied the sweet whisperings of the Spirit that might have been theirs unless they pay the price of studying, pondering, and praying about the scriptures." (In Regional Representatives' Seminar, 2 Apr. 1982, pp. 1–2.)

That same day, Elder Boyd K. Packer spoke to the stake presidents and regional representatives. He said: "Buildings and budgets, and reports and programs and procedures are very important. But, by themselves, they do not carry that essential spiritual nourishment and will not accomplish what the Lord has given us to do. . . . The right things, those with true spiritual nourishment, are centered in the scriptures." (In Meeting with Stake Presidents and Regional Representatives, 2 Apr. 1982, pp. 1–2.)

I add my voice to these wise and inspired brethren and say to you that one of the most important things you can do as priesthood leaders is to immerse yourselves in the scriptures. Search them diligently. Feast upon the words of Christ. Learn the doctrine. Master the principles that are found therein. There are few other efforts that will bring greater dividends to your calling. There are few other ways to gain greater inspiration as you serve.

But that alone, as valuable as it is, is not enough. You must also bend your efforts and your activities to stimulating meaningful scripture study among the members of the Church. Often we spend great effort in trying to increase the activity levels in our stakes. We work diligently to raise the percentages of those attending sacrament meetings. We labor to get a higher percentage of our young men on missions. We strive to improve the numbers of those marrying in the temple. All of these are commendable efforts and important to the growth of the kingdom. But when individual members and families immerse themselves in the scriptures regularly and consistently, these other areas of activity will automatically come. Testimonies will increase. Commitment will be strengthened. Families will be fortified. Personal revelation will flow.[3]

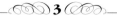

As we study God's word, we receive guidance in our daily lives, healing of the soul, and power to avoid deception and resist temptation.

The Prophet Joseph Smith said that "the Book of Mormon was the most correct of any book on earth, and the keystone of our religion, and *a man would get nearer to God by abiding by its precepts,* than by any other book." (Book of Mormon, Introduction, italics added.) Isn't that what we want for the members of our wards and stakes? Aren't we desirous that they get nearer to God? Then encourage them in every way possible to immerse themselves in this marvelous latter-day witness of Christ.

You must help the Saints see that studying and searching the scriptures is not a burden laid upon them by the Lord, but a marvelous blessing and opportunity. Note what the Lord Himself has said about the benefits of studying His word. To the great prophet-leader Joshua, He said:

"This book of the law shall not depart out of thy mouth; but thou shalt meditate therein day and night, that thou mayest observe to do according to all that is written therein: for *then thou shalt make thy way prosperous, and then thou shalt have good success."* (Josh. 1:8; italics added.)

The Lord was not promising Joshua material wealth and fame, but that his life would prosper in righteousness and that he would have success in that which matters most in life, namely the quest to find true joy. (See 2 Ne. 2:25.)

Do you have members in your stakes whose lives are shattered by sin or tragedy, who are in despair and without hope? Have you longed for some way to reach out and heal their wounds, soothe their troubled souls? The prophet Jacob offers just that with this remarkable promise: "They have come up hither to hear the pleasing word of God, yea, *the word which healeth the wounded soul."* (Jacob 2:8; italics added.)

Today the world is full of alluring and attractive ideas that can lead even the best of our members into error and deception. Students at universities are sometimes so filled with the doctrines of the world they begin to question the doctrines of the gospel. How do you as a priesthood leader help fortify your membership against such deceptive teachings? The Savior gave the answer in His great discourse on the Mount of Olives when He promised, *"And whoso treasureth up my word, shall not be deceived."* (JS—M 1:37; italics added.)

The scriptures are replete with similar promises about the value of the word. Do you have members who long for direction and guidance in their lives? The Psalms tell us, "Thy word is a lamp unto my feet, and a light unto my path" (Ps. 119:105), and Nephi promises that feasting upon the words of Christ "will tell you all things what ye should do." (2 Ne. 32:3.)

Are there members of your flock who are deep in sin and need to pull themselves back? Helaman's promise is for them: "Yea, we see that whosoever will may lay hold upon the word of God, which is quick and powerful, which shall divide asunder all the cunning and the snares and the wiles of the devil." (Hel. 3:29.)

Success in righteousness, the power to avoid deception and resist temptation, guidance in our daily lives, healing of the soul—these are but a few of the promises the Lord has given to those who will come to His word. Does the Lord promise and not fulfill? Surely if He tells us that these things will come to us if we lay hold upon His word, then the blessings can be ours. And if we do not, then the blessings may be lost. However diligent we may be in other areas, certain blessings are to be found only in the scriptures, only in coming to the word of the Lord and holding fast to it as we make our way through the mists of darkness to the tree of life.[4]

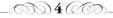 **4**

The word of the Lord is a valuable gift, and we must not treat it lightly.

And if we ignore what the Lord has given us, we may lose the very power and blessings which we seek. In a solemn warning to the early Saints, the Lord said this of the Book of Mormon: "Your minds in times past have been darkened because of unbelief, and because you have treated lightly the things you have received—

"Which vanity and unbelief have brought the whole church under condemnation.

"And this condemnation resteth upon the children of Zion, even all.

"And they shall remain under this condemnation until they repent and remember the new covenant, even the Book of Mormon." (D&C 84:54–57.)

Oh, my brethren, let us not treat lightly the great things we have received from the hand of the Lord! His word is one of the most valuable gifts He has given us. I urge you to recommit yourselves to a study of the scriptures. Immerse yourselves in them daily so you will have the power of the Spirit to attend you in your callings. Read them in your families and teach your children to love and treasure them. Then prayerfully and in counsel with others, seek every way possible to encourage the members of the Church to follow your example. If you do so, you will find, as Alma did, that "the word [has] a great tendency to lead people to do that which [is] just—yea, it [has] more powerful effect upon the minds of the people than the sword, or anything else, which [has] happened unto them." (Alma 31:5.)

Like Alma, I say unto you, "It [is] expedient that [you] should try the virtue of the word of God" (Alma 31:5).[5]

Suggestions for Study and Teaching

Questions
- Consider what President Benson said was "an answer to the great challenge of our time" (section 1). In what ways can this answer help us meet the challenges we face?

- Review the results that President Benson said will come "when individual members and families immerse themselves in the scriptures regularly and consistently" (section 2). Why do you think scripture study leads to such results?

- President Benson said that scripture study is a blessing, not a burden (see section 3). What blessings have come to you and your family through scripture study? What advice might you give to someone who feels that scripture study is a burden?

- What are some dangers of treating the word of God lightly? (See section 4.) What are some things we can do to give the word of God greater attention?

Related Scriptures

Acts 17:11; 2 Timothy 3:16–17; 1 Nephi 19:23–24; Alma 32:21–43; D&C 18:33–36; 21:4–6; 68:1–4

Study Help

"Many find that the best time to study is in the morning after a night's rest. . . . Others prefer to study in the quiet hours after the work and worries of the day are over. . . . Perhaps what is more important than the hour of the day is that a regular time be set aside for study" (Howard W. Hunter, "Reading the Scriptures," *Ensign,* Nov. 1979, 64).

Notes

1. Thomas S. Monson, in Sheri L. Dew, *Ezra Taft Benson: A Biography* (1987), 487–88.
2. "The Power of the Word," *Ensign,* May 1986, 79–80.
3. "The Power of the Word," 80–81.
4. "The Power of the Word," 81–82.
5. "The Power of the Word," 82.

The Book of Mormon—
Keystone of Our Religion

*"Is there not something deep in our hearts that longs
to draw nearer to God? . . . If so, then the Book of
Mormon will help us do so more than any other book."*

From the Life of Ezra Taft Benson

On January 5, 1986, President Ezra Taft Benson presided at a stake conference in Annandale, Virginia—his first stake conference as President of the Church. Latter-day Saints in attendance were "visibly moved" as they listened to him speak. In his sermon, "he bore testimony of the power of the Book of Mormon to change lives and lead people to Christ." He issued a "spirited challenge [to] study this book of scripture."[1]

This message was not new in President Benson's ministry. As a member of the Quorum of the Twelve Apostles, he had frequently encouraged Latter-day Saints to study the Book of Mormon and follow its teachings.[2] But as President of the Church, he was inspired to emphasize the message even more. He said: "The Lord inspired His servant Lorenzo Snow to reemphasize the principle of tithing to redeem the Church from financial bondage. . . . Now, in our day, the Lord has revealed the need to reemphasize the Book of Mormon."[3] President Benson testified of the Book of Mormon wherever he went: in missionary meetings, stake and regional conferences, general conferences, and meetings with General Authorities.[4]

In his first general conference address as President of the Church, President Benson shared one reason for the urgency of this message. "Unless we read the Book of Mormon and give heed to its teachings," he warned, "the Lord has stated in section 84 of the Doctrine and Covenants that the whole Church is under condemnation:

The Prophet Joseph Smith said that the Book of Mormon is "the keystone of our religion."

'And this condemnation resteth upon the children of Zion, even all' [D&C 84:56]. The Lord continues: 'And they shall remain under this condemnation until they repent and remember the new covenant, even the Book of Mormon and the former commandments which I have given them, not only to say, but to do according to that which I have written' [D&C 84:57]."[5]

The following quotations, all from sermons President Benson delivered as President of the Church, provide a sampling of his warnings and promises related to the Book of Mormon:

"Now we not only need to *say* more about the Book of Mormon, but we need to *do* more with it. Why? The Lord answers: 'That they may bring forth fruit meet for their Father's kingdom; otherwise there remaineth a scourge and judgment to be poured out upon the children of Zion' [D&C 84:58]. We have felt that scourge and judgment!

". . . The Book of Mormon has not been, nor is it yet, the center of our personal study, family teaching, preaching, and missionary work. Of this we must repent."[6]

"We have not been using the Book of Mormon as we should. Our homes are not as strong unless we are using it to bring our children to Christ. Our families may be corrupted by worldly trends and teachings unless we know how to use the book to expose and combat falsehoods. . . . Our missionaries are not as effective unless they are [teaching] with it. Social, ethical, cultural, or educational converts will not survive under the heat of the day unless their taproots go down to the fulness of the gospel which the Book of Mormon contains. Our Church classes are not as Spirit-filled unless we hold it up as a standard."[7]

"I bless you with increased understanding of the Book of Mormon. I promise you that from this moment forward, if we will daily sup from its pages and abide by its precepts, God will pour out upon each child of Zion and the Church a blessing hitherto unknown—and we will plead to the Lord that He will begin to lift the condemnation—the scourge and judgment. Of this I bear solemn witness."[8]

"I do not know fully why God has preserved my life to this age, but I do know this: That for the present hour He has revealed to me the absolute need for us to move the Book of Mormon forward now in a marvelous manner. You must help with this burden and with this blessing which He has placed on the whole Church, even all the children of Zion.

"Moses never entered the promised land. Joseph Smith never saw Zion redeemed. Some of us may not live long enough to see the day when the Book of Mormon floods the earth and when the Lord lifts His condemnation. (See D&C 84:54–58.) But, God willing, I intend to spend all my remaining days in that glorious effort."[9]

Teachings of Ezra Taft Benson

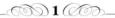

1

The Book of Mormon is the keystone of our religion.

How important is the Book of Mormon? Joseph Smith called it "the keystone of our religion." (*History of the Church,* 4:461.) "Take away the Book of Mormon and the revelations," he said, "and where is our religion? We have none." (*History of the Church,* 2:52.)[10]

A keystone is the central stone in an arch. It holds all the other stones in place, and if removed, the arch crumbles.

. . . Just as the arch crumbles if the keystone is removed, so does all the Church stand or fall with the truthfulness of the Book of Mormon. The enemies of the Church understand this clearly. This is why they go to such great lengths to try to disprove the Book of Mormon, for if it can be discredited, the Prophet Joseph Smith goes with it. So does our claim to priesthood keys, and revelation, and the restored Church. But in like manner, if the Book of Mormon be true—and millions have now testified that they have the witness of the Spirit that it is indeed true—then one must accept the claims of the Restoration and all that accompanies it.[11]

Perhaps there is nothing that testifies more clearly of the importance of this book of scripture than what the Lord Himself has said about it.

By His own mouth He has borne witness (1) that it is true (D&C 17:6), (2) that it contains the truth and His words (D&C 19:26), (3) that it was translated by power from on high (D&C 20:8), (4) that it contains the fulness of the gospel of Jesus Christ (D&C 20:9; 42:12), (5) that it was given by inspiration and confirmed by the ministering of angels (D&C 20:10), (6) that it gives evidence that the holy scriptures are true (D&C 20:11), and (7) that those who receive it in faith shall receive eternal life (D&C 20:14).[12]

2

The Book of Mormon testifies of Jesus Christ and brings us nearer to God.

The major mission of the Book of Mormon, as recorded on its title page, is "to the convincing of the Jew and Gentile that Jesus is the Christ, the eternal God, manifesting himself unto all nations."

The honest seeker after truth can gain the testimony that Jesus is the Christ as he prayerfully ponders the inspired words of the Book of Mormon.[13]

Do we remember the new covenant, even the Book of Mormon? In the Bible we have the Old Testament and the New Testament. The word *testament* is the English rendering of a Greek word that can also be translated as *covenant*. Is this what the Lord meant when He called the Book of Mormon the "new covenant"? It is indeed another testament or witness of Jesus. This is one of the reasons why we have recently added the words "Another Testament of Jesus Christ" to the title of the Book of Mormon. . . .

The Book of Mormon is the keystone in our witness of Jesus Christ, who is Himself the cornerstone of everything we do. It bears witness of His reality with power and clarity. Unlike the Bible, which passed through generations of copyists, translators, and corrupt religionists who tampered with the text, the Book of Mormon came from writer to reader in just one inspired step of translation. Therefore, its testimony of the Master is clear, undiluted, and full of power. But it does even more. Much of the Christian world today rejects the divinity of the Savior. They question His miraculous birth, His perfect life, and the reality of His glorious resurrection. The Book of Mormon teaches in plain and unmistakable terms

*In the Book of Mormon, the testimony of Jesus Christ
is "clear, undiluted, and full of power."*

about the truth of all of those. It also provides the most complete
explanation of the doctrine of the Atonement. Truly, this divinely
inspired book is a keystone in bearing witness to the world that
Jesus is the Christ.[14]

The Prophet Joseph Smith . . . said, "I told the brethren that the
Book of Mormon was the most correct of any book on earth, and
the keystone of our religion, and a man would get nearer to God
by abiding by its precepts, than by any other book" [*History of the
Church,* 4:461]. . . . Is there not something deep in our hearts that
longs to draw nearer to God, to be more like Him in our daily walk,
to feel His presence with us constantly? If so, then the Book of Mormon will help us do so more than any other book. . . .

Our beloved brother, President Marion G. Romney, . . . who
knows of himself of the power that resides in this book, testified
of the blessings that can come into the lives of those who will read
and study the Book of Mormon. He said:

"I feel certain that if, in our homes, parents will read from the
Book of Mormon prayerfully and regularly, both by themselves and

with their children, the spirit of that great book will come to permeate our homes and all who dwell therein. The spirit of reverence will increase; mutual respect and consideration for each other will grow. The spirit of contention will depart. Parents will counsel their children in greater love and wisdom. Children will be more responsive and submissive to the counsel of their parents. Righteousness will increase. Faith, hope, and charity—the pure love of Christ—will abound in our homes and lives, bringing in their wake peace, joy, and happiness" (*Ensign,* May 1980, p. 67).

These promises—increased love and harmony in the home, greater respect between parent and child, increased spirituality and righteousness—are not idle promises, but exactly what the Prophet Joseph Smith meant when he said the Book of Mormon will help us draw nearer to God.[15]

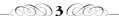

The Book of Mormon teaches true doctrine, confounds false doctrine, and exposes the enemies of Christ.

The Lord Himself has stated that the Book of Mormon contains the "fulness of the gospel of Jesus Christ" (D&C 20:9). That does not mean it contains every teaching, every doctrine ever revealed. Rather, it means that in the Book of Mormon we will find the fulness of those doctrines required for our salvation. And they are taught plainly and simply so that even children can learn the ways of salvation and exaltation. The Book of Mormon offers so much that broadens our understandings of the doctrines of salvation. Without it, much of what is taught in other scriptures would not be nearly so plain and precious.[16]

As far as preaching the gospel is concerned, the Book of Mormon contains the clearest, most concise, and complete explanation. There is no other record to compare with it. In what record do you get such a complete understanding of the nature of the Fall, the nature of physical and spiritual death, the doctrine of the Atonement, the doctrine of justice and mercy as it relates to the Atonement, and the principles and ordinances of the gospel? The Book of Mormon contains the most comprehensive account of these fundamental doctrines.[17]

The Book of Mormon . . . verifies and clarifies the Bible. It removes stumbling blocks, it restores many plain and precious things. We testify that when used together, the Bible and the Book of Mormon confound false doctrines, lay down contentions, and establish peace. (See 2 Ne. 3:12.)[18]

We . . . should know the Book of Mormon better than any other book. Not only should we know what history and faith-promoting stories it contains, but we should understand its teachings. If we really do our homework and approach the Book of Mormon doctrinally, we can expose the errors and find the truths to combat many of the current false theories and philosophies of men.

I have noted within the Church a difference in discernment, insight, conviction, and spirit between those who know and love the Book of Mormon and those who do not. That book is a great sifter.[19]

The Book of Mormon exposes the enemies of Christ. It confounds false doctrines and lays down contention. (See 2 Ne. 3:12.) It fortifies the humble followers of Christ against the evil designs, strategies, and doctrines of the devil in our day. The type of apostates in the Book of Mormon are similar to the type we have today. God, with his infinite foreknowledge, so molded the Book of Mormon that we might see the error and know how to combat false educational, political, religious, and philosophical concepts of our time.[20]

 4

The Doctrine and Covenants is the binding link between the Book of Mormon and the continuing work of the Restoration.

I would like to speak particularly about the Book of Mormon and the Doctrine and Covenants. These two great books of latter-day scripture are bound together as revelations from Israel's God for the purpose of gathering and preparing His people for the second coming of the Lord. . . .

To the Prophet Joseph Smith the Lord said, "This generation shall have my word through you" (D&C 5:10). The Book of Mormon and the Doctrine and Covenants are part of the fulfillment of that promise. Together these two great works of scripture bring great blessings to this generation. . . .

Each of these two great latter-day scriptures bears powerful and eloquent witness of the Lord Jesus Christ. Virtually every page of both the Doctrine and Covenants and the Book of Mormon teaches about the Master—His great love for His children and His atoning sacrifice—and teaches us how to live so that we can return to Him and our Heavenly Father.

Each of these two great latter-day books of scripture contains the knowledge and the power to help us live better lives in a time of great wickedness and evil. Those who carefully and prayerfully search the pages of these books will find comfort, counsel, guidance, and the quiet power to improve their lives.[21]

The Doctrine and Covenants is the binding link between the Book of Mormon and the continuing work of the Restoration through the Prophet Joseph Smith and his successors.

In the Doctrine and Covenants we learn of temple work, eternal families, the degrees of glory, Church organization, and many other great truths of the Restoration. . . .

The Book of Mormon is the "keystone" of our religion, and the Doctrine and Covenants is the capstone, with continuing latter-day revelation. The Lord has placed His stamp of approval on both the keystone and the capstone.[22]

The Doctrine and Covenants is a glorious book of scripture given directly to our generation. It contains the will of the Lord for us in these last days that precede the second coming of Christ. It contains many truths and doctrines not fully revealed in other scripture. Like the Book of Mormon, it will strengthen those who carefully and prayerfully study from its pages.

Do we, as Saints of the Most High God, treasure the word He has preserved for us at so great a cost? Are we using these books of latter-day revelation to bless our lives and resist the powers of the evil one? This is the purpose for which they were given. How can we not stand condemned before the Lord if we treat them lightly by letting them do no more than gather dust on our shelves?

My beloved brothers and sisters, I bear my solemn witness that these books contain the mind and the will of the Lord for us in these days of trial and tribulation. They stand with the Bible to give witness of the Lord and His work. These books contain the voice of the Lord to us in these latter days. May we turn to them with full purpose of heart and use them in the way the Lord wishes them to be used.[23]

Suggestions for Study and Teaching

Questions
- As you read President Benson's teachings about the Book of Mormon being the keystone of our religion (see section 1), reflect on its place in your life. What can we do to make the Book of Mormon more central in our efforts to live the gospel?

- President Benson said that the Book of Mormon testifies of Jesus Christ and brings us nearer to God (see section 2). What are some things you have learned about the Savior as you have studied the Book of Mormon? How has the Book of Mormon brought you and your family nearer to God?

- Why should we "know the Book of Mormon better than any other book"? How have the doctrines in the Book of Mormon fortified you against the "doctrines of the devil in our day"? (See section 3.)

- In what ways do the Book of Mormon and the Doctrine and Covenants work together to strengthen us? (See section 4.)

Related Scriptures
Isaiah 29:9–18; 1 Nephi 13:35–41; 2 Nephi 25:23, 26; 29:6–9; D&C 1:17–29

Teaching Help
"Most lesson manuals provide questions for getting discussions started and keeping them going. You may use these questions and prepare your own. Ask questions that encourage thoughtful comments and help individuals truly ponder the gospel" (*Teaching, No Greater Call* [1999], 63).

Notes

1. Sheri L. Dew, *Ezra Taft Benson: A Biography* (1987), 489.

2. See, for example, "The Book of Mormon Is the Word of God," *Ensign,* May 1975, 63–65; "A New Witness for Christ," *Ensign,* Nov. 1984, 6–8; see also *Ezra Taft Benson: A Biography,* 491–93.

3. "A Sacred Responsibility," *Ensign,* May 1986, 78; see also *Teachings of Presidents of the Church: Lorenzo Snow* (2012), 157–60.

4. See *Ezra Taft Benson: A Biography,* 495.

5. "Cleansing the Inner Vessel," *Ensign,* May 1986, 5.

6. "Cleansing the Inner Vessel," 5–6.

7. "The Book of Mormon Is the Word of God," *Ensign,* Jan. 1988, 5.

8. "A Sacred Responsibility," *Ensign,* May 1986, 78; italics removed from original.

9. "Flooding the Earth with the Book of Mormon," *Ensign,* Nov. 1988, 6.

10. "A New Witness for Christ," 6.

11. "The Book of Mormon—Keystone of Our Religion," *Ensign,* Nov. 1986, 5, 6.

12. "The Book of Mormon—Keystone of Our Religion," 4.

13. "Come unto Christ," *Ensign,* Nov. 1987, 83.

14. "The Book of Mormon—Keystone of Our Religion," 4, 5.

15. "The Book of Mormon—Keystone of Our Religion," 7. President Marion G. Romney served as a counselor in the First Presidency from July 1972 to November 1985.

16. "The Book of Mormon—Keystone of Our Religion," 6.

17. *The Teachings of Ezra Taft Benson* (1988), 56.

18. "A New Witness for Christ," 8.

19. "Jesus Christ—Gifts and Expectations," *Ensign,* Dec. 1988, 4.

20. "The Book of Mormon Is the Word of God," *Ensign,* Jan. 1988, 3.

21. "The Gift of Modern Revelation," *Ensign,* Nov. 1986, 79.

22. "The Book of Mormon and the Doctrine and Covenants," *Ensign,* May 1987, 83.

23. "The Gift of Modern Revelation," 80.

*Millions have come unto Christ because of the truths
in the book that Moroni delivered to Joseph Smith.*

Flooding the Earth and Our Lives with the Book of Mormon

*"There is a power in [the Book of Mormon] which
will begin to flow into your lives the moment
you begin a serious study of the book."*

From the Life of Ezra Taft Benson

In the April 1989 general conference, President Thomas S. Monson read a message from President Ezra Taft Benson to the children of the Church. In this message, President Benson said:

"I know you are reading the Book of Mormon, for I have received hundreds of personal letters from you telling me that you are reading this sacred book. It makes me weep for joy when I hear this. . . .

"How pleased I am to hear of your love for the Book of Mormon. *I* love it too, and Heavenly Father wants you to continue to learn from the Book of Mormon every day. It's Heavenly Father's special gift to you. By following its teachings, you will learn to do the will of our Father in Heaven."[1]

Throughout the Church, Latter-day Saints heeded this counsel from their prophet. The following accounts provide examples of the blessings that came to those who answered President Benson's call to "flood the earth and [their] lives with the Book of Mormon."[2]

"'He can't be serious!' thought Margo Merrill . . . when she first heard President Ezra Taft Benson's request that parents read the Book of Mormon with their children. 'My children are only six, five, and two years old. I'll just be wasting my time and patience.'

"Brother and Sister Merrill decided to try reading the Book of Mormon with their children anyway. When they came to the story of Nephi and his broken bow, six-year-old Melissa became ill with pneumonia.

"'Melissa pleaded with me to let her go back to school even though she was sick,' [said] Margo. 'She said that if she didn't go back, her friend, Pamela—who is a member of another church—wouldn't know what happened to Nephi. Then Melissa sobbed and slumped into my arms. I dried her tears and suggested she call Pamela on the telephone and tell her what had happened to Nephi.

"'As I heard Melissa relate in detail the incident regarding Nephi's broken bow, I remembered my earlier thoughts about wasting my time and patience reading the Book of Mormon to my young children. Oh, how I had underestimated their ability to learn the lessons of the Book of Mormon!'"[3]

Howard J. McOmber II pondered President Benson's exhortation to flood the earth with the Book of Mormon. He wondered, "How could I as an individual be a significant part of such a flood?

"Then one night," Brother McOmber said, "as I was pondering this problem I realized that I could give every individual on my street the opportunity to receive a copy of the Book of Mormon.

"But there was a problem—they knew me. They knew about my dog that barked too often—and too early in the morning. They knew that my yard was not the garden spot of the neighborhood. They knew my shortcomings as a neighbor; they would probably turn me away.

"I determined to have faith and go ahead anyway. I would offer them the book—even if they might throw it away, or let it collect dust on their shelves for years. Yet I found myself thinking negatively; I had almost convinced myself that nothing could come of my efforts.

"Then I remembered that I knew my neighbors at least as well as they knew me. A few had told questionable jokes at the last community development meeting, and a few had drunk too much at the last neighborhood barbecue. Some seemed to have little purpose in their lives. I wondered what I would have been like if I weren't a member of the Church, or if I'd never heard of the Book of Mormon. Clearly, this book could help those who would give it a chance.

"So I contacted everyone on my street and offered them a copy of the Book of Mormon—and they all thanked me! It went so well that I went to the next street, completed my subdivision, and then went on to the next subdivision. When I was through, I had visited 104 houses and placed forty books.

"It started to become easier to offer copies of the Book of Mormon to acquaintances.

"In time I had given all seventy-five employees at my work copies of the Book of Mormon. Twenty-three of them took the missionary discussions. Seven were later baptized, and four children belonging to my coworkers also joined the Church. One man took two discussions but then lost interest in investigating the Church. Seven months later, after he had moved on to a job at another company, he called to tell me that he had been reading the Book of Mormon and had realized that he was feeling the calm, peaceful touch of the Spirit, just as I had described it. He, too, soon finished the discussions and was baptized.

"I love the Book of Mormon. I think of it as the Lord's calling card, and I have been amazed at how easy it is to start a spiritual flood with it on a personal scale. When we do the work of the Lord, we have his help."[4]

Another member told of the transformation that occurred in his testimony as he followed President Benson's counsel to read the Book of Mormon: "When President Benson challenged us to read the Book of Mormon, I was 15 years old. I was already a faithful scripture reader, focusing mostly on the New Testament. But at President Benson's urging, I started to study the Book of Mormon every day. That was a major turning point for me. The New Testament had taught me about the earthly ministry of Jesus Christ, and I will always be grateful for that. But I needed the depth that came from a study of the Book of Mormon. While the Bible helped me know about what Jesus did for people in the Holy Land, the Book of Mormon gave me a deeper understanding of what He has done for me. Through a study of the Book of Mormon, I gained a testimony of the infinite Atonement of my Savior. And later, when I faced crises that tested my faith, I turned to the Book of Mormon for comfort and strength. Now I never let a day go by without reading the Book of Mormon."[5]

Teachings of Ezra Taft Benson

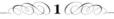 1

The Book of Mormon was written for us.

The Book of Mormon . . . was written for our day. The Nephites never had the book; neither did the Lamanites of ancient times. It was meant for us. Mormon wrote near the end of the Nephite civilization. Under the inspiration of God, who sees all things from the beginning, he abridged centuries of records, choosing the stories, speeches, and events that would be most helpful to us.

Each of the major writers of the Book of Mormon testified that he wrote for future generations. . . . If they saw our day and chose those things which would be of greatest worth to us, is not that how we should study the Book of Mormon? We should constantly ask ourselves, "Why did the Lord inspire Mormon (or Moroni or Alma) to include that in his record? What lesson can I learn from that to help me live in this day and age?"

And there is example after example of how that question will be answered. For example, in the Book of Mormon we find a pattern for preparing for the Second Coming. A major portion of the book centers on the few decades just prior to Christ's coming to America. By careful study of that time period, we can determine why some were destroyed in the terrible judgments that preceded His coming and what brought others to stand at the temple in the land of Bountiful and thrust their hands into the wounds of His hands and feet.

From the Book of Mormon we learn how disciples of Christ live in times of war. From the Book of Mormon we see the evils of secret combinations portrayed in graphic and chilling reality. In the Book of Mormon we find lessons for dealing with persecution and apostasy. We learn much about how to do missionary work. And more than anywhere else, we see in the Book of Mormon the dangers of materialism and setting our hearts on the things of the world. Can anyone doubt that this book was meant for us and that in it we find great power, great comfort, and great protection?[6]

As we study the Book of Mormon daily, the power of the book will flow into our lives.

It is not just that the Book of Mormon teaches us truth, though it indeed does that. It is not just that the Book of Mormon bears testimony of Christ, though it indeed does that, too. But there is something more. There is a power in the book which will begin to flow into your lives the moment you begin a serious study of the book. You will find greater power to resist temptation. You will find the power to avoid deception. You will find the power to stay on the strait and narrow path. The scriptures are called "the words of life" (D&C 84:85), and nowhere is that more true than it is of the Book of Mormon. When you begin to hunger and thirst after those words, you will find life in greater and greater abundance.[7]

Men may deceive each other, but God does not deceive men. Therefore, the Book of Mormon sets forth the best test for determining its truthfulness—namely, read it and then ask God if it is true [see Moroni 10:4]. . . .

This, then, is the supreme assurance for the honest in heart—to know by personal revelation from God that the Book of Mormon is true. Millions have put it to that test and know, and increasing millions will yet know.

Now the spirit, as well as the body, is in need of constant nourishment. Yesterday's meal is not enough to sustain today's needs. So also an infrequent reading of "the most correct of any book on earth," as Joseph Smith called it, is not enough. (*History of the Church,* 4:461.)

Not all truths are of equal value, nor are all scriptures of the same worth. What better way to nourish the spirit than to frequently feast from the book which the Prophet Joseph Smith said would get a man "nearer to God by abiding by its precepts, than by any other book"? (*History of the Church,* 4:461.)[8]

141

Do eternal consequences rest upon our response to this book? Yes, either to our blessing or our condemnation.

Every Latter-day Saint should make the study of this book a life-time pursuit. Otherwise, he is placing his soul in jeopardy and neglecting that which could give spiritual and intellectual unity to his whole life. There is a difference between a convert who is built on the rock of Christ through the Book of Mormon and stays hold on the iron rod, and one who [is] not.[9]

We have an increasing number who have been convinced, through the Book of Mormon, that Jesus is the Christ. Now we need an increasing number who will use the Book of Mormon to become committed to Christ. We need to be convinced and committed.

. . . My beloved brethren and sisters, let us read the Book of Mormon and be convinced that Jesus is the Christ. Let us continually reread the Book of Mormon so that we might more fully come to Christ, be committed to Him, centered in Him, and consumed in Him.

We are meeting the adversary every day. The challenges of this era will rival any of the past, and these challenges will increase both spiritually and temporally. We must be close to Christ, we must daily take His name upon us, always remember Him, and keep His commandments.[10]

3

We must flood the earth and our lives with the Book of Mormon.

We each need to get our own testimony of the Book of Mormon through the Holy Ghost. Then our testimony, coupled with the Book of Mormon, should be shared with others so that they, too, can know through the Holy Ghost of its truthfulness.[11]

Can you imagine what would happen with an increasing number of copies of the Book of Mormon in the hands of an increasing number of missionaries who know how to use it and who have been born of God? When this happens, we will get the bounteous harvest of souls that the Lord promised.[12]

"I have a vision of flooding the earth with the Book of Mormon."

I have a conviction: The more we teach and preach from the Book of Mormon, the more we shall please the Lord and the greater will be our power of speaking. By so doing, we shall greatly increase our converts, both within the Church and among those we proselyte. . . . Our commission then is to teach the principles of the gospel which are in the Bible and the Book of Mormon. "These shall be their teachings, as they shall be directed by the Spirit" (D&C 42:13).[13]

The Book of Mormon is the instrument that God designed to "sweep the earth as with a flood, to gather out [His] elect." (Moses 7:62.) This sacred volume of scripture needs to become more central in our preaching, our teaching, and our missionary work.

. . . In this age of the electronic media and the mass distribution of the printed word, God will hold us accountable if we do not now move the Book of Mormon in a monumental way.

We have the Book of Mormon, we have the members, we have the missionaries, we have the resources, and the world has the need. The time is now!

My beloved brothers and sisters, we hardly fathom the power of the Book of Mormon, nor the divine role it must play, nor the extent to which it must be moved. . . .

I challenge all of us to prayerfully consider steps that we can personally take to bring this new witness for Christ more fully into our own lives and into a world that so desperately needs it.

I have a vision of homes alerted, of classes alive, and of pulpits aflame with the spirit of Book of Mormon messages.

I have a vision of home teachers and visiting teachers, ward and branch officers, and stake and mission leaders counseling our people out of the most correct of any book on earth—the Book of Mormon.

I have a vision of artists putting into film, drama, literature, music, and paintings great themes and great characters from the Book of Mormon.

I have a vision of thousands of missionaries going into the mission field with hundreds of passages memorized from the Book of Mormon so that they might feed the needs of a spiritually famished world.

I have a vision of the whole Church getting nearer to God by abiding by the precepts of the Book of Mormon.

Indeed, I have a vision of flooding the earth with the Book of Mormon.[14]

May I commend you faithful Saints who are striving to flood the earth and your lives with the Book of Mormon. Not only must we move forward in a monumental manner more copies of the Book of Mormon, but we must move boldly forward into our own lives and throughout the earth more of its marvelous messages.[15]

Suggestions for Study and Teaching

Questions
- In section 1, review President Benson's counsel about how to study the Book of Mormon. How can this counsel help us meet challenges? What are some passages in the Book of Mormon that relate to challenges we face?

- In what ways have you seen the fulfillment of the promises listed in section 2? What are some things we can do to share the Book of Mormon with people who need these promises in their lives?

- What do you think it means to "flood the earth and [our] lives with the Book of Mormon"? (For some examples, see section 3.)

Related Scriptures

2 Nephi 27:22; Mormon 8:26–41; Moroni 1:4; 10:3–5; see also the introduction to the Book of Mormon

Study Help

As you read, "underline and mark words or phrases so that you distinguish between ideas in a single [passage]. . . . In the margins write scripture references that clarify the passages you are studying" (*Preach My Gospel* [2004], 23).

Notes

1. "To the Children of the Church," *Ensign,* May 1989, 81–82.

2. "Beware of Pride," *Ensign,* May 1989, 4.

3. LaRene Gaunt, "Does the Book of Mormon Count?" *Ensign,* June 1991, 20.

4. Howard J. McOmber II, in "Finding Truth in the Book of Mormon," *Ensign,* Jan. 1996, 10–11.

5. Name withheld, unpublished manuscript.

6. "The Book of Mormon—Keystone of Our Religion," *Ensign,* Nov. 1986, 6–7.

7. "The Book of Mormon—Keystone of Our Religion," 7.

8. "A New Witness for Christ," *Ensign,* Nov. 1984, 6–7.

9. "The Book of Mormon Is the Word of God," *Ensign,* Jan. 1988, 5.

10. "Come unto Christ," *Ensign,* Nov. 1987, 84, 85.

11. "The Book of Mormon and the Doctrine and Covenants," *Ensign,* May 1987, 84.

12. "Born of God," *Ensign,* July 1989, 4.

13. *The Teachings of Ezra Taft Benson* (1988), 58.

14. "Flooding the Earth with the Book of Mormon," *Ensign,* Nov. 1988, 4, 5–6.

15. "Beware of Pride," 4.

*Today, Latter-day Saints gather in the Conference Center
and throughout the world to listen to the living prophet.*

Follow the Living Prophet

"The most important prophet, so far as we are concerned, is the one who is living in our day and age."

From the Life of Ezra Taft Benson

One night when Ezra Taft Benson was 15 years old, he sat at the supper table with the rest of his family and listened to his father read a letter from President Joseph F. Smith and his counselors in the First Presidency. In part, the letter said: "We advise and urge the inauguration of a 'Home Evening' throughout the Church, at which time fathers and mothers may gather their boys and girls about them in the home and teach them the word of the Lord. . . . If the Saints obey this counsel, we promise that great blessings will result. Love at home and obedience to parents will increase. Faith will be developed in the hearts of the youth of Israel, and they will gain power to combat the evil influences and temptations which beset them."[1]

President Benson later recalled: "When [my father] concluded the letter, he said, 'The Presidency has spoken, and this is the word of the Lord to us!' From that time forward, we diligently held family home evenings in my boyhood home."[2]

When President Benson had a family of his own, he and his wife carried on the tradition he had learned from his parents. He said, "I testify out of this experience [in my parents' home] and the experience of family nights in my own home that great spiritual blessings can result."[3]

In 1947 the First Presidency directed Church members to renew efforts to hold home evenings. President Benson, then a member of the Quorum of the Twelve Apostles, emphasized that subject in a general conference address. He testified of the family as "a divine institution,"[4] and he reminded the Saints of the blessings that would come if they would follow the counsel of the prophet to strengthen their families and hold home evenings. He testified: "Our happiness here and hereafter is tied up with our successful discharge of this great responsibility. It merits, my brethren and sisters, our prayerful planning and attention, and I am confident in my own heart that great dividends will result, that great joy and satisfaction will come if we heed this as all other counsels given to us by the Presidency of the Church."[5]

Having experienced blessings that result from heeding the counsel of the Lord's chosen servants, Ezra Taft Benson frequently urged Latter-day Saints to keep their eyes on the living prophet. He boldly testified of the divine calling of each President of the Church with whom he served.[6] When President Spencer W. Kimball, who had been ordained an Apostle on the same day as President Benson, delivered his first address as President of the Church to a group of Church leaders, President Benson "arose and with a voice filled with emotion, echoing the feeling of all present, said, in substance: 'President Kimball, through all the years that these meetings have been held, we have never heard such an address as you have just given. Truly, there is a prophet in Israel.'"[7] And when that divine calling came to President Benson after the death of President Kimball, he accepted it with humility and determination. He said: "My wife, Flora, and I have prayed continually that President Kimball's days would be prolonged on this earth and another miracle performed on his behalf. Now that the Lord has spoken, we will do our best, under his guiding direction, to move the work forward in the earth."[8]

Teachings of Ezra Taft Benson

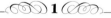 1

The President of the Church is the Lord's mouthpiece on the earth.

Learn to keep your eye on the prophet. He is the Lord's mouthpiece and the only man who can speak for the Lord today. Let his inspired counsel take precedence. Let his inspired words be a basis for evaluating the counsel of all lesser authorities. Then live close to the Spirit so you may know the truth of all things.[9]

The Lord's mouthpiece and prophet on the face of the earth today received his authority through a line of prophets going back to Joseph Smith, who was ordained by Peter, James, and John, who were ordained by Christ, who was and is the head of the Church, the Creator of this earth, and the God before whom all men must stand accountable.[10]

This Church is not being directed by the wisdom of men. I know that. The power and influence of Almighty God are directing His Church.[11]

The most important prophet for us is the living prophet.

God knows all things, the end from the beginning, and no man becomes president of the church of Jesus Christ by accident, or remains there by chance, or is called home by happenstance.

The most important prophet, so far as we are concerned, is the one who is living in our day and age. This is the prophet who has today's instructions from God to us. God's revelation to Adam did not instruct Noah how to build the ark. Every generation has need of the ancient scripture, plus the current scripture from the living prophet. Therefore, the most crucial reading and pondering that you should do is of the latest inspired words from the Lord's mouthpiece. That is why it is essential that you have access to and carefully read his words. . . .

Yes, we thank thee, O God, for a prophet to guide us in these latter days [see *Hymns,* no. 19].[12]

Beware of those who would set up the dead prophets against the living prophets, for the living prophets always take precedence.[13]

Each President has been uniquely selected for the time and situation which the world and Church needed. All were "men of the hour," as we have witnessed in President Spencer W. Kimball. Contemplate the miracle of that foreordination and preparation! Though called and given keys many years prior to the time that the mantle fell upon him, the President was always the right man in the right

*As President of the Church, Ezra Taft Benson
spoke with great love and urgency.*

place for the times. This miracle alone is one of the marks of the divinity of the Church.[14]

Let me ask, do we need a true prophet of the Lord on the earth today? Did the people in Noah's day need a prophet to warn them spiritually and temporally? Had a man refused to follow Noah, would he have been saved from the flood? Yet the Bible tells us that in the last days in which we live, the wickedness of the people will become comparable to the wickedness of the people in Noah's day when God cleansed the earth by flood [see Matthew 24:37–39]. Do you think we need a prophet today to warn us and prepare us for the cleansing that God promised will come, this time by fire?[15]

If we want to know how well we stand with the Lord then let us ask ourselves how well we stand with His mortal captain—how close do our lives harmonize with the Lord's anointed—the living Prophet—President of the Church, and with the Quorum of the First Presidency.[16]

_____ €〈3〈€_____

The living prophet tells us what we need to know, not necessarily what we want to hear.

A revealing characteristic of a true prophet is that he declares a message from God. He makes no apology for the message, nor does he fear for any social repercussions which may lead to derision and persecution.[17]

Sometimes there are those who feel their earthly knowledge on a certain subject is superior to the heavenly knowledge which God gives to his prophet on the same subject. They feel the prophet must have the same earthly credentials or training which they have had before they will accept anything the prophet has to say that might contradict their earthly schooling. How much earthly schooling did Joseph Smith have? Yet he gave revelations on all kinds of subjects. . . . We encourage earthly knowledge in many areas, but remember if there is ever a conflict between earthly knowledge and the words of the prophet, you stand with the prophet and you'll be blessed and time will show you have done the right thing.

. . . The prophet does not have to say "Thus saith the Lord" to give us scripture.

Sometimes there are those who argue about words. They might say the prophet gave us counsel but that we are not obliged to follow it unless he says it is a commandment. But the Lord says of the Prophet, "Thou shalt give heed unto all his words and commandments which he shall give unto you." (D&C 21:4.)

. . . The prophet tells us what we need to know, not always what we want to know.

"Thou has declared unto us hard things, more than we are able to bear," complained Nephi's brethren. But Nephi answered by saying, "The guilty taketh the truth to be hard, for it cutteth them to the very center." (1 Ne. 16:1–2.)

Said President Harold B. Lee:

"You may not like what comes from the authority of the Church. It may conflict with your political views. It may contradict your social views. It may interfere with some of your social life. . . . Your safety and ours depends upon whether or not we follow. . . . Let's keep our eye on the President of the Church." (Conference Report, October 1970, p. 152–153.)

But it is the living prophet who really upsets the world. "Even in the Church," said President Kimball, "many are prone to garnish the sepulchres of yesterday's prophets and mentally stone the living ones." (*Instructor,* 95:257.)

Why? Because the living prophet gets at what we need to know now, and the world prefers that prophets either be dead or worry about their own affairs. . . .

How we respond to the words of a living prophet when he tells us what we need to know, but would rather not hear, is a test of our faithfulness. . . .

The learned may feel the prophet is only inspired when he agrees with them, otherwise the prophet is just giving his opinion—speaking as a man. The rich may feel they have no need to take counsel of a lowly prophet. . . .

. . . The prophet will not necessarily be popular with the world or the worldly.

As a prophet reveals the truth it divides the people. The honest in heart heed his words but the unrighteous either ignore the prophet or fight him. When the prophet points out the sins of the world, the worldly either want to close the mouth of the prophet, or else act as if the prophet didn't exist, rather than repent of their sins. Popularity is never a test of truth. Many a prophet has been killed or cast out. As we come closer to the Lord's second coming you can expect that as the people of the world become more wicked, the prophet will be less popular with them.[18]

We will be blessed as we follow the living prophet.

To help you pass the crucial tests which lie ahead, I am going to give you . . . a grand key which, if you will honor, will crown you with God's glory and bring you out victorious in spite of Satan's fury.

. . . As a Church we sing the hymn, "We Thank Thee, O God, for a Prophet" [*Hymns,* no. 19]. Here then is the grand key—Follow the prophet. . . .

. . . The prophet is the only man who speaks for the Lord in everything.

In section 132 verse 7 of the Doctrine and Covenants the Lord speaks of the prophet—the president—and says:

"There is never but one on the earth at a time on whom this power and the keys of this priesthood are conferred."

Then in section 21 verses 4–6, the Lord states:

"Wherefore, meaning the church, thou shalt give heed unto all his words and commandments which he shall give unto you as he receiveth them, walking in all holiness before me;

"For his word ye shall receive, as if from mine own mouth, in all patience and faith.

"For by doing these things the gates of hell shall not prevail against you." [19]

The prophet will never lead the Church astray.

President Wilford Woodruff stated: "I say to Israel, The Lord will never permit me or any other man who stands as president of the Church to lead you astray. It is not in the program. It is not in the mind of God" [see *Teachings of Presidents of the Church: Wilford Woodruff* (2004), 199].

President Marion G. Romney tells of this incident which happened to him:

"I remember years ago when I was a bishop I had President Heber J. Grant talk to our ward. After the meeting I drove him home. . . . Standing by me, he put his arm over my shoulder and said: 'My boy, you always keep your eye on the President of the Church and if he ever tells you to do anything, and it is wrong, and you do it, the Lord will bless you for it.' Then with a twinkle in his eye, he said, 'But you don't need to worry. The Lord will never let his mouthpiece lead the people astray.'" (Conference Report, October 1960, p. 78.) [20]

The story is told how Brigham Young, driving through a community, saw a man building a house and simply told him to double the thickness of his walls. Accepting President Young as a prophet, the man changed his plans and doubled the walls. Shortly afterward a flood came through that town, resulting in much destruction, but this man's walls stood. While putting the roof on his house, he was heard singing, "We thank thee, O God, for a prophet!"[21]

As members of the Church we have some close quarters to pass through if we are going to get home safely. We will be given a chance to choose between conflicting counsel given by some. That's why we must learn—and the sooner we learn, the better—to keep our eye on the Prophet, the President of the Church.[22]

Suggestions for Study and Teaching

Questions
- President Benson said, "Learn to keep your eye on the prophet" (section 1). What does this mean to you?

- Why do you think the most important prophet for us is the current President of the Church? (See section 2.) What counsel have we recently received from the living prophet?

- As you review section 3, reflect on a time when you have followed the prophet's counsel even though you have not completely understood it. What can we learn from such experiences?

- Consider the "grand key" that President Benson identifies in section 4. What are some blessings you have received when you have been true to this grand key?

Related Scriptures
2 Chronicles 20:20; Amos 3:7; Ephesians 2:19–20; 4:11–15; D&C 1:14–16, 37–38; 107:91–92; Articles of Faith 1:6

Teaching Help
"Do not be afraid of silence. People often need time to think about and reply to questions or to express what they are feeling. You might pause after you have asked a question, after a spiritual experience has been shared, or when a person is having difficulty expressing himself or herself" (*Teaching, No Greater Call* [1999], 67).

Notes

1. Joseph F. Smith, Anthon H. Lund, and Charles W. Penrose, "Home Evening," *Improvement Era,* June 1915, 733–34.

2. *The Teachings of Ezra Taft Benson* (1988), 528.

3. *The Teachings of Ezra Taft Benson,* 528.

4. In Conference Report, Oct. 1947, 23.

5. In Conference Report, Oct. 1947, 27.

6. See, for example, Conference Report, Oct. 1968, 17; Conference Report, Apr. 1970, 127; *Ensign,* Jan. 1973, 57; *Ensign,* Nov. 1980, 34; *Ensign,* May 1984, 8.

7. W. Grant Bangerter, "A Special Moment in Church History," *Ensign,* Nov. 1977, 27.

8. Quoted in Don L. Searle, "President Ezra Taft Benson Ordained Thirteenth President of the Church," *Ensign,* Dec. 1985, 5.

9. *The Teachings of Ezra Taft Benson,* 134.

10. *The Teachings of Ezra Taft Benson,* 132.

11. *The Teachings of Ezra Taft Benson,* 132.

12. "Jesus Christ—Gifts and Expectations," *New Era,* May 1975, 16–17.

13. "Fourteen Fundamentals in Following the Prophet," *Tambuli,* June 1981, 3.

14. *The Teachings of Ezra Taft Benson,* 142.

15. "Listen to a Prophet's Voice," *Ensign,* Jan. 1973, 59.

16. "Fourteen Fundamentals in Following the Prophet," 8.

17. "Joseph Smith: Prophet to Our Generation," *Ensign,* Nov. 1981, 61.

18. "Fourteen Fundamentals in Following the Prophet," 3–4, 6; italics removed from original.

19. "Fourteen Fundamentals in Following the Prophet," 1–2; italics removed from original.

20. "Fourteen Fundamentals in Following the Prophet," 3; italics removed from original.

21. "Civic Standards for the Faithful Saints," *Ensign,* July 1972, 61; see also Sidney Alvarus Hanks and Ephraim K. Hanks, *Scouting for the Mormons on the Great Frontier* [1948], 78–80.

22. In Conference Report, Oct. 1966, 122.

"How do we obtain the Spirit? 'By the prayer of faith,' says the Lord."

Seek the Spirit in All You Do

"We must remain open and sensitive to the promptings of the Holy Ghost in all aspects of our lives."

From the Life of Ezra Taft Benson

When President Ezra Taft Benson counseled other General Authorities about serving in the Church, he often said, "Remember, Brethren, in this work it is the Spirit that counts."[1] And when he and these brethren ministered together, he taught this principle by example, showing that the Lord "is close to His servants, even within whispering distance."[2] Elder Robert D. Hales of the Quorum of the Twelve Apostles told of a time when he accompanied President Benson to a stake conference in which a new stake president would be called:

"After praying, interviewing, studying, and praying again, Elder Benson asked if I knew who the new president would be. I said I had not received that inspiration yet. He looked at me for a long time and replied he hadn't either. However, we *were* inspired to ask three worthy priesthood holders to speak in the Saturday evening session of conference. Moments after the third speaker began, the Spirit prompted me that he should be the new stake president. I looked over at President Benson and saw tears streaming down his face. Revelation had been given to both of us—but only by continuing to seek our Heavenly Father's will as we moved forward in faith."[3]

At the beginning of a conference for new mission presidents, President Benson shared the following counsel:

"I have said so many times to my brethren that the Spirit is the most important single element in this work. With the Spirit and magnifying your call, you can do miracles for the Lord in the mission field. Without the Spirit you will never succeed *regardless* of your talent and ability.

"You will receive excellent instruction in the next three days. Handbooks will be distributed, responsibilities and procedures will be discussed, policies will be analyzed, and all this will be most helpful to you. But the greatest help you will ever receive as a mission president will not be from handbooks or manuals. Your greatest help will come from the Lord Himself as you supplicate and plead with Him in humble prayer. As you are driven to your knees again and again, asking Him for divine help in administering your mission, you will feel the Spirit, you will get your answer from above, your mission will prosper spiritually because of your dependence and your reliance on Him."[4]

President Benson extended this counsel to all members of the Church, including young children.[5] He said: "In this work it is the Spirit that counts—wherever we serve. I know I must rely on the Spirit. Let us obtain that Spirit and be faithful members of the Church, devoted children and parents, effective home teachers, edifying instructors, inspired ward and stake leaders."[6]

Although President Benson taught this truth publicly and boldly throughout the world, his primary effort to follow it was private and quiet. It began at home, in partnership with his wife, Flora. Flora's half-sister Julia Dalley once visited the Bensons, and she later wrote a letter to Flora, commenting on the Benson family. "What on earth could be more ideal?" she said. "I admire the simplicity of your mode of living but most of all I was impressed with the fact that in your home there dwelled the Spirit of the Lord."[7]

Teachings of Ezra Taft Benson

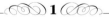 1

We should strive for the constant companionship of the Holy Ghost all the days of our lives.

One sure way we can determine whether we are on the strait and narrow path is that we will possess the Spirit of the Lord in our lives.

Having the Holy Ghost brings forth certain fruits.

The Apostle Paul said that "the fruit of the Spirit is love, joy, peace, longsuffering, gentleness, goodness, faith, meekness, [and] temperance." (Gal. 5:22–23.)

The most important thing in our lives is the Spirit. I have always felt that. We must remain open and sensitive to the promptings of the Holy Ghost in all aspects of our lives. . . . These promptings most often come when we are not under the pressure of appointments and when we are not caught up in the worries of day-to-day life.[8]

Spirituality—being in tune with the Spirit of the Lord—is the greatest need we all have. We should strive for the constant companionship of the Holy Ghost all the days of our lives. When we have the Spirit, we will love to serve, we will love the Lord, and we will love those with whom we serve, and those whom we serve.

Several years after Joseph Smith was martyred, he appeared to President Brigham Young. Hear his message:

"Tell the people to be humble and faithful, and be sure to keep the spirit of the Lord and it will lead them right. Be careful and not turn away the small still voice; it will teach you what to do and where to go; it will yield the fruits of the kingdom. Tell the brethren to keep their hearts open to conviction, so that when the Holy Ghost comes to them, their hearts will be ready to receive it." . . .

This latter-day work is spiritual. It takes spirituality to comprehend it, to love it, and to discern it. Therefore seek the Spirit in all you do. Keep it with you continually. That is our challenge.[9]

We live in a very wicked world. We are surrounded with propaganda that evil is good and good is evil. False teachings abound that affect us. Almost everything that is wholesome, good, pure, uplifting, and strengthening is being challenged as never before.

One reason we are on this earth is to discern between truth and error. This discernment comes by the Holy Ghost, not just our intellectual faculties.

When we earnestly and honestly seek for the truth, this beautiful promise finds fulfillment: "God shall give unto you knowledge by

his Holy Spirit, yea, by the unspeakable gift of the Holy Ghost."
(Doctrine and Covenants 121:26.)[10]

2

If we are humble and sensitive, the Lord will prompt us through our feelings.

Pray to Heavenly Father to bless you with His Spirit at all times.
We often call the Spirit the Holy Ghost. . . . The Holy Ghost helps
you to choose the right. The Holy Ghost will protect you from evil.
He whispers to you in a still, small voice to do right. When you *do*
good, you *feel* good, and that is the Holy Ghost speaking to you.
The Holy Ghost is a wonderful companion. He is *always* there to
help you.[11]

Ponder matters that you do not understand. As the Lord commanded Oliver Cowdery: "Study it out in your mind; then . . . ask
me if it be right, and if it is right I will cause that your bosom shall
burn within you; therefore, you shall *feel* that it is right." (D&C 9:8,
italics added.)

Did you notice that last phrase? "You shall *feel* that it is right."

We hear the words of the Lord most often by a feeling. If we are
humble and sensitive, the Lord will prompt us through our feelings.
That is why spiritual promptings move us on occasion to great
joy, sometimes to tears. Many times my emotions have been made
tender and my feelings very sensitive when touched by the Spirit.

The Holy Ghost causes our feelings to be more tender. We feel
more charitable and compassionate with each other. We are more
calm in our relationships. We have a greater capacity to love each
other. People want to be around us because our very countenances
radiate the influence of the Spirit. We are more godly in our character. As a result, we become increasingly more sensitive to the
promptings of the Holy Ghost and thus able to comprehend spiritual things more clearly.[12]

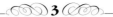

We obtain the Spirit through sincere prayer and fasting.

How do we obtain the Spirit? "By the prayer of faith," says the Lord [D&C 42:14]. Therefore, we must pray with sincerity and real intent. We must pray for increased faith and pray for the Spirit to accompany our teaching. We should ask the Lord for forgiveness.

Our prayers must be offered in the same spirit and with the same fervor as were the prayers of Enos in the Book of Mormon. Most are familiar with that inspiring story, so I will not repeat the background. I only want to draw your attention to these words. Enos testified: "I will tell you of the wrestle which I had before God, before I received a remission of my sins." He clarified that wrestle with God. Note the fervor in his petition:

"My soul hungered."

"I kneeled down before my Maker."

"I cried unto him in mighty prayer and supplication for *mine own soul.*"

"All day long did I cry unto him."

Then Enos testified, "There came a voice unto me, saying: Enos, thy sins are forgiven thee, and thou shalt be blessed. . . . Wherefore, my guilt was swept away." When he inquired of the Lord how this had been accomplished, the Lord answered him: "Because of thy faith in Christ . . . thy faith hath *made thee whole.*" (Enos 1:2, 4–8; italics added.)

Enos was spiritually healed. Through his mighty supplications to God, he experienced what the faithful of any dispensation can experience, do experience, and must experience if they are to see God and be filled with His Spirit.[13]

If you want to get the spirit of your office and calling . . . try fasting for a period. I don't mean just missing one meal, then eating twice as much the next meal. I mean really fasting, and praying during that period. It will do more to give you the real spirit of your office and calling and permit the Spirit to operate through you than anything I know.[14]

"Daily scripture study invites the Spirit."

4

Daily scripture study, including meditation on passages of scripture, invites the Spirit.

Search the scriptures diligently in personal study every day. Daily scripture study invites the Spirit.[15]

Take time to meditate. Meditation on a passage of scripture—James 1:5—led a young boy into a grove of trees to commune with his Heavenly Father. That is what opened the heavens in this dispensation.

Meditation on a passage of scripture from the book of John in the New Testament brought forth the great revelation on the three degrees of glory [see John 5:29; D&C 76].

162

Meditation on another passage of scripture from the Epistle of Peter opened the heavens to President Joseph F. Smith, and he saw the spirit world. That revelation, known as the Vision of the Redemption of the Dead, is now a part of the Doctrine and Covenants [see 1 Peter 3:18–20; 4:6; D&C 138].

Ponder the significance of the responsibility the Lord has given to us. The Lord has counseled, "Let the solemnities of eternity rest upon your minds." (D&C 43:34.) You cannot do that when your minds are preoccupied with the cares of the world.

Read and study the scriptures. The scriptures should be studied in the home with fathers and mothers taking the lead and setting the example. The scriptures are to be comprehended by the power of the Holy Ghost, for the Lord has given this promise to His faithful and obedient: "Thou mayest know the mysteries and peaceable things." (D&C 42:61.)

The following statement by President Spencer W. Kimball illustrates how we may develop more spirituality in our lives:

"I find that when I get casual in my relationships with divinity and when it seems that no divine ear is listening and no divine voice is speaking, that I am far, far away. If I immerse myself in the scriptures the distance narrows and the spirituality returns. I find myself loving more intensely those whom I must love with all my heart and mind and strength, and loving them more, I find it easier to abide their counsel." . . .

That is great counsel which I know by experience to be true.

The more familiar you are with the scriptures, the closer you become to the mind and will of the Lord and the closer you become as husband and wife and children. You will find that by reading the scriptures the truths of eternity will rest on your minds.[16]

The adversary does not want scripture study to take place in our homes, and so he will create problems if he can. But we must persist.[17]

We cannot know God and Jesus without studying about them and then doing their will. This course leads to additional revealed knowledge which, if obeyed, will eventually lead us to further truths. If we follow this pattern, we will receive further light and joy, eventually leading into God's presence, where we, with Him, will have a fulness.[18]

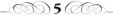

The Holy Ghost will abide with us as we honor, respect, and obey God's laws.

We have been taught that the Spirit will not dwell in unclean tabernacles [see Helaman 4:24]. Therefore, one of our first priorities is to make sure our own personal lives are in order.[19]

Let me talk about obedience. You're learning now to keep all the commandments of the Lord. As you do so, you will have His Spirit to be with you. You'll feel good about yourselves. You can't *do* wrong and *feel* right. It's impossible![20]

The temporal promise for obedience [to the Word of Wisdom] is: They "shall receive health in their navel and marrow to their bones; . . . [they] shall run and not be weary, and shall walk and not faint." (D&C 89:18, 20.)

I have always felt, however, that the greater blessing of obedience to the Word of Wisdom and all other commandments is spiritual.

Listen to the spiritual promise: "All saints who remember to keep and do these sayings, walking in obedience *to the commandments,* . . . shall find wisdom and great treasures of knowledge, even hidden treasures." (D&C 89:18, 19; italics added.)

Some have thought this promise was contingent on just keeping the provisions of the Word of Wisdom. But you will notice we must walk in obedience to *all* the commandments. Then we shall receive specific spiritual promises. This means we must obey the law of tithing, keep the Sabbath day holy, keep morally clean and chaste, and obey all other commandments.

When we do all this, the promise is: They "shall find wisdom and great treasures of knowledge, even hidden treasures." (D&C 89:19.)

What father and mother would not want the inspiration of the Lord in rearing their children? I testify these blessings can be yours. Surely parents would not want, through disobedience, to prevent their children from receiving the Lord's blessings. All fathers and mothers in Israel should qualify themselves for this promise.

Living the commandments of God is a condition of worthiness for entrance into the House of the Lord. There wisdom and "great treasures of knowledge" are given that relate to our happiness in this life and joy throughout eternity. . . .

I do not believe that a member of the Church can have an active, vibrant testimony of the gospel without keeping the commandments. A testimony is to have current inspiration to know the work is true, not something we receive only once. The Holy Ghost abides with those who honor, respect, and obey God's laws. And it is that Spirit which gives inspiration to the individual. Humbly I testify to the reality of this promise.[21]

Suggestions for Study and Teaching

Questions

- President Benson said that promptings from the Holy Ghost "most often come when we are not under the pressure of appointments and when we are not caught up in the worries of day-to-day life" (section 1). How can we remain sensitive to the Spirit even when we have such pressures?

- President Benson taught, "If we are humble and sensitive, the Lord will prompt us through our feelings" (section 2). What have you learned about recognizing such promptings?

- In section 3, President Benson encourages us to follow the example of Enos, as recorded in the Book of Mormon. What are some lessons about seeking the Spirit that we can learn from Enos?

- For you, what is the difference between reading the scriptures and "meditat[ing] on a passage of scripture"? (See section 4.) Why do you think diligent, daily scripture study helps us be open to the promptings of the Spirit?

- President Benson said, "The Holy Ghost abides with those who honor, respect, and obey God's laws" (section 5). Why do you think our ability to receive inspiration is influenced by our efforts to keep the commandments?

Related Scriptures

1 Nephi 10:17–19; 2 Nephi 4:15–16; Mosiah 2:36–37; D&C 8:2–3; 45:56–57; 76:5–10; 121:45–46

Study Help

"As you study, pay careful attention to ideas that come to your mind and feelings that come to your heart" (*Preach My Gospel* [2004], 18). Consider recording the impressions you receive, even if they seem unrelated to the words you are reading. They may be the very things the Lord wants to reveal to you.

Notes

1. Quoted by Thomas S. Monson, "A Provident Plan—A Precious Promise," *Ensign,* May 1986, 63.

2. "Seek the Spirit of the Lord," *Ensign,* Apr. 1988, 5

3. Robert D. Hales, "Personal Revelation: The Teachings and Examples of the Prophets," *Ensign,* Nov. 2007, 87–88.

4. "My Challenges to Mission Presidents," seminar for new mission presidents, June 25, 1986.

5. See "To the Children of the Church," *Ensign,* May 1989, 82.

6. "A Sacred Responsibility," *Ensign,* May 1986, 77.

7. Julia Dalley, in Sheri L. Dew, *Ezra Taft Benson: A Biography* (1988), 128.

8. "Seek the Spirit of the Lord," 2.

9. "Seek the Spirit of the Lord," 5; the statement by Brigham Young is found in *Manuscript History of Brigham Young,* Feb. 23, 1947, 2 vols., ed. Elden Jay Watson (1968, 1971), 2:529.

10. *Come unto Christ* (1983), 22.

11. "To the Children of the Church," 82.

12. "Seek the Spirit of the Lord," 4.

13. *Come unto Christ,* 92–93.

14. *The Teachings of Ezra Taft Benson* (1988), 331–32.

15. "My Challenges to Mission Presidents," seminar for new mission presidents, June 25, 1986; italics removed from original.

16. "Seek the Spirit of the Lord," 2, 4; the statement by Spencer W. Kimball is found in *Teachings of Presidents of the Church: Spencer W. Kimball* (2006), 67.

17. "A Sacred Responsibility," 78.

18. "In His Steps," *Ensign,* Sept. 1988, 5.

19. *Come unto Christ,* 92.

20. "Preparing Yourselves for Missionary Service," *Ensign,* May 1985, 36.

21. "A Principle with a Promise," *Ensign,* May 1983, 54.

Priceless Blessings of the House of the Lord

"It is in the temples that we obtain God's greatest blessings pertaining to eternal life. Temples are really the gateways to heaven."

From the Life of Ezra Taft Benson

"I am grateful to the Lord that my temple memories extend back—even to young boyhood," said President Ezra Taft Benson. "I remember so well, as a little boy, coming in from the field and approaching the old farm house in Whitney, Idaho. I could hear my mother singing 'Have I Done Any Good in the World Today?' (*Hymns*, no. 58.)

"I can still see her in my mind's eye bending over the ironing board with newspapers on the floor, ironing long strips of white cloth, with beads of perspiration on her forehead. When I asked her what she was doing, she said, 'These are temple robes, my son. Your father and I are going to the temple. . . .'

"Then she put the old flatiron on the stove, drew a chair close to mine, and told me about temple work—how important it is to be able to go to the temple and participate in the sacred ordinances performed there. She also expressed her fervent hope that some day her children and grandchildren and great-grandchildren would have the opportunity to enjoy these priceless blessings.

"These sweet memories about the spirit of temple work were a blessing in our farm home. . . . These memories have returned as I have performed the marriage of each of our children and grand-children, my mother's grandchildren and great-grandchildren, under the influence of the Spirit in the house of the Lord.

"These are choice memories to me."[1]

Los Angeles California Temple

Teachings of Ezra Taft Benson

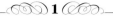

Temples are symbols of all we hold dear.

The temple is the nearest place to heaven on mortal earth.[2]

[The] temple will be a light to all in [the] area—a symbol of all we hold dear.[3]

The temple is an ever-present reminder that God intends the family to be eternal.[4]

[The temple is] a constant, visible symbol that God has not left man to grope in darkness. It is a place of revelation. Though we live in a fallen world—a wicked world—holy places are set apart and consecrated so that worthy men and women can learn the order of heaven and obey God's will.[5]

[The temple is] a standing witness that the power of God can stay the powers of evil in our midst. Many parents, in and out of the Church, are concerned about protection against a cascading avalanche of wickedness which threatens to engulf Christian principles. I find myself in complete accord with a statement made by President Harold B. Lee during World War II. Said he: "We talk about security in this day, and yet we fail to understand that . . . we have standing the holy temple wherein we may find the symbols by which power might be generated that will save this nation from destruction."[6]

At a party at the Beverly Hills Hilton Hotel in Los Angeles, [California,] I had been asked by the President of the United States [as his secretary of agriculture] to greet the president of one of our newer republics, the president of eighty-eight million people scattered on some 3,000 islands a thousand miles long, a nation that had been in existence only a few years. As we sat there at this dinner, which was sponsored in large measure by the motion picture industry and at which many movie stars were present, I could look out a beautiful bay window. Down the avenue, on the elevation, I could see the soft floodlights around our glorious Los Angeles Temple, and I had the joy of pointing it out to my guests and to friends at our table and other tables. I thought, as we sat there, "Much of what goes on tonight is simply the froth of life. The things that endure, the things that are real, the things that are important are those things represented in the temple of God."[7]

May [the temple] be a constant reminder that life is eternal and that covenants made by us in mortality can be everlasting.[8]

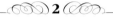

We need temple ordinances and covenants in order to enter into the fulness of the priesthood and prepare to regain God's presence.

When our Heavenly Father placed Adam and Eve on this earth, He did so with the purpose in mind of teaching them how to regain His presence. Our Father promised a Savior to redeem them from their fallen condition. He gave to them the plan of salvation and told them to teach their children faith in Jesus Christ and repentance. Further, Adam and his posterity were commanded by God to be baptized, to receive the Holy Ghost, and to enter into the order of the Son of God.

To enter into the order of the Son of God is the equivalent today of entering into the fullness of the Melchizedek Priesthood, which is only received in the house of the Lord.

Because Adam and Eve had complied with these requirements, God said to them, "Thou art after the order of him who was without beginning of days or end of years, from all eternity to all eternity." (Moses 6:67.)

Three years before Adam's death, a great event occurred. He took his son Seth, his grandson Enos, and other high priests who were his direct-line descendants, with others of his righteous posterity, into a valley called Adam-ondi-Ahman. There Adam gave to these righteous descendants his last blessing.

The Lord then appeared to them [see D&C 107:53–56]. . . .

How did Adam bring his descendants into the presence of the Lord?

The answer: Adam and his descendants entered into the priesthood order of God. Today we would say they went to the House of the Lord and received their blessings.

The order of priesthood spoken of in the scriptures is sometimes referred to as the patriarchal order because it came down from father to son. But this order is otherwise described in modern revelation as an order of family government where a man and woman enter into a covenant with God—just as did Adam and Eve—to be sealed for eternity, to have posterity, and to do the will and work of God throughout their mortality.

If a couple are true to their covenants, they are entitled to the blessing of the highest degree of the celestial kingdom. These covenants today can only be entered into by going to the House of the Lord.

Adam followed this order and brought his posterity into the presence of God. . . .

. . . This order of priesthood can only be entered into when we comply with all the commandments of God and seek the blessings of the fathers as did Abraham [see Abraham 1:1–3] by going to our Father's house. They are received in no other place on this earth!

. . . Go to the temple—our Father's house—to receive the blessings of your fathers that you may be entitled to the highest blessings of the priesthood. "For without this no man can see the face of God, even the Father, and live." (D&C 84:22.)

Our Father's house is a house of order. We go to *His* house to enter into that order of priesthood which will entitle us to all that the Father hath, if we are faithful.[9]

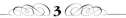

3

**Through temple ordinances and covenants,
we can receive protection and God's greatest
blessings pertaining to eternal life.**

The blessings of the house of the Lord are eternal. They are of the highest importance to us because it is in the temples that we obtain God's greatest blessings pertaining to eternal life. Temples are really the gateways to heaven.[10]

The Lord's desire is for every adult man and woman in the Church to receive the ordinances of the temple. This means that they are to be endowed and that all married couples are to be sealed for eternity. These ordinances provide a protection and blessing to their marriage. Their children also are blessed to be born in the covenant. Birth in the covenant entitles those children to a birthright blessing which guarantees them eternal parentage regardless of what happens to the parents, so long as the children remain worthy of the blessings.[11]

Is it not significant to you that today the Saints are scattered over the face of the world and, in their scattered situation, temples are being provided for them? By the ordinances that they receive in holy places, they will be armed with righteousness and endowed with the power of God in great measure.[12]

There is a power associated with the ordinances of heaven—even the power of godliness—which can and will thwart the forces of evil if we will be worthy of those sacred blessings. [Our] community will be protected, our families will be protected, our children will be safeguarded as we live the gospel, visit the temple, and live close to the Lord. . . . God bless us as Saints to live worthy of the covenants and ordinances made in this sacred place.[13]

The temple ceremony was given by a wise Heavenly Father to help us become more Christlike.[14]

We will not be able to dwell in the company of celestial beings unless we are pure and holy. The laws and ordinances which cause men and women to come out of the world and become sanctified are administered only in these holy places. They were given by revelation and are comprehended by revelation. It is for this reason that one of the Brethren has referred to the temple as the "university of the Lord."[15]

No member of the Church can be perfected without the ordinances of the temple. We have a mission to assist those who do not have these blessings to receive them.[16]

We have the privilege of opening the doors of salvation to our ancestors.

Temples are built and dedicated so that, through the priesthood, parents can be sealed to their children and children can be sealed to their parents. These sealing ordinances apply to both the living and the dead. If we fail to be sealed to our progenitors and our posterity, the purpose of this earth, man's exaltation, will be utterly wasted so far as we are concerned.[17]

It is not sufficient for a husband and wife to be sealed in the temple to guarantee their exaltation—if they are faithful—they must also be eternally linked with their progenitors and see that the work is done for those ancestors. "They without us," said the Apostle Paul, "cannot be made perfect—neither can we without our dead be made perfect" (D&C 128:15). Our members must therefore understand that they have an individual responsibility to see that they are linked to their progenitors—or, as sacred scripture designates, our "fathers." This is the meaning of section 2, verse 2, in the Doctrine and Covenants when Moroni declared that Elijah "shall plant in the hearts of the children the promises made to the fathers, and the hearts of the children shall turn to their fathers."[18]

When I think of genealogy, I see people—people I love who are waiting for our family, their posterity, to help them gain exaltation in the celestial kingdom.[19]

Ours is the privilege of opening the doors of salvation to those souls who may be imprisoned in darkness in the world of spirits, that they may receive the light of the gospel and be judged the same as we. Yes, "the works that I do"—proffering the saving ordinances of the gospel to others—"shall ye do also" [see John 14:12]. How many thousands of our kindred yet await these sealing ordinances?

It is well to ask, "Have I done all I can as an individual on this side of the veil? Will I be a savior to them—my own progenitors?"

Without them, we cannot be made perfect! Exaltation is a family affair.[20]

The veil is very thin. We are living in eternity. All is as with one day with God. I imagine that to the Lord there is no veil. It is all one great program. I am sure there is rejoicing in heaven as we meet [in the temple]. Our progenitors are rejoicing, and my hope and prayer is that we will take advantage of the opportunities now afforded us to come regularly to the temple.[21]

Those of you who have worked at your genealogies, who realize the importance of the work and have felt the excitement that comes from tying families together and learning of your noble heritage, need to share that excitement with others. Help them to see the joy and fulfillment you see in the work. We need to proselyte more of our members into this work. There is much to be done, as you all know, and there are many, many members who could do the work and who would enjoy doing the work if some of us—all of you—would just ignite that spark in them through your enthusiasm, example, and devotion.[22]

5

Children and youth need to learn about the blessings that await them in the temple.

The temple is a sacred place, and the ordinances in the temple are of a sacred character. Because of its sacredness we are sometimes reluctant to say anything about the temple to our children and grandchildren.

As a consequence, many do not develop a real desire to go to the temple, or when they go there, they do so without much background to prepare them for the obligations and covenants they enter into.

I believe a proper understanding or background will immeasurably help prepare our youth for the temple. This understanding, I believe, will foster within them a desire to seek their priesthood blessings just as Abraham sought his [see Abraham 1:1–4].[23]

When your children ask why we marry in the temple, you should teach them that temples are the only places on the earth where certain ordinances may be performed. You should also share with your children your personal feelings as you knelt together before

"God bless us to teach our children and our grandchildren what great blessings await them by going to the temple."

the sacred altar and took upon yourselves covenants which made it possible for them to be sealed to you forever.[24]

How fitting it is for mothers and fathers to point to the temple and say to their children, "That is the place where we were married for eternity." By so doing, the ideal of temple marriage can be instilled within the minds and hearts of your children while they are very young.[25]

We should share with our families our love of our forebears and our gratitude to be able to help them receive the saving ordinances, as my parents did with me. As we do so, increased bonds of appreciation and affection will develop within our families.[26]

I believe the youth are not only willing and able to do genealogical research, but they are a good means of giving life to the whole program.[27]

God bless us to teach our children and our grandchildren what great blessings await them by going to the temple.[28]

Increased temple attendance leads to increased personal revelation.

I make it a practice, whenever I perform a marriage, to suggest to the young couple that they return to the temple as soon as they can and go through the temple again as husband and wife. It isn't possible for them to understand fully the meaning of the holy endowment or the sealings with one trip through the temple, but as they repeat their visits to the temple, the beauty, the significance, and the importance of it all will be emphasized upon them. I have later had letters from some of these young couples expressing appreciation because that item was emphasized particularly. As they repeat their visits to the temple, their love for each other tends to increase and their marriage tends to be strengthened.[29]

In the course of our visits to the temple, we are given insights into the meaning of the eternal journey of man. We see beautiful and impressive symbolisms of the most important events—past, present, and future—symbolizing man's mission in relationship to God. We are reminded of our obligations as we make solemn covenants pertaining to obedience, consecration, sacrifice, and dedicated service to our Heavenly Father.[30]

I promise you that, with increased attendance in the temples of our God, you shall receive increased personal revelation to bless your life as you bless those who have died.[31]

In the peace of these lovely temples, sometimes we find solutions to the serious problems of life. Under the influence of the Spirit, sometimes pure knowledge flows to us there. Temples are places of personal revelation. When I have been weighed down by a problem or a difficulty, I have gone to the House of the Lord with a prayer in my heart for answers. These answers have come in clear and unmistakable ways.[32]

Do we return to the temple often to receive the personal blessings that come from regular temple worship? Prayers are answered, revelation occurs, and instruction by the Spirit takes place in the holy temples of the Lord.[33]

Let us make the temple a sacred home away from our eternal home.[34]

Suggestions for Study and Teaching

Questions
- President Benson said that a temple is "a symbol of all we hold dear," and he identified some truths that temples symbolize (see section 1). What do temples represent for you?

- In section 2, how do President Benson's teachings about the blessings of the priesthood apply to all family members? As you review this section, ponder your privilege and responsibility to help family members prepare to return to the presence of God.

- As you read section 3, ponder President Benson's teachings about the blessings we receive through temple ordinances. In what ways have you been blessed through temple ordinances? If you have not yet received temple ordinances, ponder what you can do to prepare to receive them.

- President Benson said, "When I think of genealogy, I see people—people I love" (section 4). How might this observation influence your approach to family history? What can we do to help more of our ancestors receive the blessings of the gospel?

- What are some things we can do to help children and youth prepare for temple ordinances and covenants? In what ways might youth give "life to the whole program" of family history? (See section 5.)

- President Benson encouraged us to "make the temple a sacred home away from our eternal home" (section 6). What does this statement mean to you? Reflect on blessings you have received as you have returned to the temple.

Related Scriptures
Isaiah 2:1–3; D&C 97:15–16; 109:8–23; 124:39–41; 138:32–34

Teaching Help

"Often a lesson will contain more material than you are able to teach in the time you are given. In such cases, you should select the material that will be most helpful for those you teach" (*Teaching, No Greater Call* [1999], 98–99).

Notes

1. "What I Hope You Will Teach Your Children about the Temple," *Ensign,* Aug. 1985, 8.

2. *The Teachings of Ezra Taft Benson* (1988), 260.

3. *The Teachings of Ezra Taft Benson,* 256.

4. "What I Hope You Will Teach Your Children about the Temple," 6.

5. *The Teachings of Ezra Taft Benson,* 252.

6. *The Teachings of Ezra Taft Benson,* 256; the statement by Harold B. Lee is found in Conference Report, Apr. 1942, 87.

7. *God, Family, Country: Our Three Great Loyalties* (1974), 85.

8. *The Teachings of Ezra Taft Benson,* 256.

9. "What I Hope You Will Teach Your Children about the Temple," 8–10.

10. *The Teachings of Ezra Taft Benson,* 255.

11. *The Teachings of Ezra Taft Benson,* 259.

12. *The Teachings of Ezra Taft Benson,* 255–56.

13. *The Teachings of Ezra Taft Benson,* 256.

14. *The Teachings of Ezra Taft Benson,* 250.

15. *The Teachings of Ezra Taft Benson,* 252; see also ElRay L. Christiansen, in Conference Report, Apr. 1968, 134.

16. *The Teachings of Ezra Taft Benson,* 252.

17. *The Teachings of Ezra Taft Benson,* 248.

18. *The Teachings of Ezra Taft Benson,* 248–49.

19. *The Teachings of Ezra Taft Benson,* 164.

20. *Come unto Christ* (1983), 126.

21. *The Teachings of Ezra Taft Benson,* 253.

22. *The Teachings of Ezra Taft Benson,* 162.

23. "What I Hope You Will Teach Your Children about the Temple," 8.

24. *The Teachings of Ezra Taft Benson,* 258.

25. "What I Hope You Will Teach Your Children about the Temple," 6, 8.

26. *Come unto Christ through Temple Ordinances and Covenants* (pamphlet, 1987), 2.

27. *The Teachings of Ezra Taft Benson,* 163.

28. "What I Hope You Will Teach Your Children about the Temple," 10.

29. *God, Family, Country,* 183.

30. *The Teachings of Ezra Taft Benson,* 251.

31. "The Book of Mormon and the Doctrine and Covenants," *Ensign,* May 1987, 85.

32. "What I Hope You Will Teach Your Children about the Temple," 8.

33. "Come unto Christ, and Be Perfected in Him," *Ensign,* May 1988, 85.

34. *The Teachings of Ezra Taft Benson,* 256.

Marriage and Family—
Ordained of God

*"The family is one of God's greatest fortresses against
the evils of our day. Help keep your family strong and
close and worthy of our Father in Heaven's blessings."*

From the Life of Ezra Taft Benson

From the beginning of their marriage, Ezra and Flora Benson made
their home and family their top priority. When their children were
young, they began emphasizing that they wanted their family to
have no "empty chairs" in the eternities.[1] President Benson emphasized this same message during his service as a Church leader.
He said:

"God intended the family to be eternal. With all my soul, I testify
to the truth of that declaration. May He bless us to strengthen our
homes and the lives of each family member so that in due time we
can report to our Heavenly Father in His celestial home that we are
all there—father, mother, sister, brother, all who hold each other
dear. Each chair is filled. We are all back home."[2]

For President and Sister Benson, the effort to strengthen their
family started with nurturing their marriage. They were loving and
devoted, loyal and true. Although they were not inclined to quarrel,
they often had frank discussions.[3] They shared an absolute trust in
each other, which they felt was one of the great strengths of their
marriage. "I have never, *never* had any question about Flora's loyalty," President Benson said.[4]

President and Sister Benson supported and strengthened each
other. "Flora has had more vision for me and my potential than
anyone else in my life. Her faith and support have been a great
blessing," President Benson said.[5] Often, when he felt inadequate

President and Sister Benson were always loyal and true to one another.

in his demanding responsibilities, Sister Benson would wipe away his tears and comfort him.[6] She sought the Lord's help in sustaining him, and she rallied the children to do the same. "There was a lot of praying and fasting for daddy," daughter Barbara said.[7]

Building on the solid foundation of their marriage, President and Sister Benson taught their children the importance of eternal family relationships. "Our parents instilled deep feelings of loyalty and love among us children," son Mark said. "I don't think that kind of atmosphere is generated naturally in a home, but is encouraged and promoted by a concerned and loving mother and father."[8]

The standard of behavior the Bensons expected, as well as the priority they gave to the family, centered in the gospel. They worked to create a home where love prevailed, where children learned and developed, and where they had fun. The Bensons wanted their home to be a sanctuary from the world. "That doesn't mean we didn't have struggles," son Reed said. "We didn't always get along. We didn't always do our chores. We tested Mother's patience to the limit at times. But, undergirding it all, was a sense of family unity that we were trying to pull together."[9] Sister Benson acknowledged: "No one is perfect. In our family it is not our objective to magnify each other's shortcomings, but to encourage one another to improve."[10]

The Bensons' children were still young when their father was called to serve in the Quorum of the Twelve Apostles, and he was concerned about how his travel schedule might affect his time with them. He wrote in his journal: "Extensive travel on Church work will take me from my family to a great extent. . . . I sincerely trust I may be true to my family, keep them close to the Church, and yet fulfil my obligations as one of the General Authorities. This I know will be no easy matter."[11]

The fact that it wasn't easy prompted President Benson to work hard to keep close to his family. "Some of the sweetest, most soul-satisfying impressions and experiences of [my] life are associated with home and family ties," he said.[12]

In 1957, as the United States secretary of agriculture, President Benson made a four-week trip around the world to develop trade opportunities. Sister Benson and daughters Beverly and Bonnie accompanied him. They went to 12 countries, where they met with government leaders and visited landmarks, refugee settlements, and agricultural operations. President Benson felt that the tour was successful in increasing trade opportunities and also in creating goodwill for the Church. When they returned home, daughter Beth was waiting as the plane landed. When she saw her parents, she began running toward them with tears in her eyes. Her father reached out and pulled her into a loving embrace. He reflected, "With all the wonders of the world [we had seen], that moment was suddenly the best of the entire trip." [13]

Teachings of Ezra Taft Benson

1

The family is the most important organization in time and in eternity.

The Church of Jesus Christ of Latter-day Saints views the family as the most important organization in time and all eternity. The Church teaches that everything should center in and around the family. It stresses that the preservation of family life in time and eternity takes precedence above all other interests. [14]

There can be no satisfactory substitute for the home. Its foundation is as ancient as the world. Its mission has been God-ordained. [15]

No nation ever rises above its homes. This Church will never rise above its homes. We are no better as a people than are our firesides, our homes. . . . The good home is the rock foundation, the cornerstone of civilization. It must be preserved. It must be strengthened. [16]

Some people ask me as a Church leader why we place so much emphasis on the home and family when there are such larger problems around us? The answer is, of course, that the larger problems are merely a reflection of individual and family problems. [17]

Marriage and family life are ordained of God. In an eternal sense, salvation is a family affair. God holds parents responsible for their stewardship in rearing their family. It is a most sacred responsibility. [18]

In happy marriages, husbands and wives love and serve God and each other.

Marriage, the home, and family are more than mere social institutions. They are divine, not man-made. God ordained marriage from the very beginning. In the record of that first marriage recorded in Genesis, the Lord makes four significant pronouncements: first, that it is not good for man to be alone; second, that woman was created to be a helpmeet for man; third, that they twain should be one flesh; and fourth, that man should leave father and mother and cleave unto his wife. (See Genesis 2:18, 24.)

Later, as though to reinforce the earlier statement, the Lord said: "What therefore God hath joined together, let not man put asunder" (Matthew 19:6). He also said, "Thou shalt love thy wife with all thy heart, and shalt cleave unto her and none else" (D&C 42:22).[19]

The scriptures tell us: "Adam began to till the earth . . . as I the Lord had commanded him. And Eve, also, his wife, did labor with him. . . . They began to multiply and to replenish the earth. . . . And Adam and Eve, his wife, called upon the name of the Lord. . . . And Adam and Eve blessed the name of God, and they made all things known unto their sons and their daughters. . . . And Adam and Eve, his wife, ceased not to call upon God." (Moses 5:1–2, 4, 12, 16.)

From this inspired record we see that Adam and Eve provided us with an ideal example of a covenant marriage relationship. They labored together; they had children together; they prayed together; and they taught their children the gospel—together. This is the pattern God would have all righteous men and women imitate.[20]

Marriage itself must be regarded as a sacred covenant before God. A married couple have an obligation not only to each other, but to God. He has promised blessings to those who honor that covenant.

Fidelity to one's marriage vows is absolutely essential for love, trust, and peace. Adultery is unequivocally condemned by the Lord. . . .

Restraint and self-control must be ruling principles in the marriage relationship. Couples must learn to bridle their tongues as well as their passions.

Prayer in the home and prayer with each other will strengthen [a couple's] union. Gradually thoughts, aspirations, and ideas will merge into a oneness until you are seeking the same purposes and goals.

Rely on the Lord, the teachings of the prophets, and the scriptures for guidance and help, particularly when there may be disagreements and problems.

Spiritual growth comes by solving problems together—not by running from them. Today's inordinate emphasis on individualism brings egotism and separation. Two individuals becoming "one flesh" is still the Lord's standard. (See Gen. 2:24.)

The secret of a happy marriage is to serve God and each other. The goal of marriage is unity and oneness, as well as self-development. Paradoxically, the more we serve one another, the greater is our spiritual and emotional growth.[21]

The counsel from the Apostle Paul is most beautiful and to the point. He said simply, "Husbands, love your wives, even as Christ also loved the church" (Ephesians 5:25).

In latter-day revelation the Lord speaks again of this obligation. He said, "Thou shalt love thy wife with all thy heart, and shalt cleave unto her and none else" (D&C 42:22). To my knowledge there is only one other thing in all scripture that we are commanded to love with all our hearts, and that is God Himself. Think what that means!

This kind of love can be shown for your wives in so many ways. First and foremost, nothing except God Himself takes priority over your wife in your life—not work, not recreation, not hobbies. Your wife is your precious, eternal helpmate—your companion.

What does it mean to love someone with all your heart? It means to love with all your emotional feelings and with all your devotion. Surely when you love your wife with all your heart, you cannot demean her, criticize her, find fault with her, or abuse her by words, sullen behavior, or actions.

"The secret of a happy marriage is to serve God and each other."

What does it mean to "cleave unto her"? It means to stay close to her, to be loyal and faithful to her, to communicate with her, and to express your love for her.[22]

Husbands and wives who love each other will find that love and loyalty are reciprocated. This love will provide a nurturing atmosphere for the emotional growth of children. Family life should be a time of happiness and joy that children can look back on with fond memories and associations.[23]

 **3**

Strong families cultivate love, respect, and support for each family member.

Let us strengthen the family. Family and individual prayers morning and evening can invite the blessings of the Lord on our households. Mealtime provides a wonderful time to review the activities of the day and to not only feed the body but to feed the spirit as well, with members of the family taking turns reading the scriptures, particularly the Book of Mormon. Nighttime is a great time for the busy father to go to the bedside of each of his children, to talk with them, answer their questions, and tell them how much they are loved.[24]

The family is one of God's greatest fortresses against the evils of our day. Help keep your family strong and close and worthy of our Father in Heaven's blessings. As you do, you will receive faith and strength which will bless your lives forever.[25]

One great thing the Lord requires of each of us is to provide a home where a happy, positive influence for good exists. In future years the costliness of home furnishings or the number of bathrooms will not matter much, but what will matter significantly is whether our children felt love and acceptance in the home. It will greatly matter whether there was happiness and laughter, or bickering and contention.[26]

Successful families have love and respect for each family member. Family members know they are loved and appreciated. Children feel they are loved by their parents. Thus, they are secure and self-assured.

Strong families cultivate an attribute of effective communication. They talk out their problems, make plans together, and cooperate toward common objectives. Family home evening and family councils are practiced and used as effective tools toward this end.

Fathers and mothers in strong families stay close to their children. They talk. Some fathers formally interview each child, others do so informally, and others take occasion to regularly spend time alone with each child.

Every family has problems and challenges. But successful families try to work together toward solutions instead of resorting to criticism and contention. They pray for each other, discuss, and give encouragement. Occasionally these families fast together in support of one of the family members.

Strong families support each other.[27]

The home is the best place for children to learn the principles and practices of the gospel.

The family is the most effective place to instill lasting values in its members. Where family life is strong and based on principles and practices of the gospel of Jesus Christ, . . . problems do not as readily appear.[28]

Successful parents have found that it is not easy to rear children in an environment polluted with evil. Therefore, they take deliberate steps to provide the best of wholesome influences. Moral principles are taught. Good books are made available and read. Television watching is controlled. Good and uplifting music is provided. But most importantly, the scriptures are read and discussed as a means to help develop spiritual-mindedness.

In successful Latter-day Saint homes, parents teach their children to understand faith in God, repentance, baptism, and the gift of the Holy Ghost. (See D&C 68:25.)

Family prayer is a consistent practice in these families. Prayer is the means to acknowledge appreciation for blessings and to humbly recognize dependence on Almighty God for strength, sustenance, and support.

It is a wise and true maxim that families that kneel together stand upright before the Lord![29]

Children need to know who they are in the eternal sense of their identity. They need to know that they have an eternal Heavenly Father on whom they can rely, to whom they can pray, and from whom they can receive guidance. They need to know from whence they came so that their lives will have meaning and purpose.

Children must be taught to pray, to rely on the Lord for guidance, and to express appreciation for the blessings that are theirs. I recall kneeling at the bedsides of our young children, helping them with their prayers.

Children must be taught right from wrong. They can and must learn the commandments of God. They must be taught that it is wrong to steal, lie, cheat, or covet what others have.

Children must be taught to work at home. They should learn there that honest labor develops dignity and self-respect. They should learn the pleasure of work, of doing a job well.

The leisure time of children must be constructively directed to wholesome, positive pursuits.[30]

Designed to strengthen and safeguard the family, the Church's home evening program establishes one night each week that is to be set apart for fathers and mothers to gather their sons and daughters around them in the home.[31]

Gospel principles may be instilled through effective family home evenings where youth will be fortified so that they have no need to fear for their future. Such teaching must be done in faith, testimony, and optimism.[32]

Setting your home in order is keeping the commandments of God. This brings harmony and love. . . . It is daily family prayer. It is teaching your family to understand the gospel of Jesus Christ. It is each family member keeping the commandments of God. It is . . . being worthy to receive a temple recommend, all family members receiving the ordinances of exaltation, and your family being sealed together for eternity. It is being free from excessive debt, with family members paying honest tithes and offerings.[33]

5

God has revealed that the family may endure beyond the grave.

The love we know here is not a fleeting shadow, but the very substance that binds families together for time and eternity.[34]

It was through Joseph Smith that the God of Heaven revealed the truth that the family may endure beyond the grave—that our sympathies, affections, and love for each other may exist forever.[35]

No sacrifice is too great to have the blessings of an eternal marriage. To most of us, a temple is easily accessible, perhaps so conveniently that the blessing is taken too casually. As with other matters of faithfulness in gospel living, being married the Lord's way takes a willingness to deny yourself ungodliness—worldliness—and a determination to do our Father's will. By this act of faith, we show our love to God and our regard for a posterity yet unborn. As our family is our greatest source of joy in this life, so it may well be in the eternity.[36]

Home and family. What sweet memories surge up in our breasts at the mere mention of these cherished words! May I wish for you prayerfully, and with all the fervor of my soul, that you may know the unspeakable joy and satisfaction of honorable parenthood. You will miss one of the deepest joys of this life and eternity if you willfully avoid the responsibilities of parenthood and home-building. As revealed through the Prophet Joseph Smith, the glorious concept of home and the enduring family relationship lies at the very basis of our happiness here and hereafter.[37]

Suggestions for Study and Teaching

Questions

- President Benson taught, "In an eternal sense, salvation is a family affair" (section 1). What does this mean to you? What can family members do for each other's salvation?

- As you study President Benson's counsel in section 2, ponder how it all relates to what he called "the secret of a happy marriage." Why do you think this "secret" leads to happiness?

- In section 3, consider what President Benson said about the practices of successful families. In what ways do these practices strengthen families? Ponder what you can do to follow this counsel.

- Why do you think the family is "the most effective place to instill lasting values"? (See section 4, noting President Benson's specific counsel about teaching in the family.) When have you seen family members help each other learn gospel principles?

- President Benson testified that families can "endure beyond the grave" (section 5). What are your thoughts and feelings as you ponder this truth? What are some "sweet memories" that come to you at the mention of home and family?

Related Scriptures

Psalm 127:3–5; 1 Corinthians 11:11; 3 Nephi 18:21; D&C 49:15; 132:18–19; see also "The Family: A Proclamation to the World," *Ensign,* Nov. 2010, 129

Study Help

"Your gospel study is most effective when you are taught by the Holy Ghost. Always begin your gospel study by praying for the Holy Ghost to help you learn" (*Preach My Gospel* [2004], 18).

Notes

1. In Sheri L. Dew, *Ezra Taft Benson: A Biography* (1987), 363.
2. *The Teachings of Ezra Taft Benson* (1988), 493.
3. See *Ezra Taft Benson: A Biography,* 126.
4. In Derin Head Rodriguez, "Flora Amussen Benson: Handmaiden of the Lord, Helpmeet of a Prophet, Mother in Zion," *Ensign,* Mar. 1987, 20.
5. In "Flora Amussen Benson: Handmaiden of the Lord, Helpmeet of a Prophet, Mother in Zion," 14.
6. See *Ezra Taft Benson: A Biography,* 179.
7. Barbara Benson Walker, in *Ezra Taft Benson: A Biography,* 179.
8. Mark Amussen Benson, in "Flora Amussen Benson: Handmaiden of the Lord, Helpmeet of a Prophet, Mother in Zion," 20.
9. Reed Amussen Benson, in *Ezra Taft Benson: A Biography,* 140.
10. Flora Amussen Benson, in *Ezra Taft Benson: A Biography,* 133.
11. In *Ezra Taft Benson: A Biography,* 178.
12. In *Ezra Taft Benson: A Biography,* 126.
13. In *Ezra Taft Benson: A Biography,* 327.
14. *The Teachings of Ezra Taft Benson,* 489.
15. In Conference Report, Apr. 1949, 198.
16. In Conference Report, Oct. 1953, 122.
17. *The Teachings of Ezra Taft Benson,* 521.
18. "Fundamentals of Enduring Family Relationships," *Ensign,* Nov. 1982, 59.
19. *The Teachings of Ezra Taft Benson,* 534.
20. *The Teachings of Ezra Taft Benson,* 534.
21. "Fundamentals of Enduring Family Relationships," 59, 60.
22. *Sermons and Writings of President Ezra Taft Benson* (2003), 209–10.
23. "Fundamentals of Enduring Family Relationships," 59.
24. *The Teachings of Ezra Taft Benson,* 491.
25. "To the 'Youth of the Noble Birthright,'" *Ensign,* May 1986, 43.
26. "Great Things Required of Their Fathers," *Ensign,* May 1981, 34.
27. "Counsel to the Saints," *Ensign,* May 1984, 6.
28. "Fundamentals of Enduring Family Relationships," 59.
29. "Counsel to the Saints," 6–7.
30. "Fundamentals of Enduring Family Relationships," 60.
31. *The Teachings of Ezra Taft Benson,* 528.
32. "May the Kingdom of God Go Forth," *Ensign,* May 1978, 33.
33. "Great Things Required of Their Fathers," 36.
34. *The Teachings of Ezra Taft Benson,* 492.
35. *The Teachings of Ezra Taft Benson,* 490.
36. "This Is a Day of Sacrifice," *Ensign,* May 1979, 33–34.
37. *The Teachings of Ezra Taft Benson,* 491–92.

The Sacred Callings of Fathers and Mothers

"May we be faithful to this great obligation of parenthood, this sacred obligation."

From the Life of Ezra Taft Benson

By word and example, at home and around the world, in Church and civic settings, President Ezra Taft Benson taught the importance of being good parents. "Nurture your children with love and the admonitions of the Lord," he said.[1] "God holds parents responsible for their stewardship in rearing their family. It is a most sacred responsibility."[2]

President Benson and his wife, Flora, worked closely together in fulfilling their sacred responsibilities as parents. They "approached the task of nurturing their family unit with energy and enthusiasm."[3] They frequently counseled together about their children and other matters. "I could see that I had a spiritually perceptive woman at my side," President Benson said.[4]

They worked together to create a home where their children could grow and learn—and where their children wanted to be. "I would have rather been home than anywhere," their son Mark said. "It was a refuge from the storm. Mother was the protective element, and Dad was there with his strength."[5]

President and Sister Benson approached their responsibilities as parents prayerfully. Mark said: "Mother had more faith than any woman I've ever known. . . . I've never seen more praying in my life. At the drop of a hat she'd be on her knees, praying for the children, whether it was about a test or a fight on the school grounds, it didn't matter. She and Dad both had that simple faith."[6]

Ezra Taft Benson with his sons, Reed and Mark

President Benson was frequently away from home because of his work and Church duties, so Flora assumed much of the responsibility for nurturing and teaching their six children. She relished her role of motherhood. "The home is the center of our mortal affections," she said.[7] Mark recalled, "Mother absolutely loved home. And she loved us—not because it was her duty to, but because that was her life."[8] Expressing her feelings about the importance of being a mother, Flora wrote: "If you want to find greatness, don't go to the throne, go to the cradle. There is mighty power in a mother. She is the one who molds hearts, lives, and shapes character."[9]

When President Benson was away from home, he always sought ways to watch over and strengthen his family. He maintained regular contact with them through phone calls and letters. When he was home, he spent as much time with them as possible. He often cited the story of "a busy father who explained the hours he spent playing ball with his son by saying, 'I'd sooner have a backache now than a heartache later.'"[10]

He also spent extended time individually with his children. Mark recalled his father taking him to Salt Lake City, Utah, to see a medical specialist: "How fun it was to be with Dad, just him and me! We talked about anything I wanted to talk about. Even as a boy, I knew Dad loved me, because he was with me and helping me get better."[11]

When he could, President Benson took his children with him during his travels. In March 1948 he took his daughter Bonnie, who was seven years old at the time, to an agriculture meeting in Nebraska. "The press was so intrigued by the poise of the little girl, and by the anomalous example of a father bringing such a young child on such a long trip to attend such a distinguished function, that a picture of Bonnie was featured on the front page [of the newspaper] the next morning. But to Elder Benson the incident was not an anomaly. He frequently took the children with him on out-of-town trips, both as a means of cementing good relations and of educating them."[12]

Teachings of Ezra Taft Benson

 **1**

A father's calling is eternal.

Fathers, yours is an eternal calling from which you are never released. Callings in the Church, as important as they are, by their very nature are only for a period of time, and then an appropriate release takes place. But a father's calling is eternal, and its importance transcends time. It is a calling for both time and eternity.[13]

Our pattern, or model, for fatherhood is our Heavenly Father. How does He work with His children? Well, in order to know that, of course, [fathers] will need to know something about the gospel, the great plan of the Lord.[14]

For a man, there is no calling as high as that of a righteous patriarch, married in the house of the Lord, presiding over His children. Even the very Elohim has us address Him as "our Father who art in heaven" (Matthew 6:9; 3 Nephi 13:9).[15]

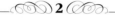 **2**

Fathers are to provide spiritual leadership in their families.

The father must hunger and thirst and yearn to bless his family, go to the Lord, ponder the words of the Lord, and live by the Spirit to know the mind and will of the Lord and what he must do to lead his family.[16]

[Fathers,] you have a sacred responsibility to provide spiritual leadership in your family.

In a pamphlet published some years ago by the Council of the Twelve, we said the following: "Fatherhood is leadership, the most important kind of leadership. It has always been so; it always will be so. Father, with the assistance and counsel and encouragement of your eternal companion, you preside in the home" (*Father, Consider Your Ways* [pamphlet, 1973], 4–5). . . .

With love in my heart for the fathers in Israel, may I suggest 10 specific ways that fathers can give spiritual leadership to their children:

1. Give father's blessings to your children. Baptize and confirm your children. Ordain your sons to the priesthood. These will become spiritual highlights in the lives of your children.

2. Personally direct family prayers, daily scripture reading, and weekly family home evenings. Your personal involvement will show your children how important these activities really are.

3. Whenever possible, attend Church meetings together as a family. Family worship under your leadership is vital to your children's spiritual welfare.

4. Go on daddy-daughter dates and father-and-sons' outings with your children. . . .

5. Build traditions of family vacations and trips and outings. These memories will never be forgotten by your children.

6. Have regular one-on-one visits with your children. Let them talk about what they would like to. Teach them gospel principles. Teach them true values. Tell them you love them. Personal time with your children tells them where Dad puts his priorities.

7. Teach your children to work, and show them the value of working toward a worthy goal. . . .

8. Encourage good music and art and literature in your homes. Homes that have a spirit of refinement and beauty will bless the lives of your children forever.

9. As distances allow, regularly attend the temple with your wife. Your children will then better understand the importance of temple marriage and temple vows and the eternal family unit.

10. Have your children see your joy and satisfaction in service to the Church. This can become contagious to them, so they, too, will want to serve in the Church and will love the kingdom.

Oh, husbands and fathers in Israel, you can do so much for the salvation and exaltation of your families! Your responsibilities are so important.[17]

We sometimes hear accounts of men, even in the Church, who think that being head of the home somehow puts them in a superior role and allows them to dictate and make demands upon their family.

"Have regular one-on-one visits with your children."

The Apostle Paul points out that "the husband is the head of the wife, *even as* Christ is the head of the church" (Ephesians 5:23; italics added). That is the model we are to follow in our role of presiding in the home. We do not find the Savior leading the Church with a harsh or unkind hand. We do not find the Savior treating His Church with disrespect or neglect. We do not find the Savior using force or coercion to accomplish His purposes. Nowhere do we find the Savior doing anything but that which edifies, uplifts, comforts, and exalts the Church. Brethren, I say to you with all soberness, He is the model we must follow as we take the spiritual lead in our families.[18]

As the patriarch in your home, you have a serious responsibility to assume leadership in working with your children. You must help create a home where the Spirit of the Lord can abide. . . .

Your homes should be havens of peace and joy for your family. Surely no child should fear his own father—especially a priesthood father. A father's duty is to make his home a place of happiness and joy. . . . The powerful effect of righteous fathers in setting an example, disciplining and training, nurturing and loving is vital to the spiritual welfare of [their] children.[19]

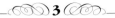

3

A mother's role is ordained by God.

[Mothers] are, or should be, the very heart and soul of the family. No more sacred word exists in secular or holy writ than that of *mother*. There is no more noble work than that of a good and God-fearing mother.

In the eternal family, God established that fathers are to preside in the home. Fathers are to provide, to love, to teach, and to direct. A mother's role is also God-ordained. Mothers are to conceive, to bear, to nourish, to love, and to train. So declare the revelations.[20]

We realize that some women, through no fault of their own, are not able to bear children. To these lovely sisters, every prophet of God has promised that they will be blessed with children in the eternities and that posterity will not be denied them.

Through pure faith, pleading prayers, fasting, and special blessings, many of these same lovely sisters, with their noble companions at their sides, have had miracles take place in their lives and have been blessed with children. Others have prayerfully chosen to adopt children. We salute these wonderful couples for the sacrifices and love you have given to those children you have chosen to call your own.[21]

God bless our wonderful mothers. We pray for you. We sustain you. We honor you as you bear, nourish, train, teach, and love for eternity. I promise you the blessings of heaven and "all that [the] Father hath" (see D&C 84:38) as you magnify the noblest calling of all—a mother in Zion.[22]

4

Mothers should love, teach, and spend effective time with their children.

Mothers in Zion, your God-given roles are so vital to your own exaltation and to the salvation and exaltation of your family. A child needs a mother more than all the things money can buy. Spending time with your children is the greatest gift of all.[23]

With love in my heart for the mothers in Zion, I would now like to suggest 10 specific ways our mothers may spend effective time with their children.

[First,] whenever possible, be at the crossroads when your children are either coming or going—when they leave and return from school, when they leave or return from dates, when they bring friends home. Be there at the crossroads whether your children are 6 or 16. . . .

Second, mothers, take time to be a real friend to your children. Listen to your children, really listen. Talk with them, laugh and joke with them, sing with them, play with them, cry with them, hug them, honestly praise them. Yes, regularly spend one-on-one time with each child. Be a real friend to your children.

Third, take time to read to your children. Starting from the cradle, read to your sons and daughters. . . . You will plant a love for good literature and a real love for the scriptures if you will read to your children regularly.

Fourth, take time to pray with your children. Family prayers, under the direction of the father, should be held morning and night. Have your children feel of your faith as you call down the blessings of heaven upon them. . . . Have your children participate in family and personal prayers, and rejoice in their sweet utterances to their Father in Heaven.

Fifth, take time to have a meaningful weekly home evening. Have your children actively involved. Teach them correct principles. Make this one of your family traditions. . . .

Sixth, take time to be together at mealtimes as often as possible. This is a challenge as the children get older and lives get busier. But happy conversation, sharing of the day's plans and activities, and special teaching moments occur at mealtime because parents and children work at it.

Seventh, take time daily to read the scriptures together as a family. . . . Reading the Book of Mormon together as a family will especially bring increased spirituality into your home and will give both parents and children the power to resist temptation and to have the

"Take time to read to your children."

Holy Ghost as their constant companion. I promise you that the Book of Mormon will change the lives of your family.

Eighth, take time to do things as a family. Make family outings and picnics and birthday celebrations and trips special times and memory builders. Whenever possible, attend, as a family, events where one of the family members is involved, such as a school play, a ball game, a talk, a recital. Attend Church meetings together, and sit together as a family when you can. Mothers who help families pray and play together will [help them] stay together and will bless children's lives forever.

Ninth, mothers, take time to teach your children. Catch the teaching moments at mealtime, in casual settings, or at special sit-down times together, at the foot of the bed at the end of the day, or during an early-morning walk together. . . .

A mother's love and prayerful concern for her children are the most important ingredients in teaching her own. Teach children gospel principles. Teach them it pays to be good. Teach them there is no safety in sin. Teach them a love for the gospel of Jesus Christ and a testimony of its divinity.

Teach your sons and daughters modesty, and teach them to respect manhood and womanhood. Teach your children sexual purity, proper dating standards, temple marriage, missionary service, and the importance of accepting and magnifying Church callings.

Teach them a love for work and the value of a good education.

Teach them the importance of the right kind of entertainment, including appropriate movies, videos, music, books, and magazines. Discuss the evils of pornography and drugs, and teach them the value of living the clean life.

Yes, mothers, teach your children the gospel in your own home, at your own fireside. This is the most effective teaching that your children will ever receive. . . .

Tenth and finally, mothers, take the time to truly love your little children. A mother's unqualified love approaches Christlike love.

Your teenage children also need that same kind of love and attention. It seems easier for many mothers and fathers to express their love to their children when they are young, but more difficult when they are older. Work at this prayerfully. There need be no generation gap. And the key is love. Our young people need love and attention, not indulgence. They need empathy and understanding, not indifference from mothers and fathers. They need the parents' time. A mother's kindly teachings and her love for and confidence in a teenage son or daughter can literally save them from a wicked world.[24]

Do you know one reason why righteous mothers love their children so much? Because they sacrifice so much for them. We love what we sacrifice for and we sacrifice for what we love.[25]

Parents should work together in unity and love in raising their children.

Husbands and wives, as co-creators, should eagerly and prayerfully invite children into their homes. . . . Blessed is the husband and wife who have a family of children. The deepest joys and blessings in life are associated with family, parenthood, and sacrifice. To have those sweet spirits come into the home is worth practically any sacrifice.[26]

When parents, in companionship, love, and unity, fulfill their heaven-imposed responsibility and children respond with love and obedience, great joy is the result.[27]

God help us to support one another. May it start in the home as we support our families. May there be a spirit of loyalty, unity, love, and mutual respect. May husbands be loyal to their wives, true to them, love them, strive to ease their burdens, and share the responsibility for the care, training, and the rearing of the children. May mothers and wives show a spirit of helpfulness to their husbands, uphold and sustain them in their priesthood duties, and be loyal and true to the calls that come to them from the priesthood of God.[28]

May we be faithful to this great obligation of parenthood, this sacred obligation, that we may build our homes solidly upon eternal principles, that we may have no regrets. May we never be recreant [unfaithful] to the great trust which has been imposed in us. May we always keep in mind that these spirits that have entered our homes are choice spirits.[29]

Suggestions for Study and Teaching

Questions
- President Benson said, "Our pattern, or model, for fatherhood, is our Heavenly Father" (section 1). In what ways can earthly fathers follow the pattern Heavenly Father has set?

- Consider President Benson's list of "10 specific ways that fathers can give spiritual leadership to their children" (section 2). How do you think each of these recommendations might influence children?

- President Benson declared, "There is no more noble work than that of a good and God-fearing mother" (section 3). What examples have you seen of noble motherhood? As worldly attitudes about motherhood change, what can we do to uphold the noble and sacred responsibilities of mothers?

- What are some benefits that come when parents and children spend time together? (For some examples, see section 4.)

- What are some blessings that come to a home when parents are unified in their responsibilities? (See section 5.) What can fathers and mothers do to be more unified? In what ways can single parents receive the strength they need to fulfill these responsibilities?

Related Scriptures

Proverbs 22:6; Ephesians 6:4; Mosiah 4:14–15; Alma 56:45–48; 3 Nephi 22:13; see also "The Family: A Proclamation to the World," *Ensign,* Nov. 2010, 129

Teaching Help

"As you prepare yourself spiritually and acknowledge the Lord in your teaching, you will become an instrument in His hands. The Holy Ghost will magnify your words with power" (*Teaching, No Greater Call* [1999], 41).

Notes

1. "Fundamentals of Enduring Family Relationships," *Ensign,* Nov. 1982, 60; italics removed from original.

2. "Fundamentals of Enduring Family Relationships," 59.

3. Sheri L. Dew, *Ezra Taft Benson: A Biography* (1987), 127.

4. In *Ezra Taft Benson: A Biography,* 141.

5. Mark Amussen Benson, in *Ezra Taft Benson: A Biography,* 133.

6. Mark Amussen Benson, in *Ezra Taft Benson: A Biography,* 139.

7. Flora Amussen Benson, in *Ezra Taft Benson: A Biography,* 134.

8. Mark Amussen Benson, in *Ezra Taft Benson: A Biography,* 133.

9. Flora Amussen Benson, in *Ezra Taft Benson: A Biography,* 130.

10. In *Ezra Taft Benson: A Biography,* 134.

11. Mark Amussen Benson, in *Ezra Taft Benson: A Biography,* 138.

12. Francis M. Gibbons, *Ezra Taft Benson: Statesman, Patriot, Prophet of God* (1996), 165.

13. *Sermons and Writings of President Ezra Taft Benson* (2003), 205.

14. *The Teachings of Ezra Taft Benson* (1988), 503.

15. *The Teachings of Ezra Taft Benson,* 496.

16. *The Teachings of Ezra Taft Benson,* 511.

17. *Sermons and Writings of President Ezra Taft Benson,* 208, 212–13.

18. *Sermons and Writings of President Ezra Taft Benson,* 209.

19. *Sermons and Writings of President Ezra Taft Benson,* 211.

20. *Sermons and Writings of President Ezra Taft Benson,* 215.

21. *Sermons and Writings of President Ezra Taft Benson,* 216.

22. *Sermons and Writings of President Ezra Taft Benson,* 222.

23. *Sermons and Writings of President Ezra Taft Benson,* 217.

24. *Sermons and Writings of President Ezra Taft Benson,* 218–21.

25. "Jesus Christ—Gifts and Expectations," *Ensign,* Dec. 1988, 6.

26. *Sermons and Writings of President Ezra Taft Benson,* 216.

27. "Counsel to the Saints," *Ensign,* May 1984, 6.

28. In Conference Report, Oct. 1951, 155.

29. In Conference Report, Oct. 1953, 123.

The Elderly in the Church

*"May these golden years be your very best years as you
fully live and love and serve. And God bless those who
minister to your needs—your family, your friends,
and your fellow Church members and leaders."*

From the Life of Ezra Taft Benson

Ezra Taft Benson was 86 years old when he became President
of the Church. He understood the joys and challenges that come
during the later years of life. One joy for him was his continued
association with his wife, Flora. The couple celebrated their 60th
wedding anniversary during his first year as President. They enjoyed
each other's company and attended the temple together nearly every Friday morning. At his 87th birthday party, someone asked President Benson the secret to his long, happy life. "Before he could
answer, Sister Benson said, teasingly but with meaning, 'He has a
good wife.'"[1]

In their senior years, President and Sister Benson loved to spend
time with their children and their grandchildren, and their family
continued to learn from their example. "One granddaughter lived
with her grandparents during much of his first eighteen months as
president, and at their request often traveled with them to assist
them and attend to their personal needs. And she observed first-
hand her grandparents at home—their dates to an ice cream parlor;
sitting on the couch and holding hands as they reminisced, sang,
and laughed together; the warm visits they had with the home
teachers and others who came calling."[2]

The grandchildren realized what a blessing it was to have the
influence of wise and loving grandparents. "A granddaughter
wrote her thanks after President Benson had counseled her and

*"I hold special feelings for the elderly. . . . I feel that in some
measure I understand them, for I am one of them."*

her husband regarding a difficult decision. 'We asked you what you thought and you said, "Pray about it. I have faith that you will make the right decision." Your faith in us gave us extra confidence.'"³

For the general conference that immediately followed his 90th birthday, President Benson prepared an address directed "to the elderly in the Church and to their families and to those who minister to their needs." In the introduction, he expressed his personal connection to the topic: "I hold special feelings for the elderly—for this marvelous group of men and women. I feel that in some measure I understand them, for I am one of them."⁴

Teachings of Ezra Taft Benson

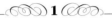

The Lord knows and loves the elderly and has bestowed many of His greatest responsibilities upon them.

The Lord knows and loves the elderly among His people. It has always been so, and upon them He has bestowed many of His greatest responsibilities. In various dispensations He has guided His people through prophets who were in their advancing years. He has needed the wisdom and experience of age, the inspired direction from those with long years of proven faithfulness to His gospel.

The Lord blessed Sarah, in her old age, to bear Abraham a child. Perhaps King Benjamin's greatest sermon was given when he was very elderly and nigh unto death. He was truly an instrument in the hands of the Lord as he was able to lead and establish peace among his people.

Many other men and women throughout the ages have accomplished great things as they went forth to serve the Lord and His children, even in their elderly years.

In our dispensation, of [those] prophets who have been called of the Lord, many were called when they were in their seventies or eighties, or even older. How the Lord knows and loves His children who have given so much through their years of experience!

We love you who are the elderly in the Church. You are the fastest-growing segment of our population in the world today, as well as within the Church.

Our desires are that your golden years will be wonderful and rewarding. We pray that you will feel the joy of a life well spent and one filled with fond memories and even greater expectations through Christ's atonement. We hope you will feel of the peace the Lord promised those who continue to strive to keep His commandments and follow His example. We hope your days are filled with things to do and ways in which you can render service to others who are not as fortunate as you. Older almost always means better, for your wealth of wisdom and experience can continue to expand and increase as you reach out to others.[5]

2

We can make the most of our senior years.

May we suggest eight areas in which we can make the most of our senior years:

1. *Work in the temple and attend often.* We who are older should use our energies not only to bless our predecessors, but to ensure that, insofar as possible, all of our posterity might receive the ordinances of exaltation in the temple. Work with your families; counsel with and pray for those who may yet be unwilling to prepare themselves.

We urge all who can to attend the temple frequently and accept calls to serve in the temple when health and strength and distance will permit. We rely on you to help in temple service. With the increasing number of temples, we need more of our members to prepare themselves for this sweet service. Sister Benson and I are grateful that almost every week we can attend the temple together. What a blessing this has been in our lives!

2. *Collect and write family histories.* We call on you to pursue vigorously the gathering and writing of personal and family histories. In so many instances, you alone have within you the history, the memory of loved ones, the dates and events. In some situations you *are* the family history. In few ways will your heritage be better preserved than by your collecting and writing your histories.

3. *Become involved in missionary service.* We need increasing numbers of senior missionaries in missionary service. Where health

and means make it possible, we call upon hundreds more of our couples to set their lives and affairs in order and to go on missions. How we need you in the mission field! You are able to perform missionary service in ways that our younger missionaries cannot.

I'm grateful that two of my own widowed sisters were able to serve as missionary companions together in England. They were sixty-eight and seventy-three years of age when they were called, and they both had a marvelous experience.

What an example and a blessing it is to a family's posterity when grandparents serve missions. Most senior couples who go are strengthened and revitalized by missionary service. Through this holy avenue of service, many are sanctified and feel the joy of bringing others to the knowledge of the fulness of the gospel of Jesus Christ. . . .

4. *Provide leadership by building family togetherness.* We urge all senior members, when possible, to call their families together. Organize them into cohesive units. Give leadership to family gatherings. Establish family reunions where fellowship and family heritage can be felt and learned. Some of the sweetest memories I have are of our own family reunions and gatherings. Foster wonderful family traditions which will bind you together eternally. In doing so, we can create a bit of heaven right here on earth within individual families. After all, eternity will be but an extension of righteous family life.

5. *Accept and fulfill Church callings.* We trust that all senior members who possibly can will accept callings in the Church and fulfill them with dignity. I am grateful to personally know brethren who are in their seventies and eighties who are serving as bishops and branch presidents. How we need the counsel and influence of you who have walked the pathway of life! We all need to hear of your successes and how you have risen above heartache, pain, or disappointment, having become stronger for experiencing them.

There are rich opportunities for you to serve in most of the organizations of the Church. You have the time and solid gospel foundation which enable you to render a great work. In so many ways you lead out in faithful service in the Church. We thank you for all

*"May these golden years be your very best years
as you fully live and love and serve."*

that you have done and pray that the Lord will strengthen you to do more.

6. *Plan for your financial future.* As you move through life toward retirement and the decades which follow, we invite all of our senior members to plan frugally for the years following full-time employment. Let us avoid unnecessary debt. We also advise caution in cosigning financial notes, even with family members, when retirement income might be jeopardized.

Be even more cautious in advancing years about "get-rich" schemes, mortgaging homes, or investing in uncertain ventures. Proceed cautiously so that the planning of a lifetime is not disrupted by one or a series of poor financial decisions. Plan your financial future early, then follow the plan.

7. *Render Christlike service.* Christlike service exalts. Knowing this, we call on all senior members who are able to thrust in their sickles in service to others. This can be part of the sanctifying process. The Lord has promised that those who lose their lives serving others will find themselves. The Prophet Joseph Smith told us that

we should "wear out our lives" in bringing to pass the Lord's purposes (D&C 123:13).

Peace and joy and blessings will follow those who render service to others. Yes, we commend Christlike service to all, but it is especially sweet in the lives of the elderly.

8. *Stay physically fit, healthy, and active.* We are thrilled with the efforts being made by so many of the elderly to ensure good health in advancing years. . . .

How we love to see our elderly remain vigorous and active! Through keeping active, both the mind and the body function better.[6]

 **3**

Serving others helps heal those who have lost loved ones or who dread being alone.

To those who have lost your spouses, we should also like to express our love. Sometimes there is for some of you a feeling of uselessness and aloneness which can be almost overwhelming. In so many instances, this need not be so. In addition to the eight suggestions just mentioned, here is a sampling of activities that have proved helpful to others.

Some who are alone keep busy by quilting blankets for each new grandchild to be married or each new baby born into the family. Others write letters on birthdays or attend school and athletic events of grandchildren when they can. Some compile albums of pictures of each grandchild to give on birthdays. . . .

We see numerous others of our widows who volunteer . . . at the hospitals or render other kinds of community service. So many find fulfillment helping in these ways.

The key to overcoming aloneness and a feeling of uselessness for one who is physically able is to step outside yourself by helping others who are truly needy. We promise those who will render this kind of service that, in some measure, you will be healed of the loss of loved ones or the dread of being alone. The way to feel better about your own situation is to improve someone else's circumstances.[7]

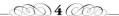

In times of illness and pain, we can remain strong in attitude and spirit.

To those who are ill and suffering pain and the vicissitudes of this life, we extend particular love and concern. Our hearts and prayers go out to you. Remember what father Lehi said in blessing his son Jacob, who had suffered at the hands of his older brothers Laman and Lemuel. He said, "Thou knowest the greatness of God; and he shall consecrate thine afflictions for thy gain" (2 Nephi 2:2). And so he will for you.

We pray that you will continue to strive to remain strong in attitude and spirit. We know it is not always easy. We pray that those who now do for you tasks that you no longer are able to do for yourself will do so in love, in gentleness, and with a caring spirit.

We hope that you will continue to generate good thoughts and feelings in your heart and mind and quickly dismiss those which are harmful and destructive to you. We trust your prayers are being offered daily and even hourly, if needed. As the Book of Mormon teaches, "Live in thanksgiving daily, for the many mercies and blessings which [God] doth bestow upon you" (Alma 34:38).

You will find that the daily reading of the Book of Mormon will lift your spirit, draw you nearer to your Savior, and help you to be a student of the gospel who can share great truths with others.[8]

It is important that families give their elderly parents and grandparents the love, care, and respect they deserve.

Now for a few minutes may I speak to the families of the elderly. We repeat a scripture from Psalms: "Cast me not off in the time of old age; forsake me not when my strength faileth" (Psalm 71:9).

We encourage families to give their elderly parents and grandparents the love, care, and attention they deserve. Let us remember the scriptural command that we must care for those of our own house lest we be found "worse than an infidel" (1 Timothy 5:8). I am so grateful for my own dear family and for the loving care they have given their parents over so many years.

Remember that parents and grandparents are our responsibility, and we are to care for them to the very best of our ability. When the elderly have no families to care for them, priesthood and Relief Society leaders should make every effort to meet their needs in the same loving way. We submit a few suggestions to families of the elderly.

Ever since the Lord etched the Ten Commandments into the tablets of stone, His words from Sinai have echoed down through the centuries to "honour thy father and thy mother" (Exodus 20:12).

To honor and respect our parents means that we have a high regard for them. We love and appreciate them and are concerned about their happiness and well-being. We treat them with courtesy and thoughtful consideration. We seek to understand their point of view. Certainly obedience to parents' righteous desires and wishes is a part of honoring.

Furthermore, our parents deserve our honor and respect for giving us life itself. Beyond this they almost always made countless sacrifices as they cared for and nurtured us through our infancy and childhood, provided us with the necessities of life, and nursed us through physical illnesses and the emotional stresses of growing up. In many instances, they provided us with the opportunity to receive an education, and, in a measure, they educated us. Much of what we know and do we learned from their example. May we ever be grateful to them and show that gratitude.

Let us also learn to be forgiving of our parents, who, perhaps having made mistakes as they reared us, almost always did the best they knew how. May we ever forgive them as we would likewise wish to be forgiven by our own children for mistakes we make.

Even when parents become elderly, we ought to honor them by allowing them freedom of choice and the opportunity for independence as long as possible. Let us not take away from them choices which they can still make. Some parents are able to live and care for themselves well into their advancing years and would prefer to do so. When they can, let them.

If they become less able to live independently, then family, Church, and community resources may be needed to help them.

211

When the elderly become unable to care for themselves, even with supplemental aid, care can be provided in the home of a family member when possible. Church and community resources may also be needed in this situation.

The role of the care-giver is vital. There is great need for support and help to be given to such a person. Usually this is an elderly spouse or a middle-aged daughter with children of her own to care for as well as caring for the elderly parent.[9]

6

Those who are blessed with a closeness to grandparents and other elderly people have a rich companionship and association.

We also hope that you would include the elderly in family activities when possible. What a joy it is for us to see lively, sweet grandchildren with a loving grandparent in the midst of them. Children love such occasions. They love to have their grandparents visit them and to have them over for dinner, for family home evenings, and for other special events. This provides opportunities for teaching ways to honor, love, respect, and care for those who are in their later years.

Grandparents can have a profound influence on their grandchildren. Their time is generally not as encumbered and busy as the parents', so books can be opened and read, stories can be told, and application of gospel principles can be taught. Children then obtain a perspective of life which not only is rewarding but can bring them security, peace, and strength. It is possible to send letters, [recordings], and pictures, particularly where distances are great and it is not possible to see one another often. Those who are blessed with a closeness to grandparents and other elderly people have a rich companionship and association. There might be times when they can attend graduations, weddings, temple excursions, . . . and other special events with family members.

We enjoy watching our children and grandchildren grow and achieve in special ways as we share in many of their joys and rejoice in their victories. Happiness blesses our lives as our children strive and achieve in their own lives. In 3 John 1:4 we read, "I have

"Grandparents can have a profound influence on their grandchildren."

no greater joy than to hear that my children walk in truth." And knowing this can bring a renewal of love and courage to continue in our own struggles.[10]

―――――――――――― 7 ――――――――――――

Church leaders should prayerfully seek the Spirit in helping members meet the needs of the elderly.

We . . . urge priesthood leaders of the elderly to be sensitive to the Spirit of our Father in Heaven in assessing and meeting the spiritual, physical, emotional, and financial needs of the elderly. We trust you will utilize your counselors, Melchizedek Priesthood quorum leaders, and Relief Society leaders, home teachers, and visiting teachers in this great responsibility, for we must fulfill these duties without reluctance or hesitation.

We hope that priesthood and auxiliary leaders will continue to give the elderly callings in which they can use their reservoirs of wisdom and counsel. We hope, where possible, that each can be a home teacher or visiting teacher. Even those who are somewhat confined to their beds and homes can sometimes assist in this watch-care through telephone calls, writing notes, or other special assignments.

A priesthood leader can do much to assist and encourage individuals and couples as they prepare to serve missions. The temple extraction [now called family history indexing] and welfare programs are blessed greatly by those who are in their senior years and have opportunities to serve in these areas.

We hope each of the elderly individuals and couples has sensitive and caring home teachers and visiting teachers assigned to them. Great comfort and peace can come to those who know they have someone to whom they can turn in time of emergency or need. It is important that tact, diplomacy, and sincerity be evident in assessing and addressing such needs.

We hope you will involve the independent elderly in compassionate service assignments. Include them also in stake and ward social activities, especially single members and those with dependent spouses. So many times they are forgotten. Especially at the time of the death of a spouse, loving care can be given. This is a very tender time for most.

At times temporary relief is very much needed and appreciated by family members who provide constant physical and emotional care to those with special needs. It is important to help the family maintain its functions as a family with periodic freedom from the heavy responsibilities that long-term or terminal illness can impose. All need loving support and relief from the overwhelming duties of serious illness or problems.

Transportation is often a great concern to the elderly. We can assist by providing a way for them to attend their Sunday meetings, visit loved ones, shop, and go to the doctor or clinic.

Again, we should prayerfully seek inspiration and direction in caring for the elderly. There is always a great diversity of individuals and individual needs.[11]

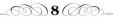

8

Our later years can be our best years.

God bless the elderly in the Church. I love you with all my heart. I am one of you.

You have so much to live for. May these golden years be your very best years as you fully live and love and serve. And God bless those who minister to your needs—your family, your friends, and your fellow Church members and leaders.

I leave you my testimony of the joy of living—of the joys of *full* gospel living and of going through the Refiner's fire and the sanctification process that takes place. As the Apostle Paul so well said, "We know that all things work together for good to them that love God" (Romans 8:28).

I leave my blessing upon you. The Savior lives. This is His church. The work is true, and in the words of our Lord and Savior, "Look unto me, and endure to the end, and ye shall live; for unto him that endureth to the end will I give eternal life" (3 Nephi 15:9).[12]

Suggestions for Study and Teaching

Questions

- How have you benefited from the "wisdom and experience" of people older than you? (See section 1.)

- In section 2, President Benson lists eight things elderly people can do to "make the most of [their] senior years." Consider each suggestion. How can these suggestions enrich our lives regardless of our age?

- Why do you think service is "the key to overcoming aloneness and a feeling of uselessness"? (See section 3.) When have you seen that this is true?

- Ponder President Benson's counsel for us when we experience illness and pain (see section 4). How can this counsel help us "remain strong in attitude and spirit"?

- Consider President Benson's teachings in section 5. In what ways can children and grandchildren honor their elderly parents and grandparents?

- When have you seen young people and elderly people enjoy each other's company? (See section 6.) What can we do in our families and in the Church to nurture such relationships?

- What are some ways Church leaders and ward or branch members can help meet the needs of the elderly? (For some examples, see section 7.)

- What does it mean to you to experience "the joys of full gospel living"? (See section 8.) What examples have you seen of people enduring faithfully to the end?

Related Scriptures

Proverbs 20:29; Isaiah 46:3–4; Luke 2:36–38; Ephesians 6:1–3; Titus 2:1–5; James 1:27; D&C 121:7–8

Study Help

"Acting on what you have learned will bring added and enduring understanding (see John 7:17)" (*Preach My Gospel* [2004], 19). Consider asking yourself how you can apply gospel teachings at home, at work, and in your Church responsibilities.

Notes

1. Sheri L. Dew, *Ezra Taft Benson: A Biography* (1987), 502.

2. Sheri L. Dew, *Ezra Taft Benson: A Biography,* 504.

3. Sheri L. Dew, *Ezra Taft Benson: A Biography,* 504–5.

4. In Conference Report, Oct. 1989, 3; see also *Ensign,* Nov. 1989, 4.

5. In Conference Report, Oct. 1989, 3; see also *Ensign,* Nov. 1989, 4.

6. In Conference Report, Oct. 1989, 3–5; see also *Ensign,* Nov. 1989, 4–6.

7. In Conference Report, Oct. 1989, 5; see also *Ensign,* Nov. 1989, 6.

8. In Conference Report, Oct. 1989, 5–6; see also *Ensign,* Nov. 1989, 6.

9. In Conference Report, Oct. 1989, 6–7; see also *Ensign,* Nov. 1989, 6–7.

10. In Conference Report, Oct. 1989, 7; see also *Ensign,* Nov. 1989, 7.

11. In Conference Report, Oct. 1989, 7–8; see also *Ensign,* Nov. 1989, 7–8.

12. In Conference Report, Oct. 1989, 8; see also *Ensign,* Nov. 1989, 8.

Keeping the Law of Chastity

"The moral code of heaven for both men and women is complete chastity before marriage and full fidelity after marriage."

From the Life of Ezra Taft Benson

Traveling widely as a religious and political leader, President Ezra Taft Benson was keenly aware of the steady moral decline throughout the world, especially with regard to the law of chastity. He took a strong stand against this decline, teaching that "the law of chastity is a principle of eternal significance."[1] He declared that "in the Church and kingdom of God, chastity will never be out-of-date, regardless of what the world may do or say."[2] He further taught: "We must be *in* the amoral and immoral world, . . . but not *of* it. We must be able to drop off to sleep at night without having to first sing lullabies to our conscience."[3]

To illustrate the importance of staying clean from the immoral influences of the world, President Benson shared the following story:

"I am reminded of a story of a young girl who, with her date, was going to a place of questionable reputation, against the wise counsel of her parents. Her question was, 'What harm is there in just going in to see what goes on there?' Her parents apparently gave in to her and suggested that she wear her lovely white dress for the occasion. Before her young man arrived, her father said, 'Would you do me a favor before you go and go out to the smokehouse and bring in a side of bacon?'

"The girl was aghast at this request and said, 'In my best dress? I would never get rid of that awful smell.' Her mother said, 'That is right, you can't go into the smokehouse without absorbing some of the influence there. We think you are smart enough not to go into a

Obedience to the law of chastity brings a
"significant sense of joy and happiness."

place where you would come out any less beautiful and clean than when you went in.' With that wise counsel, this young girl made the right decision to keep herself unspotted and clean from evil influences in the world."[4]

Teachings of Ezra Taft Benson

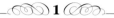 1

God has established the standard of chastity for His children.

In this dispensation the Lord reiterated the commandment given at Sinai when He said, "Thou shalt not . . . commit adultery, . . . *nor do anything like unto it*" (D&C 59:6, emphasis added). From the beginning of time, the Lord has set a clear and unmistakable standard of sexual purity. It always has been, it is now, and it always will be the same. That standard is the law of chastity. It is the same for all—for men and women, for old and young, for rich and poor.[5]

The Church has no double standard of morality. The moral code of heaven for both men and women is complete chastity before marriage and full fidelity after marriage.[6]

In the Book of Mormon, the prophet Jacob tells us that the Lord delights in the chastity of His children (see Jacob 2:28). Do you hear that, my brothers and sisters? The Lord is not just pleased when we are chaste; He *delights* in chastity. Mormon taught the same thing to his son Moroni when he wrote that chastity and virtue are "most dear and precious above all things" (Moroni 9:9).[7]

The natural desire for men and women to be together is from God. But such association is bounded by his laws. Those things properly reserved for marriage, when taken within the bonds of marriage, are right and pleasing before God and fulfil the commandment to multiply and replenish the earth. But those same things when taken outside the bonds of marriage are a curse.[8]

Go to the marriage altar pure and clean. Reserve for the marriage relationship those sweet and intimate associations which the God of Heaven intended should be a part of marriage and not be indulged in outside of the marriage covenant. I care not what the world says, but these are the standards of the kingdom of God.[9]

The plaguing sin of this generation is sexual immorality.

The plaguing sin of this generation is sexual immorality. This, the Prophet Joseph said, would be the source of more temptations, more buffetings, and more difficulties for the elders of Israel than any other.[10]

Sexual immorality is a viper that is striking not only in the world, but in the Church today. Not to admit it is to be dangerously complacent or is like putting one's head in the sand. In the category of crimes, only murder and denying the Holy Ghost come ahead of illicit sexual relations, which we call fornication when it involves an unmarried person, or the graver sin of adultery when it involves one who is married. I know the laws of the land do not consider unchastity as serious as God does, nor punish as severely as God does, but that does not change its abominableness. In the eyes of God there is but one moral standard for men and women. In the eyes of God chastity will never be out of date. . . .

No sin is causing the loss of the Spirit of the Lord among our people more today than sexual promiscuity. It is causing our people to stumble, damning their growth, darkening their spiritual powers, and making them subject to other sins.[11]

There is a grave danger in building your premarital associations on a physical basis. . . . The harmful effects of such unlawful associations are carried over into married life, bringing disappointment, heartache, and the weakening of the structure of the home.[12]

Moral purity is an eternal principle. The Spirit of God "cannot dwell in an unclean tabernacle" [see Helaman 4:24]. Purity is life-giving; impurity is deadly. God's holy laws cannot be broken with impunity. Great nations have fallen when they became morally corrupt, because the sins of immorality left their people scarred and misshapen creatures who were unable to face the challenge of their times.[13]

Unchastity is the most damning of all evils, while moral purity is one of the greatest bulwarks of successful homemaking. Happy and successful homes cannot be built on immorality.[14]

Some would justify their immorality with the argument that restrictions against it are merely religious rules, rules that are meaningless because in reality there is no God. This you will recognize is merely an untruthful rationalization designed to justify one's carnal appetite, lust, and passion. God's law is irrevocable. It applies to all, whether they believe in God or not. Everyone is subject to its penalties, no matter how one tries to rationalize or ignore them.

Immorality . . . always brings with it attendant remorse. A person cannot indulge in promiscuous relations without suffering ill effects from it. He cannot do wrong and feel right—it is impossible. Anytime one breaks a law of God, he pays a penalty in heartache, in sadness, in remorse, in lack of self-respect, and he removes himself from contact with the Spirit of God.[15]

 **3**

To stay morally clean, we need to prepare ourselves to resist temptation.

Most people fall into sexual sin in a misguided attempt to fulfill basic human needs. We all have a need to feel loved and worthwhile. We all seek to have joy and happiness in our lives. Knowing this, Satan often lures people into immorality by playing on their basic needs. He promises pleasure, happiness, and fulfillment.

But this is, of course, a deception. As the writer of Proverbs says: "Whoso committeth adultery with a woman lacketh understanding: he that doeth it destroyeth his own soul" (Proverbs 6:32). Samuel the Lamanite taught the same thing when he said, "Ye have sought for happiness in doing iniquity, which thing is contrary to the nature of . . . righteousness" (Helaman 13:38). Alma said it more simply: "Wickedness never was happiness" (Alma 41:10).[16]

There is an old saying that states: It is better to prepare and prevent than it is to repair and repent. How true that is of the law of chastity. The first line of defense in keeping ourselves morally clean is to prepare ourselves to resist temptation and prevent ourselves from falling into sin.[17]

Clean thoughts

Control your thoughts. No one steps into immorality in an instant. The first seeds of immorality are always sown in the mind. When we allow our thoughts to linger on lewd or immoral things, the first step on the road to immorality has been taken. I especially warn you against the evils of pornography. Again and again we hear from those caught in deep sin that often the first step on their road to transgression began with pornographic materials. The Savior taught that even when a man looks upon a woman to lust after her, or in other words, when he lets his thoughts begin to get out of control, he has already committed adultery with her in his heart (see Matt. 5:28; D&C 63:16).[18]

Those who think clean thoughts do not do dirty deeds. You are not only responsible before God for your acts but also for controlling your thoughts. So live that you would not blush with shame if your thoughts and acts could be flashed on a screen in your church. The old adage is still true that you sow thoughts and you reap acts, you sow acts and you reap habits, you sow habits and you reap a character, and your character determines your eternal destiny. "As a man thinketh, so is he." (See Prov. 23:7.)[19]

Consider carefully the words of the prophet Alma to his errant son, Corianton, "Forsake your sins, and go no more after the lusts of your eyes." (Alma 39:9.)

"The lusts of your eyes." In our day, what does that expression mean?

Movies, television programs, and video recordings that are both suggestive and lewd.

Magazines and books that are obscene and pornographic.

We counsel you . . . not to pollute your minds with such degrading matter, for the mind through which this filth passes is never the same afterwards.[20]

Be clean. Be virtuous in your thoughts and actions. Read good books. Never let your minds be subjected to pornography. . . . In the words of the Lord, "Let virtue garnish thy thoughts unceasingly; then shall thy confidence wax strong in the presence of God. The Holy Ghost shall be thy constant companion." (D&C 121:45–46.)[21]

Prayers for strength

Always pray for the power to resist temptation. Temptation will come to all of us. It will take many forms and appear in many disguises, but the Lord has given us the key for resisting it. He said to the Prophet Joseph Smith: "Pray always, that you may come off conqueror; yea, that you may conquer Satan, and that you may escape the hands of the servants of Satan that do uphold his work" (D&C 10:5). It should be part of our daily prayers to ask the Lord for constant strength to resist temptation, especially temptations that involve the law of chastity.[22]

There is no temptation placed before you which you cannot shun. Do not allow yourself to get in positions where it is easy to fall. Listen to the promptings of the Spirit. If you are engaged in things where you do not feel you can pray and ask the Lord's blessings on what you are doing, then you are engaged in the wrong kind of activity.[23]

Avoidance of improper situations

Men and women who are married sometimes flirt and tease with members of the opposite sex. So-called harmless meetings are arranged, or inordinate amounts of time are spent together. In all of these cases, people rationalize by saying that these are natural expressions of friendship. But what may appear to be harmless teasing or simply having a little fun with someone of the opposite sex can easily lead to more serious involvement and eventual infidelity.

A good question to ask ourselves is this: Would my spouse be pleased if he or she knew I was doing this?[24]

If you are married, avoid being alone with members of the opposite sex wherever possible. Many of the tragedies of immorality begin when a man and woman are alone in the office, or at church, or driving in a car. At first there may be no intent or even thought of sin. But the circumstances provide a fertile seedbed for temptation. One thing leads to another, and very quickly tragedy may result. It is so much easier to avoid such circumstances from the start so that temptation gets no chance for nourishment.[25]

Modesty

Be modest. Modesty in dress and language and deportment is a true mark of refinement and a hallmark of a virtuous Latter-day Saint. . . . Shun the low and the vulgar and the suggestive.[26]

"For those who are single and dating, carefully plan positive and constructive activities."

Healthful, positive activities

Overcome evil with good. You can overcome many evil inclinations through good physical exertion and healthful activities. A healthy soul, free of the body-and-spirit-dulling influences of alcohol and tobacco, is in better condition to overthrow the devil.[27]

For those who are single and dating, carefully plan positive and constructive activities so that you are not left to yourselves with nothing to do but share physical affection. . . . This is the principle of filling one's life with positive activities so that the negative has no chance to thrive.[28]

Fill your lives with positive sources of power. It is not enough simply to try to resist evil or empty our lives of sin. We must also fill our lives with righteousness. We must engage in activities that bring spiritual power.

I speak of such activities as immersing ourselves in the scriptures. There is a power that flows into our lives when we read and study the scriptures on a daily basis that cannot be found in any other way. Daily prayer is another source of great power. Fasting for specific strength or special blessings can strengthen us beyond our normal ability. Christian service, church attendance, service in the kingdom—all can add to our storehouse of strength and power.

We must do more than simply remove the negative influences from our lives. We must replace them with righteous activities that fill us with the strength and determination to live as we should.[29]

Through proper repentance, those who are entangled in sexual sin can become clean again.

There may be some for whom the counsel to prepare and prevent is too late. You may already be deeply entangled in serious sin. If this is the case, there is no choice now but to repair your lives and repent of your sins. To you I would suggest five important things you can do to come back to a state of moral purity. Flee immediately from any situation you are in that is either causing you to sin or that may cause you to sin. Plead with the Lord for the power to overcome. Let your priesthood leaders help you resolve the transgression and come back into full fellowship with the Lord. Drink from the divine fountain and fill your lives with positive sources of power. Remember that through proper repentance, you can become clean again.

For those who pay the price required by true repentance, the promise is sure. You can be clean again. The despair can be lifted. The sweet peace of forgiveness will flow into your lives. In this dispensation the Lord spoke with clarity when he said, "Behold, he who has repented of his sins, the same is forgiven, and I, the Lord, remember them no more" (D&C 58:42).[30]

Parents should teach their children to live the law of chastity.

Parents should give their children specific instructions on chastity at an early age, both for their physical and moral protection.[31]

If parents love and respect each other, and if in their sacred partnership there are full support and unquestioned fidelity, these essentials will be translated into the homes of tomorrow. Conversely, if there are bickering, quarreling, and lack of harmony at home, and

*President Ezra Taft Benson counseled parents
to teach their children about the law of chastity.*

participation in the dangerous practice of flirtations with others when away, then the homes of tomorrow will be weakened thereby. . . .

. . . Our homes must become bulwarks of strength through enthroning righteousness and bringing into them the peace, unity, and unselfishness engendered by personal purity, unquestioned fidelity, and simple family devotion. Parents must accept marriage as a divine institution, and honor parenthood. Children must be inspired by precept and example in preparation for marriage, to guard against unchastity as against a loathsome disease, and to practice the other fundamental Christian virtues.[32]

6

God has given us the law of chastity to bring us joy.

Our Heavenly Father desires nothing for us but to be happy. He tells us only those things that will bring us joy. And one of the surest principles given by God to help us find that joy is the law of chastity. I pray with all my heart that you will consider most solemnly the joyful consequences of keeping this law, and the tragic consequences of violating it.[33]

A reason for virtue—which includes personal chastity, clean thoughts and practices, and integrity—is that we must have the Spirit and the power of God in our lives to do God's work. Without that power and influence we are no better off than individuals in other organizations. That virtue shines through and will influence others toward a better life and cause nonmembers to inquire of our faith.[34]

Be true to God's holy laws. Remember, they cannot be broken with impunity. If you would be happy and successful in your earthly association, courtship, and home building, conform your lives to the eternal laws of heaven. There is no other way.[35]

There is no lasting happiness in immorality. There is no joy to be found in breaking the law of chastity. Just the opposite is true. There may be momentary pleasure. For a time it may seem like everything is wonderful. But quickly the relationship will sour. Guilt and shame set in. We become fearful that our sins will be discovered. We must sneak and hide, lie and cheat. Love begins to die. Bitterness, jealousy, anger, and even hate begin to grow. All of these are the natural results of sin and transgression.

On the other hand, when we obey the law of chastity and keep ourselves morally clean, we will experience the blessings of increased love and peace, greater trust and respect for our marital partners, deeper commitment to each other, and therefore a deep and significant sense of joy and happiness.[36]

Suggestions for Study and Teaching

Questions
- President Benson said that the Lord's standard of sexual purity is "clear and unmistakable" (section 1). How does this standard differ from the messages of the world?

- What are some of the consequences of violating the law of chastity? (For some examples, see section 2.)

- What are some specific things we can do to guard ourselves and our families from sexual temptation? (For some examples, see section 3.)

- Review President Benson's counsel to those "in serious sin" (section 4). What are your thoughts and feelings as you ponder the Lord's promise to welcome the repentant "back into full fellowship"?

• Why do you think it is important for parents to "give their children specific instructions on chastity at an early age"? How do parents' faithfulness to each other influence their children's feelings about marriage and the law of chastity? (See section 5.)

• What are some of the "joyful consequences" of keeping the law of chastity? (For some examples, see section 6.)

Related Scriptures

Genesis 39:7–21; 1 Corinthians 6:18–20; Galatians 5:16; Alma 38:12; 39:3–5; 3 Nephi 12:27–30; D&C 42:22–25

Teaching Help

"Encourage those you teach to come to class prepared to learn and participate. When they are striving individually to learn the gospel, they are more likely to contribute to the learning atmosphere during lessons" (*Teaching, No Greater Call* [1999], 80).

Notes

1. "The Law of Chastity," *New Era*, Jan. 1988, 4.
2. "To 'the Rising Generation,'" *New Era*, June 1986, 6.
3. *The Teachings of Ezra Taft Benson* (1988), 285.
4. *The Teachings of Ezra Taft Benson*, 282–83.
5. "The Law of Chastity," 4.
6. "To 'the Rising Generation,'" 5–6.
7. "The Law of Chastity," 4.
8. In Conference Report, Oct. 1964, 59.
9. *The Teachings of Ezra Taft Benson*, 281.
10. "Cleansing the Inner Vessel," *Ensign*, May 1986, 4; the statement by Joseph Smith is quoted in Brigham Young, "Instructions to Missionaries," *Deseret News*, June 13, 1860, 113.
11. In Conference Report, Oct. 1964, 59.
12. "Your Charge: To Increase in Wisdom and Favor with God and Man," *New Era*, Sept. 1979, 43.
13. In Conference Report, Oct. 1959, 113.
14. In Conference Report, Apr. 1949, 196.
15. *This Nation Shall Endure* (1977), 97.
16. "The Law of Chastity," 4–5.
17. "The Law of Chastity," 6.
18. "The Law of Chastity," 6.
19. In Conference Report, Oct. 1964, 60.
20. "To the 'Youth of the Noble Birthright,'" *Ensign*, May 1986, 45; see also "To the Young Women of the Church," *Ensign*, Nov. 1986, 81.
21. *The Teachings of Ezra Taft Benson*, 285.
22. "The Law of Chastity," 6.
23. In Conference Report, Oct. 1964, 60.
24. "The Law of Chastity," 6.
25. "The Law of Chastity," 6.
26. "To the Young Women of the Church," *Ensign*, Nov. 1986, 83.
27. In Conference Report, Oct. 1964, 60.
28. "The Law of Chastity," 6.
29. "The Law of Chastity," 7.
30. *The Teachings of Ezra Taft Benson*, 284.
31. In Conference Report, Oct. 1964, 59.
32. In Conference Report, Apr. 1949, 197, 198.
33. "The Law of Chastity," 7.
34. *The Teachings of Ezra Taft Benson*, 278.
35. "Your Charge: To Increase in Wisdom and Favor with God and Man," 43.
36. "The Law of Chastity," 5.

Beware of Pride

"Pride is the universal sin, the great vice.
The antidote for pride is humility."

From the Life of Ezra Taft Benson

In his first general conference address as President of the Church, President Ezra Taft Benson taught about differences between pride and humility:

"Pride does not look up to God and care about what is right. It looks sideways to man and argues who is right. . . .

"Pride is characterized by 'What do I want out of life?' rather than by 'What would God have me do with my life?' It is self-will as opposed to God's will. It is the fear of man over the fear of God.

"Humility responds to God's will—to the fear of His judgments and to the needs of those around us. To the proud, the applause of the world rings in their ears; to the humble, the applause of heaven warms their hearts."[1]

These teachings were familiar to the men who had served with President Benson in the Quorum of the Twelve Apostles. They knew that as President of their quorum, he never worried about his personal views—only about learning and following God's will. President Boyd K. Packer, who later served as President of the Quorum of the Twelve himself, told of President Benson's approach to discussions in quorum meetings: "You could disagree with President Benson without worrying that there was anything personal to it. We had full discussions on matters without worrying what his viewpoint might be."[2] Elder Russell M. Nelson, who served in the Quorum of the Twelve for two years under President Benson's leadership, said: "In any consideration, even if it was not his opinion, President Benson measured a situation against only one

The Savior, who is "meek and lowly in heart"
(Matthew 11:29), is our great example of humility.

standard—What's best for the kingdom? If it meant a wrinkle might have to be folded in a way he wouldn't have done it, so be it. He wanted only what was best for the kingdom."[3]

As a government leader, President Benson was equally dedicated to doing what was best for the kingdom of God. When he served as the United States secretary of agriculture, he received much "applause of the world,"[4] along with a large amount of harsh criticism. He did not allow either to ring in his ears. Instead, he was true to a reminder he frequently received from his wife, Flora: "Don't worry about the world's opinion of you as long as you're right with the Lord."[5] Content with the quiet "applause of heaven,"[6] he always sought to respond to God's will.

Teachings of Ezra Taft Benson

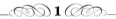

The Lord has warned us to beware of pride.

The Doctrine and Covenants tells us that the Book of Mormon is the "record of a fallen people." (D&C 20:9.) Why did they fall? This is one of the major messages of the Book of Mormon. Mormon gives the answer in the closing chapters of the book in these words: "Behold, the pride of this nation, or the people of the Nephites, hath proven their destruction." (Moro. 8:27.) And then, lest we miss that momentous Book of Mormon message from that fallen people, the Lord warns us in the Doctrine and Covenants, "Beware of pride, lest ye become as the Nephites of old." (D&C 38:39.)

I earnestly seek an interest in your faith and prayers as I strive to bring forth light on this Book of Mormon message—the sin of pride. This message has been weighing heavily on my soul for some time. I know the Lord wants this message delivered now.

In the premortal council, it was pride that felled Lucifer, "a son of the morning." (2 Ne. 24:12–15; see also D&C 76:25–27; Moses 4:3.) At the end of this world, when God cleanses the earth by fire, the proud will be burned as stubble and the meek shall inherit the earth. (See 3 Ne. 12:5; 25:1; D&C 29:9; JS—H 1:37; Mal. 4:1.)

Three times in the Doctrine and Covenants the Lord uses the phrase "beware of pride," including a warning to the second elder of the Church, Oliver Cowdery, and to Emma Smith, the wife of the Prophet. (D&C 23:1; see also 25:14; 38:39.)[7]

2

The central feature of pride is enmity toward God and our fellowmen.

Pride is a very misunderstood sin, and many are sinning in ignorance. (See Mosiah 3:11; 3 Ne. 6:18.) In the scriptures there is no such thing as righteous pride—it is always considered a sin. Therefore, no matter how the world uses the term, we must understand how God uses the term so we can understand the language of holy writ and profit thereby. (See 2 Ne. 4:15; Mosiah 1:3–7; Alma 5:61.)

Most of us think of pride as self-centeredness, conceit, boastfulness, arrogance, or haughtiness. All of these are elements of the sin, but the heart, or core, is still missing.

The central feature of pride is enmity—enmity toward God and enmity toward our fellowmen. *Enmity* means "hatred toward, hostility to, or a state of opposition." It is the power by which Satan wishes to reign over us.

Pride is essentially competitive in nature. We pit our will against God's. When we direct our pride toward God, it is in the spirit of "my will and not thine be done." As Paul said, they "seek their own, not the things which are Jesus Christ's." (Philip. 2:21.)

Our will in competition to God's will allows desires, appetites, and passions to go unbridled. (See Alma 38:12; 3 Ne. 12:30.)

The proud cannot accept the authority of God giving direction to their lives. (See Hel. 12:6.) They pit their perceptions of truth against God's great knowledge, their abilities versus God's priesthood power, their accomplishments against His mighty works.

Our enmity toward God takes on many labels, such as rebellion, hard-heartedness, stiff-neckedness, unrepentant, puffed up, easily offended, and sign seekers. The proud wish God would agree with them. They aren't interested in changing their opinions to agree with God's.

Another major portion of this very prevalent sin of pride is enmity toward our fellowmen. We are tempted daily to elevate ourselves above others and diminish them. (See Hel. 6:17; D&C 58:41.)

The proud make every man their adversary by pitting their intellects, opinions, works, wealth, talents, or any other worldly measuring device against others. In the words of C. S. Lewis: "Pride gets no pleasure out of having something, only out of having more of it than the next man. . . . It is the comparison that makes you proud: the pleasure of being above the rest. Once the element of competition has gone, pride has gone." (*Mere Christianity,* New York: Macmillan, 1952, pp. 109–10.)

In the pre-earthly council, Lucifer placed his proposal in competition with the Father's plan as advocated by Jesus Christ. (See Moses 4:1–3.) He wished to be honored above all others. (See 2 Ne. 24:13.) In short, his prideful desire was to dethrone God. (See D&C 29:36; 76:28.)

The scriptures abound with evidences of the severe consequences of the sin of pride to individuals, groups, cities, and nations. "Pride goeth before destruction." (Prov. 16:18.) It destroyed the Nephite nation and the city of Sodom. (See Moro. 8:27; Ezek. 16:49–50.)[8]

The proud stand more in fear of men's judgment than of God's judgment.

It was through pride that Christ was crucified. The Pharisees were wroth because Jesus claimed to be the Son of God, which was a threat to their position, and so they plotted His death. (See John 11:53.)

Saul became an enemy to David through pride. He was jealous because the crowds of Israelite women were singing that "Saul hath slain his thousands, and David his ten thousands." (1 Sam. 18:6–8.)

The proud stand more in fear of men's judgment than of God's judgment. (See D&C 3:6–7; 30:1–2; 60:2.) "What will men think of me?" weighs heavier than "What will God think of me?"

King Noah was about to free the prophet Abinadi, but an appeal to his pride by his wicked priests sent Abinadi to the flames.

King Noah's pride led to Abinadi's death and to his own death.

(See Mosiah 17:11–12.) Herod sorrowed at the request of his wife to behead John the Baptist. But his prideful desire to look good to "them which sat with him at meat" caused him to kill John. (Matt. 14:9; see also Mark 6:26.)

Fear of men's judgment manifests itself in competition for men's approval. The proud love "the praise of men more than the praise of God." (John 12:42–43.) Our motives for the things we do are where the sin is manifest. Jesus said He did "always those things" that pleased God. (John 8:29.) Would we not do well to have the pleasing of God as our motive rather than to try to elevate ourselves above our brother and outdo another?

Some prideful people are not so concerned as to whether their wages meet their needs as they are that their wages are more than someone else's. Their reward is being a cut above the rest. This is the enmity of pride.

When pride has a hold on our hearts, we lose our independence of the world and deliver our freedoms to the bondage of men's judgment. The world shouts louder than the whisperings of the Holy Ghost. The reasoning of men overrides the revelations of God, and the proud let go of the iron rod. (See 1 Ne. 8:19–28; 11:25; 15:23–24.)[9]

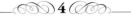

4

Pride is manifest in many ways.

Pride is a sin that can readily be seen in others but is rarely admitted in ourselves. Most of us consider pride to be a sin of those on the top, such as the rich and the learned, looking down at the rest of us. (See 2 Ne. 9:42.) There is, however, a far more common ailment among us—and that is pride from the bottom looking up. It is manifest in so many ways, such as faultfinding, gossiping, backbiting, murmuring, living beyond our means, envying, coveting, withholding gratitude and praise that might lift another, and being unforgiving and jealous.

Disobedience is essentially a prideful power struggle against someone in authority over us. It can be a parent, a priesthood leader, a teacher, or ultimately God. A proud person hates the fact that someone is above him. He thinks this lowers his position.

Selfishness is one of the more common faces of pride. "How everything affects me" is the center of all that matters—self-conceit, self-pity, worldly self-fulfillment, self-gratification, and self-seeking.

Pride results in secret combinations which are built up to get power, gain, and glory of the world. (See Hel. 7:5; Ether 8:9, 16, 22–23; Moses 5:31.) This fruit of the sin of pride, namely secret combinations, brought down both the Jaredite and the Nephite civilizations and has been and will yet be the cause of the fall of many nations. (See Ether 8:18–25.)

Another face of pride is contention. Arguments, fights, unrighteous dominion, generation gaps, divorces, spouse abuse, riots, and disturbances all fall into this category of pride.

Contention in our families drives the Spirit of the Lord away. It also drives many of our family members away. Contention ranges from a hostile spoken word to worldwide conflicts. The scriptures tell us that "only by pride cometh contention." (Prov. 13:10; see also Prov. 28:25.)

The scriptures testify that the proud are easily offended and hold grudges. (See 1 Ne. 16:1–3.) They withhold forgiveness to keep another in their debt and to justify their injured feelings.

The proud do not receive counsel or correction easily. (See Prov. 15:10; Amos 5:10.) Defensiveness is used by them to justify and rationalize their frailties and failures. (See Matt. 3:9; John 6:30–59.)

The proud depend upon the world to tell them whether they have value or not. Their self-esteem is determined by where they are judged to be on the ladders of worldly success. They feel worth-while as individuals if the numbers beneath them in achievement, talent, beauty, or intellect are large enough. Pride is ugly. It says, "If you succeed, I am a failure."

If we love God, do His will, and fear His judgment more than men's, we will have self-esteem.[10]

 **5**

Pride limits or stops progression.

Pride is a damning sin in the true sense of that word. It limits or stops progression. (See Alma 12:10–11.) The proud are not easily taught. (See 1 Ne. 15:3, 7–11.) They won't change their minds to accept truths, because to do so implies they have been wrong.

Pride adversely affects all our relationships—our relationship with God and His servants, between husband and wife, parent and child, employer and employee, teacher and student, and all mankind. Our degree of pride determines how we treat our God and our brothers and sisters. Christ wants to lift us to where He is. Do we desire to do the same for others?

Pride fades our feelings of sonship to God and brotherhood to man. It separates and divides us by "ranks," according to our "riches" and our "chances for learning." (3 Ne. 6:12.) Unity is impossible for a proud people, and unless we are one we are not the Lord's. (See Mosiah 18:21; D&C 38:27; 105:2–4; Moses 7:18.)

Humility brings unity and strength to marriages and families.

Think of what pride has cost us in the past and what it is now costing us in our own lives, our families, and the Church.

Think of the repentance that could take place with lives changed, marriages preserved, and homes strengthened, if pride did not keep us from confessing our sins and forsaking them. (See D&C 58:43.)

Think of the many who are less active members of the Church because they were offended and their pride will not allow them to forgive or fully sup at the Lord's table.

Think of the tens of thousands of additional young men and couples who could be on missions except for the pride that keeps them from yielding their hearts unto God. (See Alma 10:6; Hel. 3:34–35.)

Think how temple work would increase if the time spent in this godly service were more important than the many prideful pursuits that compete for our time.[11]

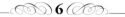

The antidote for pride is humility.

Pride affects all of us at various times and in various degrees. Now you can see why the building in Lehi's dream that represents the pride of the world was large and spacious and great was the multitude that did enter into it. (See 1 Ne. 8:26, 33; 11:35–36.)

Pride is the universal sin, the great vice. Yes, pride *is* the universal sin, the great vice.

The antidote for pride is humility—meekness, submissiveness. (See Alma 7:23.) It is the broken heart and contrite spirit. (See 3 Ne. 9:20; 12:19; D&C 20:37; 59:8; Ps. 34:18; Isa. 57:15; 66:2.) As Rudyard Kipling put it so well:

> *The tumult and the shouting dies;*
> *The captains and the kings depart.*
> *Still stands thine ancient sacrifice,*
> *An humble and a contrite heart.*
> *Lord God of Hosts, be with us yet,*
> *Lest we forget, lest we forget. . . .*

God will have a humble people. Either we can choose to be humble or we can be compelled to be humble. Alma said, "Blessed are they who humble themselves without being compelled to be humble." (Alma 32:16.)

Let us choose to be humble.

We can choose to humble ourselves by conquering enmity toward our brothers and sisters, esteeming them as ourselves, and lifting them as high or higher than we are. (See D&C 38:24; 81:5; 84:106.)

We can choose to humble ourselves by receiving counsel and chastisement. (See Jacob 4:10; Hel. 15:3; D&C 63:55; 101:4–5; 108:1; 124:61, 84; 136:31; Prov. 9:8.)

We can choose to humble ourselves by forgiving those who have offended us. (See 3 Ne. 13:11, 14; D&C 64:10.)

We can choose to humble ourselves by rendering selfless service. (See Mosiah 2:16–17.)

We can choose to humble ourselves by going on missions and preaching the word that can humble others. (See Alma 4:19; 31:5; 48:20.)

We can choose to humble ourselves by getting to the temple more frequently.

We can choose to humble ourselves by confessing and forsaking our sins and being born of God. (See D&C 58:43; Mosiah 27:25–26; Alma 5:7–14, 49.)

We can choose to humble ourselves by loving God, submitting our will to His, and putting Him first in our lives. (See 3 Ne. 11:11; 13:33; Moro. 10:32.)

Let us choose to be humble. We can do it. I know we can.

My dear brethren and sisters, we must prepare to redeem Zion. It was essentially the sin of pride that kept us from establishing Zion in the days of the Prophet Joseph Smith. It was the same sin of pride that brought consecration to an end among the Nephites. (See 4 Nephi 1:24–25.)

Pride is the great stumbling block to Zion. I repeat: Pride *is* the great stumbling block to Zion.

We must cleanse the inner vessel by conquering pride. (See Alma 6:2–4; Matthew 23:25–26.)

We must yield "to the enticings of the Holy Spirit," put off the prideful "natural man," become "a saint through the atonement of Christ the Lord," and become "as a child, submissive, meek, humble." (Mosiah 3:19; see also Alma 13:28.)

That we may do so and go on to fulfill our divine destiny is my fervent prayer.[12]

Suggestions for Study and Teaching

Questions
- President Benson pointed out that pride led to the destruction of the Nephite people (see section 1.) Why do you think pride has such destructive power?

- In what ways might people "pit [their] will against God's will"? (See section 2.) What are some blessings that come to us when we follow God's will?

- Why do you think we sometimes ask "What will other people think of me?" rather than "What will God think of me?" (See section 3.) How do our lives change when our greatest desire is to please God?

- Review the manifestations of pride that are listed in section 4. How can we avoid these manifestations of pride in our lives?

- President Benson said, "Pride adversely affects all our relationships"—with God and with others (section 5). Why is this true? In what ways do our relationships improve when we are humble?

- In section 6, President Benson lists ways we can choose to be humble. Why do you think it is better to choose to be humble than to be compelled to be humble?

Related Scriptures

Matthew 23:12; Luke 18:9–14; James 4:6; Alma 5:27–28; D&C 112:10; 121:34–40

Study Help

To liken the words of a prophet to yourself, think about how his teachings relate to you (see *Teaching, No Greater Call* [1999], 170). Consider asking yourself how those teachings can help you with concerns, questions, and challenges in your life.

Notes

1. "Cleansing the Inner Vessel," *Ensign,* May 1986, 6–7.
2. Boyd K. Packer, in Sheri L. Dew, *Ezra Taft Benson: A Biography* (1987), 429–30.
3. Russell M. Nelson, in *Ezra Taft Benson: A Biography,* 430.
4. "Cleansing the Inner Vessel," 7.
5. Flora Amussen Benson, in *Ezra Taft Benson: A Biography,* 293.
6. "Cleansing the Inner Vessel," 7.
7. "Beware of Pride," *Ensign,* May 1989, 4.
8. "Beware of Pride," 4–5.
9. "Beware of Pride," 5.
10. "Beware of Pride," 5–6.
11. "Beware of Pride," 6.
12. "Beware of Pride," 6–7; hymn text for "God of Our Fathers, Known of Old" by Rudyard Kipling in *Hymns,* no. 80.

Leadership

"If you are to provide future leadership for the Church, [your] country, and your own homes, you must stand firm in the faith, unwavering in the face of evil."

From the Life of Ezra Taft Benson

Ezra Taft Benson began learning to be a leader in his youth. When he was almost 13 years old, his father was called to serve a mission. As the oldest child in the family, Ezra assumed many leadership responsibilities on the family farm during his father's absence. Several years later, when he was called to the British Mission, he served as a branch president and as president of the Newcastle Conference (similar to a district today). Later, he served in three stake presidencies—once as a counselor, once for a short time as stake president, and once for a longer period as stake president. During his professional career, he worked in many leadership positions in the agriculture industry. Because he became a leader and expert in the field of agriculture, President Dwight D. Eisenhower asked him to serve in the highest agriculture position in the United States. For eight years he worked with President Eisenhower as the United States secretary of agriculture.

Before he became President of the Church, President Benson served for 12 years as President of the Quorum of the Twelve Apostles. Quorum members had great respect for him as their leader. Elder Bruce R. McConkie "often told family members he had never seen President Benson's administrative equal in the Church."[1]

In leading the Twelve, President Benson encouraged quorum members to express their thoughts candidly, even if he had a different opinion. When Elder Russell M. Nelson was a new member of the quorum, he thought perhaps he should not speak up. "But

*President Ezra Taft Benson and his counselors in the First Presidency:
President Gordon B. Hinckley (left) and President Thomas S. Monson (right)*

[President Benson] wouldn't have that," he said. "In fact, if I was silent on something he would draw it out."[2]

Although President Benson solicited opinions from all, he did not let discussions wander. President Howard W. Hunter said he "knew how to get open and frank discussion from [the] Brethren and [was] able to direct and control it and arrive at a unanimous decision with everyone united."[3] When "he felt that adequate discussion had taken place, he typically said, 'I think we've got enough hay down now. Let's bale a little,' bringing the issue to resolution."[4]

President Benson cared for those he led, and he taught by example. "I know of no man more considerate of his associates or more concerned for their well-being," President Gordon B. Hinckley said. "He does not ask others to do that which he is unwilling to do himself, but rather sets an example of service for others of us to follow."[5] President Benson was also effective in delegating work to others, teaching and building them through that process.

In the general conference when President Benson was sustained as President of the Church, President Gordon B. Hinckley expressed his conviction that the Lord had selected and prepared President Benson to lead the Church:

"I give you my testimony that it is the Lord who selected Ezra Taft Benson to become a member of the Council of the Twelve almost forty-three years ago. It is the Lord who over these years has tested and disciplined him, schooled and prepared him. . . .

"As one who knows him and who stands at his side, I bear witness that he is a man of faith, of tested leadership, of profound love for the Lord and His work, of love for the sons and daughters of God everywhere. He is a man of proven capacity."[6]

Teachings of Ezra Taft Benson

 1

Effective leaders stand firm in the faith and set a good example.

The power of Christ's leadership grew from the challenge of His example. His clarion call was, "Come, follow me!" . . . His [success in gaining] the loyalty and devotion of men to principles of righteousness depend[ed] upon love as the great motivating factor. He helped us realize that the godlike qualities in each of us clamoring for expression can become glorious living realities. His example continues as the greatest hope and strength of mankind.[7]

If you are to provide future leadership for the Church, [your] country, and your own homes, you must stand firm in the faith, unwavering in the face of evil, and as Paul said, "Put on the whole armour of God, that ye may be able to stand against the wiles of the devil. For we wrestle not against flesh and blood, but against principalities, against powers, against the rulers of the darkness of this world, against spiritual wickedness in high places." (Ephesians 6:11–12.)[8]

Our young people need fewer critics and more models. You are the models to which they will look for a pattern in life to which they can follow and adhere. They will need the inspiration which can come from you as you square your lives fully with the teachings of the gospel.[9]

 **2**

People respond to effective leadership.

Humility

One of the marks of great leadership always has been and ever will be the humble spirit.[10]

Spiritual strength

Spiritual strength promotes positive thinking, positive ideals, positive habits, positive attitudes, and positive efforts. These are the qualities which promote wisdom, physical and mental well-being, and enthusiastic acceptance and response by others.[11]

Only the wholesome have the capacity to lift and encourage one another to greater service, to greater achievement, to greater strength.[12]

Inspiration is essential to properly lead. . . . We must have the spirit of inspiration whether we are teaching (D&C 50:13–14) or administering the affairs of the kingdom (D&C 46:2).[13]

There is no satisfactory substitute for the Spirit.[14]

Knowledge

A genuine leader tries to stay well informed. He is a person who acts on principle rather than expediency. He tries to learn from all human experience measured against revealed principles of divine wisdom.[15]

One of the best ways for leaders to understand correct principles is to have a thorough knowledge and understanding of the scriptures and the appropriate handbook. Most situations have already arisen before, perhaps many times, and policy and procedure have already been determined to handle the problem. It is always wise, therefore, to refer to and be familiar with existing written instructions and Church policy on questions as they arise.[16]

Leaders are counseled to study the doctrines of the Church so as to be able to adequately represent our doctrines to others. To use the Apostle Paul's phraseology, we expect you to be a "workman that needeth not to be ashamed" (2 Timothy 2:15).[17]

Loyalty

A good leader expects loyalty. He in turn gives his loyalty. He backs up those to whom he has given a job. The loyalty extends to matters beyond the call of duty. He is loyal when honors come to those with whom he serves. He takes pride in their successes. He does not overrule unless he first confers with him whose decision he overrules. He does not embarrass an associate before others. He is frank and open with him.[18]

Unity

There is a "union required by the law of the celestial kingdom; And Zion cannot be built up unless it is by the principles of the law of the celestial kingdom." (D&C 105:4–5.) Among the required principles and attributes is a unity of mind and heart. "I say unto you, be one; and if ye are not one ye are not mine," is the Savior's injunction to His modern Church (D&C 38:27; John 17:20–23). Nowhere is this requirement more essential than among those whom He has called to preside throughout His kingdom.[19]

"A love of people is essential to effective leadership."

Love and expressions of confidence

A love of people is essential to effective leadership. Do you love those whom you work with? Do you realize the worth of souls is great in the sight of God (see D&C 18:10)? Do you have faith in youth? Do you find yourself praising their virtues, commending them for their accomplishments? Or do you have a critical attitude toward them because of their mistakes?[20]

Even harder to bear than criticism, oftentimes, is no word from our leader on the work to which we have been assigned. Little comments or notes, which are sincere and specific, are great boosters along the way.[21]

We know . . . that the time a leader spends in personal contact with members is more productive than time spent in meetings and administrative duties. Personal contact is the key to converting the inactive member.[22]

In the Church especially, asking produces better results than ordering—better feeling, too. Remember to tell why. Follow up to see how things are going. Show appreciation when people carry out instructions well. Express confidence when it can be done honestly.

When something gets fouled up, it is well to check back and find out where you slipped up—and don't be afraid to admit that you did. Remember, our people are voluntary, free-will workers. They also love the Lord and His work. Love them. Appreciate them. When you are tempted to reprimand a fellow worker, don't. Try an interesting challenge and a pat on the back instead. Our Father's children throughout the world are essentially good. He loves them. We should also.[23]

People do not like to be forced to do anything, even if it is for their own good. But people do respond to effective leadership.[24]

 **3**

Good leaders delegate wisely.

The Savior's example of delegation

The very foundations of the world were laid by delegated authority. Many times Jesus reminded people that His mission on earth was one through delegated authority. The restoration of His Church had its very beginning with delegated authority.

In speaking to the Jews in the synagogue, Jesus told them that He had been delegated by His Father: "For I came down from heaven, not to do mine own will, but the will of him that sent me" (John 6:38).[25]

Jesus gives us the master example of good administration through proper delegating. . . . Many of His delegated missionaries traveled without purse or scrip. Men suffered great hardships in carrying out His instructions. Some of them died cruel deaths in His service. But his delegated disciples went forth into the world bold as lions through His charge. They accomplished things they had never dreamed of. No leader ever motivated men and women as did He.[26]

The Church of Jesus Christ builds leaders through involving people delegated through authority. When [Jesus] was on earth, he called twelve apostles to assist him in administering the church. He also called the seventy. He delegated [to] others. There were to be no spectators in his church. All were to be involved in helping build the kingdom. And as they built the kingdom, they built themselves.

*During His mortal ministry, Jesus Christ delegated
authority to His Twelve Apostles.*

Jesus aimed to exalt the individual. . . .

Jesus aimed to make of every man a king, to build him in leadership into eternity. On that memorable night after the last supper, He said to the eleven . . . , "Verily, verily, I say unto you, He that believeth in me, the works that I do shall he do also; and greater works than these shall he do; because I go unto my Father." (John 14:12.) Through delegating, Jesus desired to lift, rather than suppress, the individual. And all through the Church today, men and women are growing in stature through positions delegated to them.[27]

Delegating in our organizations

Good management means delegating authority. Delegating part of the workload helps you and your organization. Effective management is the art of multiplying yourself through others.[28]

Wise delegation requires prayerful preparation, as does effective teaching or preaching. The Lord makes this clear in these words: "And the Spirit shall be given unto you by the prayer of faith; and if ye receive not the Spirit ye shall not teach" (D&C 42:14). And we might add, ye shall not delegate without the Spirit.[29]

A wise administrator in the Church today will not try to do the job himself, giving the impression that no one else is quite qualified. And as he delegates, he will give an assurance that he who has been delegated has his full backing.[30]

When responsibility has been given, the leader does not forget the person assigned nor his assignment. He follows with interest but does not "look over the shoulder." He gives specific praise when it is deserved. He gives helpful encouragement when needed. When he feels that the job is not being done and a change is needed, he acts with courage and firmness but with kindness. When the tenure of an office has been completed, he gives recognition and thanks.[31]

No wise leader believes that all good ideas originate with himself. He invites suggestions from those he leads. He lets them feel that they are an important part of decision making. He lets them feel that they are carrying out their policies, not just his.[32]

4

Church leaders are instruments in God's hands and should seek the Spirit in leading and building others.

In the Church today a leader generally gets in performance what he truly expects. He needs to think tall. He should assure those to whom he gives assignments that in the service of the Lord they have even greater powers than in ordinary responsibilities. There can be no failure in the work of the Lord when [we] do [our] best. We are but instruments; this is the Lord's work. This is His church, His gospel plan. These are His children we are working with. He will not permit us to fail if we do our part. He will magnify us even beyond our own talents and abilities when necessary. This I know.[33]

We must remember that . . . the Church . . . is not the business world. Its success is measured in terms of souls saved, not in profit and loss. We need, of course, to be efficient and productive, but we also need to keep our focus on eternal objectives. Be cautious about imposing secular methods and terminology on sacred priesthood functions. Remember that rational problem-solving procedures, though helpful, will not be solely sufficient in the work of the kingdom. God's work must be done by faith, prayer, and by the Spirit, "and if it be by some other way it is not of God" (D&C 50:18).[34]

The whole purpose of the Church is to build men and women who will be godlike in their attitudes and in their attributes and in their ideals.[35]

Suggestions for Study and Teaching

Questions

- President Benson taught that leaders should set a righteous example (see section 1). Why is example such a powerful influence? How have the righteous examples of leaders influenced you?

- Study the characteristics of good leaders that are explained in section 2. Why do you think people "respond to [such] leadership"? Think about what you can do to develop these characteristics.

- President Benson taught that Church leaders should follow the Savior's example as a delegator (see section 3). How does delegation help build the kingdom of God? In what ways have you benefited from responsibilities that have been delegated to you?

- How might our Church service change as we remember that "this is the Lord's work" and that "these are His children we are working with"? (See section 4.) What have you experienced when you have acted as an instrument in the Lord's hands to help other people?

Related Scriptures

Exodus 18:13–26; Matthew 5:13–16; Luke 22:31–32; Alma 17:1–11; D&C 38:23–27

Teaching Help

"Individuals are touched when their contributions are acknowledged. You might make a special effort to acknowledge each person's comment and, if possible, make the comments part of class discussions" (*Teaching, No Greater Call* [1999], 35–36).

Notes

1. In Sheri L. Dew, *Ezra Taft Benson: A Biography* (1987), 429.

2. In *Ezra Taft Benson: A Biography,* 430.

3. In *Ezra Taft Benson: A Biography,* 430.

4. In *Ezra Taft Benson: A Biography,* 429.

5. In *Ezra Taft Benson: A Biography,* 474–75.

6. Gordon B. Hinckley, "Come and Partake," *Ensign,* May 1986, 47.

7. *The Teachings of Ezra Taft Benson* (1988), 345.

8. *The Teachings of Ezra Taft Benson,* 372.

9. *The Teachings of Ezra Taft Benson,* 375–76.

10. *The Teachings of Ezra Taft Benson,* 371.

11. *The Teachings of Ezra Taft Benson,* 371.

12. *The Teachings of Ezra Taft Benson,* 455.

13. *God, Family, Country: Our Three Great Loyalties* (1974), 126.

14. *The Teachings of Ezra Taft Benson,* 375.

15. *The Teachings of Ezra Taft Benson,* 377.

16. *The Teachings of Ezra Taft Benson,* 375.

17. *The Teachings of Ezra Taft Benson,* 375.

18. *The Teachings of Ezra Taft Benson,* 371.

19. *The Teachings of Ezra Taft Benson,* 372.

20. *The Teachings of Ezra Taft Benson,* 370.

21. *The Teachings of Ezra Taft Benson,* 371.

22. *The Teachings of Ezra Taft Benson,* 147.

23. *The Teachings of Ezra Taft Benson,* 376–77.

24. *The Teachings of Ezra Taft Benson,* 345.

25. *The Teachings of Ezra Taft Benson,* 378.

26. *The Teachings of Ezra Taft Benson,* 378.

27. *God, Family, Country,* 135–36.

28. *The Teachings of Ezra Taft Benson,* 379.

29. *The Teachings of Ezra Taft Benson,* 379–80.

30. *The Teachings of Ezra Taft Benson,* 379.

31. *God, Family, Country,* 140.

32. *The Teachings of Ezra Taft Benson,* 371.

33. *The Teachings of Ezra Taft Benson,* 372.

34. *The Teachings of Ezra Taft Benson,* 372–73.

35. *The Teachings of Ezra Taft Benson,* 373.

"Now is the time to apply the Savior's teaching of the good shepherd."

"Feed My Sheep"

"We must all learn to be true shepherds. We must manifest the same love to others that the Good Shepherd has for all of us. Each soul is precious to Him."

From the Life of Ezra Taft Benson

President Ezra Taft Benson told of an experience he had when he was serving as a counselor in a stake presidency:

"At a stake presidency meeting in Boise, Idaho, years ago, we were trying to select a president for the weakest and smallest elders quorum in the stake. Our clerk had brought a list of all the elders of that quorum, and on the list was the name of a man whom I had known for some years. He came from a strong Latter-day Saint family, but he wasn't doing much in the Church.

"If the bishop made a call to do some work on the chapel, he would usually respond, and if the elders wanted to play softball, you would sometimes find him out playing with them. He did have leadership ability; he was president of a service club and was doing a fine job.

"I said to the stake president, 'Would you authorize me to go out and meet this man and challenge him to square his life with the standards of the Church and take the leadership of his quorum? I know there is some hazard in it, but he has the ability.'

"The stake president said, 'You go ahead, and the Lord bless you.'

". . . I went to this man's home. I'll never forget the look on his face as he opened the door and saw a member of his stake presidency standing there. He hesitantly invited me in; his wife was preparing dinner, and I could smell the aroma of coffee coming from the kitchen. I asked him to have his wife join us, and when we were seated, I told him why I had come. 'I'm not going to ask you for your answer today,' I told him. 'All I want you to do is to promise me that you will think about it, pray about it, think about it in terms of what it will mean to your family, and then I'll be back to see you next week. If you decide not to accept, we'll go on loving you,' I added.

"The next Sunday, as soon as he opened the door I saw there had been a change. He was glad to see me, and he quickly invited me in and called to his wife to join us. He said, 'Brother Benson, we have done as you said. We've thought about it and we've prayed about it, and we've decided to accept the call. If you brethren have that much confidence in me, I'm willing to square my life with the standards of the Church, a thing I should have done long ago.'

"He also said, 'I haven't had any coffee since you were here last week, and I'm not going to have any more.'

"He was set apart as elders quorum president, and attendance in his quorum began going up—and it kept going up. He went out, put his arm around the less-active elders, and brought them in. A few months later I moved from the stake.

"Years passed, and one day on Temple Square in Salt Lake City, a man came up to me, extended his hand, and said, 'Brother Benson, you don't remember me, do you?'

"'Yes, I do,' I said, 'but I don't remember your name.'

"He said, 'Do you remember coming to the home of a delinquent elder in Boise seven years ago?' And then, of course, it all came back to me. Then he said, 'Brother Benson, I'll never live long enough to thank you for coming to my home that Sunday afternoon. I am now a bishop. I used to think I was happy, but I didn't know what real happiness was.'"[1]

Having been inspired by this experience and others, President Benson encouraged faithful Latter-day Saints to reach out to members of the Church who lived "apart from the Church and the influence of the gospel."[2] In the April 1984 general conference, he said: "We are pleased with the activation of many of our brethren and sisters. We encourage priesthood and auxiliary leaders to continue this great effort."[3] That same week, he spoke to a group of priesthood leaders about the need to fellowship men in the Church who have not yet been ordained elders:

"My heart goes out to those men, heads of families. . . . I don't believe we have a greater challenge in the Church today than to activate those men and bring them to the point where they can take their families to the house of the Lord and have opened to them the richest blessings known to men and women in this world and in the world to come.

"Brethren, our hope and prayer is that you will see this activation effort as more than just a temporary program. We hope that when this period of our Church history is recorded, it will be said that this marked a time when many wandering and lost souls were reclaimed by the Church of God."[4]

Teachings of Ezra Taft Benson

1

As followers of the Lord, part of our mission is to reach out to our brothers and sisters who have separated themselves from the Church.

The purpose of the Lord's church is to further the progress of every son and daughter of God toward the ultimate blessings of eternal life. . . .

I wish to discuss our mission to perfect the Saints, particularly the challenge of activating those who have separated themselves from full activity in the Church. These members, who are our brothers and sisters, at present live apart from the Church and the influence of the gospel.

In this group of less-active members are many non-attenders who may be indifferent and non-caring. Also included are those who are temporarily lost because we do not know their whereabouts. Some of these are new converts who apparently did not receive the nurturing attention and teachings that would have caused them to be "fellow citizens with the Saints." (See Eph. 2:19.) Many are single adults.

To all such individuals, we, as members of the Church and followers of the Lord, must extend and renew our love and heartfelt invitation to come back. "Come back. Come back and feast at the table of the Lord, and taste again the sweet and satisfying fruits of fellowship with the Saints." (*Ensign,* March 1986, p. 88.)

The challenge before us is great. . . . We must exercise great faith, energy, and commitment if we are to reach these brothers and sisters. But we must do it. The Lord expects us to do it. And we will![5]

2

As we seek to nurture those who have gone astray, we are to apply the Savior's teaching of the good shepherd.

Now is the time to apply the Savior's teaching of the good shepherd to the challenge before us of retrieving lost sheep and wayward lambs.

"How think ye? if a man have an hundred sheep, and one of them be gone astray, doth he not leave the ninety and nine, and goeth into the mountains, and seeketh that which is gone astray?

"And if [it] so be that he find it, verily I say unto you, he rejoiceth more of that sheep, than of the ninety and nine which went not astray." (Matt. 18:12–13.)

In Jesus' time, the Palestinian shepherd knew each of his sheep. The sheep knew his voice and trusted him. They would not follow a stranger. Thus, when called, the sheep would come to him. (See John 10:1–5, 14.)

At night, the shepherds would lead their sheep to a corral or a sheepfold. High walls surrounded the sheepfold, and thorns were placed on top of the walls to prevent wild animals and thieves from climbing over. Sometimes, however, a wild animal driven by hunger would leap over the walls into the midst of the sheep, frightening and threatening them.

Such a situation separated the true shepherd—one who loved his sheep—from the hireling who worked only for pay out of duty. The true shepherd was willing to give his life for the sheep. He would go in among the sheep and fight for their welfare. The hireling, on the other hand, valued his own personal safety above the sheep and would usually flee from the danger.

*As we nurture friendships in our wards and branches,
we help each other stay in the fold of the Good Shepherd.*

Jesus used this common illustration of His day to declare that He was the Good Shepherd, the True Shepherd. Because of His love for His brothers and sisters, He would willingly and voluntarily lay down His life for them. (See John 10:11–18.)

Eventually the Good Shepherd did give His life for the sheep—for you and me, for us all.

The symbolism of the good shepherd is not without significant parallel in the Church today. The sheep need to be led by watchful shepherds. Too many are wandering. Some are being enticed away by momentary distractions. Others have become completely lost.

We realize, as in times past, that some of the sheep will rebel and are "as a wild flock which fleeth from the shepherd." (Mosiah 8:21.) But most of our problems stem from lack of loving and attentive shepherding, and more shepherds must be developed.

With a shepherd's care, our new members, those newly born into the gospel, must be nurtured by attentive friendshipping as they increase in gospel knowledge and begin living new standards. Such attention will help ensure that they will not return to old habits.

257

With a shepherd's loving care, our young people, our young lambs, will not be as inclined to wander. And if they do, the crook of the shepherd's staff—a loving arm and an understanding heart—will help retrieve them.

With a shepherd's care, many of those who are now independent of the flock can still be reclaimed. Many who have married outside the Church and have assumed the life-styles of the world may respond to an invitation to return to the fold.[6]

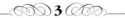

3

Latter-day Saints who have strayed need real, heartfelt concern from true and loving shepherds.

There are no *new* solutions to this *old* problem of sheep straying elsewhere for food. The charge Jesus gave to Peter, which He emphasized by repeating it three times, is the proven solution: "Feed my lambs. Feed my sheep. Feed my sheep." (See John 21:15–17.)

As in the glorious admonition of the Book of Mormon, those baptized into the church of Christ must be constantly "remembered and nourished by the good word of God." (Moro. 6:4.)

The answer, then, is found in prayerfully shepherding and feeding the flock—in other words, personal watchcare. There must be real, heartfelt concern by a true and loving shepherd, not just the shallow concern that a hireling might show.

As we discuss the concept of a true shepherd, we recognize that the Lord has given this responsibility to priesthood holders. But sisters also have callings of "shepherding" in the charitable and loving service they render to one another, and to others. Thus, we must all learn to be true shepherds. We must manifest the same love to others that the Good Shepherd has for all of us. Each soul is precious to Him. His invitation beckons every member—every son and daughter of God.

"Behold, he sendeth an invitation unto all men, for the arms of mercy are extended towards them, and he saith: Repent, and I will receive you. . . .

"Come unto me and ye shall partake of the fruit of the tree of life; . . .

"Yea, come unto me and bring forth works of righteousness." (Alma 5:33–35.)

None are denied His invitation. All are welcome who will receive His gracious invitation to partake of His gospel. The sheep—some distracted, some indifferent, some preoccupied—must be found and loved back into activity. Every priesthood and auxiliary resource must be used to assist in this effort.

This challenge will never be met until stake, ward, quorum, and auxiliary leaders and faithful members everywhere exercise their will and faith to bring the less active back into full activity in the Church.

As you earnestly strive to accomplish this worthy goal, we urge you to give renewed emphasis to effective priesthood home teaching and effective Relief Society visiting teaching. Home teaching and visiting teaching are inspired programs. They are designed to reach each member of the Church each month, both the active and the less active. Please give home teaching and visiting teaching an increased emphasis.[7]

4

As we continue to minister to our brothers and sisters, we can help them receive all the blessings and ordinances of the gospel.

Our prayers today must be of the same intensity and concern as were the prayers of Alma as he sought to reclaim the wandering Zoramites who had strayed from the Lord:

"O Lord, wilt thou grant unto us that we may have success in bringing them *again* unto thee in Christ.

"Behold, O Lord, their souls are precious, and many of them are our brethren; therefore, give unto us, O Lord, power and wisdom that we may bring these, our brethren, *again* unto thee." (Alma 31:34–35; italics added.) . . .

The principles to activate souls do not change. They are:

1. The lost or less active must be found and contacted.

2. Loving concern must be demonstrated. They must feel of our love.

3. They must be taught the gospel. They must feel the power of the Holy Ghost through the teachers.

4. They must be included in our fellowship.

5. They must have meaningful Church responsibilities.

In the words of the Book of Mormon, we are to "continue to minister." (3 Ne. 18:32.)

We are particularly concerned that new converts be integrated into full fellowship in the Church. They must be welcomed with opened arms.

Let us be united in our efforts to bring the less active back into full activity in the Church. In doing so, we will all be more fitly joined together in accomplishing the mission of the Church—to bring the gospel, with all of its blessings and ordinances, more fully into the lives of all Church members. The Church "hath need of every member" (D&C 84:110), and every member has need of the gospel, the Church, and all its ordinances.

May we all seek the blessings of the Lord to strengthen us and give us the necessary power and influence we will need as we work together in this great labor of love.[8]

Suggestions for Study and Teaching

Questions

- What are your feelings as you think about family members or friends who "live apart from the Church and the influence of the gospel"? What can we do to reach out to them? (See section 1.)

- Ponder President Benson's teachings about the differences between a hireling and a shepherd (see section 2). What can we do to be better shepherds?

- President Benson reminded us that people need "real, heartfelt concern from a true and loving shepherd" (section 3). How can we develop heartfelt concern for others? As you ponder this question, think about your service as a home teacher or visiting teacher.

- What do you think it means to "continue to minister"? (3 Nephi 18:32). Consider the five principles President Benson shared to help us serve those who need to return to Church activity (see section 4). In what ways can each of these principles help someone receive the blessings of the gospel?

Related Scriptures

Matthew 9:10–12; Luke 15; 22:32; 1 Peter 5:2–4; Moroni 6:4; D&C 18:10–16; 84:106

Study Help

"Reading, studying, and pondering are not the same. We read words and we may get ideas. We study and we may discover patterns and connections in scripture. But when we ponder, we invite revelation by the Spirit. Pondering, to me, is the thinking and the praying I do after reading and studying in the scriptures carefully" (Henry B. Eyring, "Serve with the Spirit," *Ensign* or *Liahona,* Nov. 2010, 60).

Notes

1. "Feed My Sheep," *Ensign,* Sept. 1987, 4–5.
2. "Feed My Sheep," 3.
3. "Counsel to the Saints," *Ensign,* May 1984, 8.
4. *The Teachings of Ezra Taft Benson* (1988), 234.
5. "Feed My Sheep," 3.
6. "Feed My Sheep," 3–4.
7. "Feed My Sheep," 4.
8. "Feed My Sheep," 4, 5.

Elder Ezra Taft Benson, right, with President Max Zimmer, acting president of the Swiss Mission, checking welfare supplies in Geneva, Switzerland, 1946

Principles of Temporal and Spiritual Welfare

"Everything that concerns the economic, social, and spiritual welfare of the human family is and ever will be the concern of the Church of Jesus Christ of Latter-day Saints."

From the Life of Ezra Taft Benson

In 1936, as people all over the world struggled with the economic challenges of the Great Depression, the First Presidency introduced a new welfare program. This program, called the Church Security Plan, was established not to provide handouts for people in need but "to help the people to help themselves."[1] As the First Presidency and other Church leaders established this program, they taught foundational principles of hard work, self-reliance, and service. They encouraged Church members to pay tithing and fast offerings, produce and store food, avoid unnecessary debt, and save money for future needs.

At that time, President Ezra Taft Benson was serving as a counselor in a stake presidency in Boise, Idaho. He was also an economist, marketing specialist, and farm management specialist for the state of Idaho. He accepted an assignment from his stake president to attend a meeting in which the Church Security Plan would be introduced. He later recalled: "My soul responded wholeheartedly to everything that I heard that day. I went back to the Boise Stake and expressed to my brethren that this program which had been announced is economically, socially, and spiritually sound, and expressed the confidence that the people of the Church would respond to it wholeheartedly as something that is not only sound but also needed."[2]

Two months after President Benson introduced the program to his stake, "numerous welfare projects were underway: one ward had planted a multi-acre garden, another had sown fifteen acres of sugar beets, and the Relief Society in another was canning food and making quilts and clothing. [One ward] even built a small cannery."[3]

President Benson saw the expansive influence of the welfare program 10 years later. As a member of the Quorum of the Twelve Apostles, he was assigned to preside over the Church in Europe just after World War II. In those war-torn lands, he led the Church's effort to provide goods that would help people regain their self-sufficiency. He recounted his experience when the Church's first shipment of welfare supplies arrived in Berlin, Germany:

"I took with me the acting president of the mission, President Richard Ranglack. We walked to the old battered warehouse which, under armed guard, housed the precious welfare goods. At the far end of the warehouse we saw the boxes piled almost to the ceiling.

"'Are those boxes of food?' Richard said. 'Do you mean to tell me those are boxes full of food?'

"'Yes, my brother,' I replied, 'food and clothing and bedding—and, I hope, a few medical supplies.'

"Richard and I took down one of the boxes. We opened it. It was filled with the commonest of common foods—dried beans. As that good man saw it, he put his hands into it and ran it through his fingers, then broke down and cried like a child with gratitude.

"We opened another box, filled with cracked wheat, nothing added or taken away, just as the Lord made it and intended it to be. He touched a pinch of it to his mouth. After a moment he looked at me through his tearful eyes—and mine were wet, too—and he said, while slowly shaking his head, 'Brother Benson, it is hard to believe that people who have never seen us could do so much for us.'

"That's the Lord's system! Voluntary donations motivated by brotherly love and willing sacrifice, and assisting others to help themselves. Such ensures dignity and self-respect."[4]

Teachings of Ezra Taft Benson

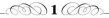 **1**

The Lord is anxious and willing to bless His people temporally and spiritually.

I realize, my brethren and sisters, that in discussing temporal matters, the Lord has said:

". . . all things unto me are spiritual, and not at any time have I given unto you a law which was temporal. . . ." [D&C 29:34.]

The objective, of course, is spiritual. We live, however, in a material, physical, temporal world. . . .

. . . Man is a dual being, temporal and spiritual, and in the early revelations to this people, the Lord took occasion, many times, to give direction and commandment regarding temporal matters. He directed the Saints and the leaders of the Church in the purchase of land and other property; in the construction of temples; even in the establishment of a printing press, and a store, and in the building of a boardinghouse for the "weary traveler" [see D&C 124:22–23]. In the great revelation known as the Word of Wisdom, he not only indicated what is good and what is not good for man, but he outlined a plan for the feeding of livestock, which, through more than a hundred years, has gradually been sustained through the scientific investigation of man [see D&C 89]. Whatever affects human welfare has always been and ever will be the concern of the Church. Our people have always been counseled in temporal affairs. . . .

It is important that we keep our thinking straight, my brothers and sisters. Let us ever keep in mind that all material things are but a means to an end, that the end is spiritual, although the Lord is anxious and willing to bless his people temporally. He has so indicated in many of the revelations. He has pointed out, time and time again, that we should pray over our crops, over our livestock, over our households, our homes, and invoke the Lord's blessings upon our material affairs. And he has promised that he will be there and ready and willing to bless us. . . .

. . . The Lord will not do for us what we can and should do for ourselves. But it is his purpose to take care of his Saints. Everything that concerns the economic, social, and spiritual welfare of the human family is and ever will be the concern of the Church of Jesus Christ of Latter-day Saints.[5]

As we administer any aspect of the welfare program, the primary purpose for which it was established must be kept before us. That stated purpose is "to set up, insofar as it might be possible, a system under which the curse of idleness would be done away with, the evils of a dole abolished, and independence, industry, thrift, and self-respect be once more established amongst our people. The aim of the Church is to help the people to help themselves. Work is to be re-enthroned as the ruling principle of the lives of our Church membership."[6]

The strength of the Church welfare program lies in every family following the inspired direction of the Church leaders to be self-sustaining through adequate preparation. God intends for his Saints to so prepare themselves "that the church [as the Lord has said] may stand independent above all other creatures beneath the celestial world." (D&C 78:14.)[7]

The scriptural parable of the five wise and the five foolish virgins [see Matthew 25:1–13] is a reminder that one can wait too long before he attempts to get his spiritual and temporal house in order. Are we prepared?[8]

2

Through energetic, purposeful, unselfish work, we obtain life's necessities and grow in godly attributes.

One of the first principles revealed to father Adam when he was driven out of the Garden of Eden was this: "In the sweat of thy face shalt thou eat bread, till thou return unto the ground" (Gen. 3:19). All we obtain in life of a material nature comes as a product of labor and the providence of God. Work alone produces life's necessities.[9]

Man is commanded by God to live by the sweat of his own brow, not someone else's.[10]

Ours is a gospel of work—purposeful, unselfish and rendered in the spirit of the true love of Christ. Only thus may we grow in godly attributes. Only thus may we become worthy instruments in the hands of the Lord for blessing others through that power which can lead to changing the lives of men and women for the better.

We should be humbly grateful for this challenge, this heritage, this opportunity for service and its abundant rewards. How fortunate are those who may follow the Lord's plan to develop this power and use it for the blessing of others. That is what the Christ did. That is what we are privileged to do.[11]

Welfare recipients should work to the extent of their ability to earn commodity or fast offering assistance. When meaningful jobs are not provided, when people are not encouraged to work, a demoralizing Church dole would develop, and the purpose for which the welfare program was established would be undermined. It is a law of heaven, and one we haven't learned fully here on earth, that you cannot help people permanently by doing for them what they can do, and should do, for themselves.[12]

We should ask the Lord's blessings on all our doings and should never do anything upon which we cannot ask His blessings. We should not expect the Lord to do for us what we can do for ourselves. I believe in faith and works, and that the Lord will bless more fully the man who works for what he prays for than He will the man who only prays.[13]

Energetic, purposeful work leads to vigorous health, praiseworthy achievement, a clear conscience, and refreshing sleep. Work has always been a boon to man. May you have a wholesome respect for labor whether with head, heart, or hand. May you ever enjoy the satisfaction of honest toil. . . . You will never wish or dream yourself into heaven. You must pay the price in toil, in sacrifice, and righteous living.[14]

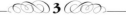

When we produce and store food, we reap immediate benefits and prepare for future needs.

Have you ever paused to realize what would happen to your community or nation if transportation were paralyzed or if we had a war or depression? How would you and your neighbors obtain food? How long would the corner grocery store—or supermarket—sustain the needs of the community?

All family members can participate in the effort to produce food.

Shortly after World War II, I was called by the First Presidency to go to Europe to reestablish our missions and set up a program for the distribution of food and clothing to the Saints. Vivid in my memory are the people who got on trains each morning with all kinds of bric-a-brac in their arms to go out to the countryside to trade their possessions for food. At evening time, the train station was filled with people with arms full of vegetables and fruits, and a menagerie of squealing pigs and chickens. You never heard such a commotion. These people were, of course, willing to barter practically anything for that commodity which sustains life—food.

An almost forgotten means of economic self-reliance is the home production of food. We are too accustomed to going to stores and purchasing what we need. By producing some of our food we reduce, to a great extent, the impact of inflation on our money. More importantly, we learn how to produce our own food and involve all family members in a beneficial project. . . .

. . . May I suggest you do what others have done. Get together with others and seek permission to use a vacant lot for a garden, or rent a plot of ground and grow your gardens. Some elders quorums have done this as a quorum, and all who have participated have reaped the benefits of a vegetable and fruit harvest and the blessings of cooperation and family involvement. Many families have dug up lawn space for gardens.

We encourage you to be more self-reliant so that, as the Lord has declared, "notwithstanding the tribulation which shall descend upon you, . . . the church may stand independent above all other creatures beneath the celestial world" (D&C 78:14). The Lord wants us to be independent and self-reliant because these will be days of tribulation. He has warned and forewarned us of the eventuality. . . .

Food production is just one part of the repeated emphasis that you store a provision of food . . . wherever it is legally permissible to do so. The Church has not told you what foods should be stored. This decision is left up to individual members. . . .

. . . The revelation to produce and store food may be as essential to our temporal welfare today as boarding the ark was to the people in the days of Noah. . . .

. . . Plan to build up your food supply just as you would a savings account. Save a little for storage each pay-check. Can or bottle fruit and vegetables from your gardens and orchards. Learn how to preserve food through drying and possibly freezing. Make your storage a part of your budget. Store seeds and have sufficient tools on hand to do the job. If you are saving and planning for a second car or a TV set or some item which merely adds to your comfort or pleasure, you may need to change your priorities. We urge you to do this prayerfully and *do it now*. . . .

Too often we bask in our comfortable complacency and rationalize that the ravages of war, economic disaster, famine, and earthquake cannot happen here. Those who believe this are either not acquainted with the revelations of the Lord, or they do not believe them. Those who smugly think these calamities will not happen, that they somehow will be set aside because of the righteousness of the Saints, are deceived and will rue the day they harbored such a delusion.

The Lord has warned and forewarned us against a day of great tribulation and given us counsel, through His servants, on how we can be prepared for these difficult times. Have we heeded His counsel? . . .

Be faithful, my brothers and sisters, to this counsel and you will be blessed—yes, the most blessed people in all the earth. You are good people. I know that. But all of us need to be better than we are. Let us be in a position so we are able to not only feed ourselves through the home production and storage, but others as well.

May God bless us to be prepared for the days which lie ahead, which may be the most severe yet.[15]

Peace and contentment come into our hearts when we save a portion of our earnings and avoid unnecessary debt.

I would respectfully urge you to live by the fundamental principles of work, thrift, and self-reliance and to teach your children by your example. . . . Live within your own earnings. Put a portion of those earnings regularly into savings. Avoid unnecessary debt. Be wise by not trying to expand too rapidly. Learn to manage well what you have before you think of expanding further.[16]

Unfortunately, there has been fostered in the minds of some an expectation that when we experience hard times, when we have been unwise and extravagant with our resources and have lived beyond our means, we should look to either the Church or government to bail us out. Forgotten by some of our members is an underlying principle of the Church welfare plan that "no true Latter-day Saint will, while physically able, voluntarily shift from himself the burden of his own support." . . .

More than ever before, we need to learn and apply the principles of economic self-reliance. We do not know when the crisis involving sickness or unemployment may affect our own circumstances. We do know that the Lord has decreed global calamities for the future and has warned and forewarned us to be prepared. For this reason the Brethren have repeatedly stressed a "back to basics" program for temporal and spiritual welfare.[17]

Living beyond our means can create "a world of heartache."

The Lord desires his Saints to be free and independent in the critical days ahead. But no man is truly free who is in financial bondage.[18]

In the book of Kings we read about a woman who came weeping to Elisha, the prophet. Her husband had died, and she owed a debt that she could not pay. The creditor was on his way to take her two sons and sell them as slaves.

By a miracle Elisha enabled her to acquire a goodly supply of oil. Then he said to her: "Go, sell the oil, and pay thy debt, and live thou and thy children of the rest." (See 2 Kgs. 4:1–7.)

"Pay thy debt, and live." How fruitful these words have ever been! What wise counsel they are for us today! . . .

Many people do not believe that serious recession will ever come again. Feeling secure in their expectations of continuing employment and a steady flow of wages and salaries, they obligate their future income without thought of what they would do if they should lose their jobs or if their incomes were stopped for some other reason. But the best authorities have repeatedly said that we are not yet smart enough to control our economy without downward adjustments. Sooner or later these adjustments will come.

Another reason for increase in debt is even deeper and causes greater concern. This is the rise of materialism, as contrasted with commitment to spiritual values. Many a family, in order to make a "proper showing," will commit itself for a larger and more expensive house than is needed, in an expensive neighborhood. . . . With the rising standard of living, that temptation increases with each new gadget that comes on the market. The subtle, carefully planned techniques of modern advertising are aimed at the weakest points of consumer resistance. As a result, there is a growing feeling, unfortunately, that material things should be had now, without waiting, without saving, without self-denial.

Worse still, a large proportion of families with personal debt have no liquid assets [savings] whatsoever to fall back upon. What troubles they invite if their income should be suddenly cut off or seriously reduced! We all know of families who have obligated themselves for more than they could pay. There is a world of heartache behind such cases.[19]

Now I do not mean to say that all debt is bad. Of course not. Sound business debt is one of the elements of growth. Sound mortgage credit is a real help to a family that must borrow for a home.[20]

In the long run, it is easier to live within our income and resist borrowing from future reserves except in cases of necessity—never for luxuries. It is not fair to ourselves or our communities to be so improvident in our spending that the day our income stops we must turn to relief agencies or the Church for financial aid.

Do not, I solemnly urge you, tie yourselves to payment of carrying charges that are often exorbitant. Save now and buy later, and you will be much further ahead. You will spare yourselves high interest and other payments, and the money you save may provide opportunity for you to buy later at substantial cash discounts.

. . . Resist the temptation to plunge into property far more pretentious or spacious than you really need.

How much better off you will be, especially young families just starting out, if first you buy a small house which you can expect to pay for in a relatively short time. . . .

Do not leave yourself or your family unprotected against financial storms. Forgo luxuries, for the time being at least, to build up savings. How wise it is to provide for the future education of your children and for your old age. . . .

Brothers and sisters, peace and contentment come into our hearts when we live within our means. God grant us the wisdom and the faith to heed the inspired counsel of the priesthood to get out of debt, to live within our means, and to pay as we go—in short, to "pay thy debt, and live."[21]

Suggestions for Study and Teaching

Questions

- In section 1, President Benson outlines the foundational principles of the Church's welfare program. In what ways do these principles contribute to our temporal well-being? In what ways do they contribute to our spiritual well-being?

- What are some benefits of "energetic, purposeful work"? (For some examples, see section 2.) What are some things you enjoy about work? What can we do to help children and youth learn to enjoy work?

- What are some blessings that will come as we follow President Benson's counsel in section 3? Think about what you will do, considering your current circumstances, to follow this counsel.

- Why do you think wise use of money leads to "peace and contentment"? In contrast, what can we experience when we do not "live within [our] own earnings"? (See section 4.)

Related Scriptures

Jacob 2:17–19; Alma 34:19–29; D&C 19:35; 42:42; 75:28–29; 104:78; Moses 5:1

Teaching Help

"To help learners prepare to answer questions, you may want to tell them before something is read or presented that you will be asking for their responses. . . . For example, you could say, 'Listen as I read this passage so that you can share what most interests you about it'" (*Teaching, No Greater Call* [1999], 69).

Notes

1. Heber J. Grant, in Conference Report, Oct. 1936, 3.

2. "Church Welfare—Economically Socially Spiritually Sound," in Welfare Agricultural Meeting, Oct. 7, 1972, 5.

3. Sheri Dew, *Ezra Taft Benson: A Biography* (1987), 119.

4. "Ministering to Needs through the Lord's Storehouse System," *Ensign*, May 1977, 84.

5. In Conference Report, Oct. 1945, 160, 163, 164.

6. "Ministering to Needs through the Lord's Storehouse System," 83; quoting Heber J. Grant, in Conference Report, Oct. 1936, 3.

7. "Prepare Ye," *Ensign*, Jan. 1974, 81.

8. In Conference Report, Apr. 1967, 61.

9. "Prepare for the Days of Tribulation," *Ensign*, Nov. 1980, 32.

10. *The Teachings of Ezra Taft Benson*, 481.

11. *The Teachings of Ezra Taft Benson*, 484.

12. "Ministering to Needs through the Lord's Storehouse System," 83.

13. *The Teachings of Ezra Taft Benson*, 485.

14. *The Teachings of Ezra Taft Benson*, 481.

15. "Prepare for the Days of Tribulation," 32–33, 34.

16. "The Ten Commandments: America at the Crossroads," *New Era*, July 1978, 39.

17. "Prepare for the Days of Tribulation," 32; quoting the *Welfare Plan Handbook* (1952), 2, as quoted by Marion G. Romney, in "Church Welfare—Some Fundamentals," *Ensign*, Jan. 1974, 91.

18. "Prepare Ye," 69.

19. "Pay Thy Debt, and Live," *Ensign*, June 1987, 3–4.

20. In Conference Report, Apr. 1957, 54.

21. "Pay Thy Debt, and Live," 4, 5.

Carrying the Gospel to the World

"We are happy to be engaged in a partnership with our Heavenly Father in the great work of the salvation and exaltation of his children."

From the Life of Ezra Taft Benson

For President Ezra Taft Benson, missionary work was a family tradition. "My father's family consisted of eleven children," he explained. "All eleven of us have filled missions. My wife also filled a mission and had the pleasure of her widowed mother serving with her for the last six months [of her mission]. When my own father went on a mission, I remember, as the eldest son, the letters that he wrote from the mission field in the Midwest. There came into that home a spirit of missionary work that has never left it, for which I am humbly grateful."[1]

President Benson served as a full-time missionary in the British Mission from 1921 to 1923, and the "spirit of missionary work" continued with him well beyond those two and a half years. For example, as United States secretary of agriculture from 1953 to 1961, he interacted with many people of other faiths. During general conference in April 1961, he told the Saints: "I have the names of some 9,000 men, approximately, with whom I have had personal contact in an official capacity. I hope to give referral cards for them. I would like to have every one of them hear the gospel. I wish that all of our Father's children might enjoy the blessings that come through an acceptance and living of the gospel of Jesus Christ."[2]

President Benson's enthusiasm for missionary work continued in his later years, and he was eager for all members of the Church to adopt the same enthusiasm. He spoke directly to young men

*"Willingly we give of our time and the means with which
[the Lord] may bless us to the establishment of his kingdom."*

about preparing themselves for full-time missionary service. "Prepare now," he said. "Prepare yourselves physically, mentally, socially, and spiritually."[3] He urged parents to guide their sons in this preparation. He also counseled young sisters and older members of the Church to seriously consider full-time missionary service. And he exhorted all members of the Church to share the gospel with their neighbors.

President Thomas S. Monson told of a time when President Benson's love for missionary work inspired a future missionary: "One Friday, he and Sister Benson followed their usual practice of attending a session at the Jordan River Temple. While there, President Benson was approached by a young man who greeted him with joy in his heart and announced that he had been called to fill a full-time mission. President Benson took the newly called missionary by the hand and, with a smile on his lips, declared, 'Take me with you! Take me with you!' That missionary testified that, in a way, he *took* President Benson with him on his mission, since this greeting demonstrated President Benson's abiding love, his devotion to missionary work, and his desire to ever be found in the service of the Lord."[4]

Love for all of Heavenly Father's children was at the heart of President Benson's dedication to sharing the gospel: "Our Father's children need the gospel. . . . I know the Lord loves them, and as his humble servant I have a love in my heart for the teeming millions of this world."[5] Reflecting on the power of the Savior's love, he testified, "Our blessings multiply as we share his love with our neighbor."[6]

From a lifetime of participating in missionary work and encouraging his fellow Saints to do likewise, President Benson could affirm: "I have tasted the joy of missionary work. There is no work in all the world that can bring an individual greater joy and happiness."[7]

Teachings of Ezra Taft Benson

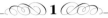

1

The world is hungry for true religion, and we have it.

Following the glorious appearance of God the Father and his Son Jesus Christ to Joseph Smith, it appears that the first great responsibility placed upon the restored Church was to carry the gospel to the world—to all our Father's children.

It has truly been a great drama of transcendent importance—a drama of sacrifice, joy, hardship, courage, and above all, love of fellowmen. Nowhere upon the face of the earth will you find a human drama to equal it. Yes, it has cost blood, sweat, and tears to carry forth this labor of love. And why have we done it? Because the God of heaven has commanded it; because he loves his children, and it is his will that the teeming millions of the earth shall have opportunity to hear and, of their own free will, accept and live the glorious saving and exalting principles of the gospel of Jesus Christ.[8]

It is my conviction that the world needs, as it needs no other thing, the gospel of Jesus Christ, and the people of the world want what the gospel will give, but they do not realize it. They want the anchor which the gospel provides, which gives them the answers to the problems that face them; that brings them a feeling of security and a feeling of inner peace. The gospel is the only answer to the problems of the world, my brethren and sisters.[9]

Only the gospel will save the world from the calamity of its own self-destruction. Only the gospel will unite men of all races and nationalities in peace. Only the gospel will bring joy, happiness, and salvation to the human family.[10]

The world is hungry for true religion, and we have it.[11]

This is the glorious message we desire to share with the world, that through God the Father and His Son Jesus Christ, the kingdom of God has been restored. It is the greatest message since the resurrection of Jesus Christ.[12]

We accept humbly, gratefully, this major responsibility placed upon the Church. We are happy to be engaged in a partnership with our Heavenly Father in the great work of the salvation and exaltation of his children. Willingly we give of our time and the means with which he may bless us to the establishment of his kingdom in the earth. This we know is our first duty and our great opportunity. This spirit has characterized the missionary work of the Church of Jesus Christ in all ages. It has been an outstanding mark of the ushering in of the dispensation of the fulness of times—our time. Wherever faithful Latter-day Saints are to be found, this spirit of unselfish sacrifice for the greatest cause in all the earth exists.[13]

We have a great mission. We must be prepared, both young and old. We must stand as a leaven among the nations, true to the principles of righteousness.[14]

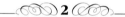

We can all be missionaries, whatever our circumstances or station in life.

As members of the Lord's Church, we must take missionary work seriously. If you are laboring as you should, if you love this work, you will be helping to save the souls of the children of men.[15]

Not only should sharing the gospel be regarded as a priesthood duty, but we should all look forward to this experience with great joy and anticipation. The real purpose in sharing the gospel is to bring souls unto Christ, to teach and baptize our Heavenly Father's children so that we may rejoice with them (see D&C 18:15) in the kingdom of our Father.[16]

We all share this great responsibility. We cannot avoid it. Let no man or woman think that because of where we live, or because of our place in society, or because of our occupation or status, we are exempt from this responsibility.[17]

Young men and young women

We hope that every young man has plans to be a messenger for the Lord.[18]

How do you build in boys a great desire to serve? You do not wait . . . to help them decide to serve a mission. You help them decide to go when they are nine, ten, or eleven! The home is the seedbed for the preparation of young men. And *every* young man should be prepared in his home to serve.

Early preparation consists of teaching a young boy how to pray, reading him stories from the Book of Mormon and other scriptures, having home evenings and giving him a portion of the lesson [to teach], teaching him principles of moral cleanliness, starting a savings account for his future mission, teaching him how to work, and providing opportunities to serve others.[19]

We want young men entering the mission field who can enter the mission field "on the run," who have the faith born of personal righteousness and clean living that they can have a great and productive mission.[20]

The Lord wants every young man to serve a full-time mission. . . . A young man can do nothing more important. School can wait. Scholarships can be deferred. Occupational goals can be postponed. Yes, even temple marriage should wait until after a young man has served an honorable full-time mission for the Lord.

. . . Young women . . . may also have the opportunity to serve a full-time mission. I am grateful my own eternal companion served a mission in Hawaii before we were married in the Salt Lake Temple, and I am pleased that I have had three granddaughters serve full-time missions. Some of our finest missionaries are young sisters.[21]

Senior missionaries

We need increasing numbers of senior missionaries in missionary service.[22]

Many older couples could serve missions. In so doing, they will find that a mission blesses their children, their grandchildren, and their great-grandchildren in a way that could not otherwise be done. It will set a great example for their posterity.[23]

Many couples can attest that their missionary service was among their happiest times together because they were completely dedicated to one purpose—missionary work.[24]

Member missionaries

We must emphasize the need for more member-missionary work. Experience has proven this is the most fruitful missionary work. Member-missionary work is one of the great keys to the individual

"The Lord expects us to be missionaries."

growth of our members. It is my conviction that member-missionary work will raise the spirituality in any ward where applied.[25]

How long has it been since you have invited a neighbor to sacrament meeting or to a stake conference, to come into your home for a home evening? How long has it been since you had a real gospel conversation? These are choice experiences.[26]

The Lord will sustain members in their missionary responsibility if they just have the faith to try.[27]

It is time to raise our sights, to get a vision of the magnitude of this great work. The Lord expects it of us. It is not enough just to be members in the Church and go to sacrament meeting, pay our tithing, support the welfare program. That is all good—but that is not enough. The Lord expects us to be missionaries, to live the gospel—yes, wholly, and to help to build up His kingdom.[28]

The Book of Mormon is the great standard we are to use in our missionary work.

The Book of Mormon is for both member and nonmember. Combined with the Spirit of the Lord, the Book of Mormon is the greatest tool which God has given us to convert the world. If we are to have the harvest of souls, we must use the instrument which God has designed for the task—the Book of Mormon.

And reading the Book of Mormon is one of the greatest persuaders to get us on missions. We need more missionaries. But we also need better-prepared missionaries coming out of the wards and branches and homes where they know and love the Book of Mormon. We need missionaries who have a burning testimony of its divinity, and who by the Spirit can challenge their investigators to read and ponder its pages, knowing with complete assurance that the Lord will manifest the truth of it to them by the power of the Holy Ghost. We need missionaries to match our message.[29]

The Book of Mormon is the great standard we are to use in our missionary work. It shows that Joseph Smith was a prophet. It contains the words of Christ, and its great mission is to bring men to Christ. All other things are secondary. The golden question of the Book of Mormon is "Do you want to learn more of Christ?" The Book of Mormon is the great finder of the golden contact. It does not contain things which are "pleasing unto the world," and so the worldly are not interested in it. It is a great sieve. (See 1 Nephi 6:5.)

There is a difference between a convert who is built on the rock of Christ through the Book of Mormon and stays hold of the iron rod, and one who is not.[30]

We must not forget that the Lord Himself provided the Book of Mormon as His chief witness. The Book of Mormon is still our most powerful missionary tool. Let us use it.[31]

To be successful in missionary work, we must obtain the Spirit, acquire humility, love the people, and work diligently.

Missionaries sometimes ask, "How can I be successful? How does one become effective in missionary work?" Here are four proven keys to successful missionary work for both missionaries and members alike.

First, strive to obtain the Spirit.

To be successful, we must have the Spirit of the Lord. We have been taught that the Spirit will not dwell in unclean tabernacles. Therefore, one of our first priorities is to make sure our own personal lives are in order. The Lord declared, "Be ye clean that bear the vessels of the Lord." (Doctrine and Covenants 38:42.)

The Savior has given us His law about teaching His gospel: "The Spirit shall be given unto you by the prayer of faith; and if ye receive not the Spirit ye shall not teach." (Doctrine and Covenants 42:14.)[32]

If there is one message I have repeated to my brethren of the Twelve, it is that it's the Spirit that counts. It is the Spirit that matters. I do not know how often I have said this, but I never tire of saying it—it is the Spirit that matters most.[33]

Second, acquire humility.

The Lord has said that no one can assist with this work unless he is humble and full of love. (See Doctrine and Covenants 12:8.) But humility does not mean weakness. It does not mean timidity; it does not mean fear. [We] can be humble and also fearless. [We] can be humble and also courageous. Humility is the recognition of our dependence upon a higher power, a constant need for the Lord's support in His work.[34]

We cannot do this work alone. This is His work. This is His gospel. We must have His help. Plead for it, live for it, pour out your soul to the Lord to receive it.[35]

Third, love the people.

We must develop a love for people. Our hearts must go out to them in the pure love of the gospel, in a desire to lift them, to build them up, to point them to a higher, finer life and eventually to exaltation in the celestial kingdom of God. We emphasize the fine qualities of the people with whom we associate, and love them as children of God whom the Lord loves. . . .

We will never be effective until we learn to have sympathy for all our Father's children—until we learn to love them. People can feel when love is extended to them. Many yearn for it. When we sympathize with their feelings, they in turn will reciprocate good will to us. We will have made a friend.[36]

We . . . have a great obligation to love our neighbors. It is the second of the two great commandments. Many of our neighbors are not yet members of the Church. We must be good neighbors. We must love all our Father's children and associate with them.

How I pray that we will be filled with the love of God for our fellowman![37]

Fourth, work diligently.

If we want to keep the Spirit, we must work. There is no greater exhilaration or satisfaction than to know, after a hard day of work, that we have done our best.

One of the greatest secrets of missionary work is *work*. If a missionary works, he will get the Spirit; if he gets the Spirit, he will teach by the Spirit; if he teaches by the Spirit, he will touch the hearts of the people, and he will be happy. . . . Work, work, work—there is no satisfactory substitute, especially in missionary work.[38]

I know that God lives. This is His work. He has again spoken from the heavens with a message for the entire world; not for a handful of Latter-day Saints only, but for all our brothers and sisters, both in and out of the Church. May God give us strength to carry that message to the world, to live the Gospel, to maintain the standards of the Church, that we may be entitled to the promised blessings.[39]

Suggestions for Study and Teaching

Questions

- Why does the world need the gospel "as it needs no other thing"? (For some examples, see section 1.) What are some restored truths that you believe "the world is hungry for"?

- As you review section 2, consider the counsel that applies to you and your family. In what ways can each of us, regardless of our circumstances, share the gospel? What can we do to prepare for full-time missionary service? What can we do to help others prepare for full-time missionary service?

- President Benson said that the Book of Mormon is "the greatest tool which God has given us to convert the world" (section 3). When have you seen people become converted through a study of the Book of Mormon? In what ways might we improve our efforts to share the Book of Mormon?

- President Benson shared "four proven keys to successful missionary work" (section 4). Why do you think these keys lead to success in missionary work? What examples have you seen of people following these principles?

Related Scriptures

Mark 16:15; 1 Timothy 4:12; Alma 17:2–3; 26:1–16; D&C 4; 12:7–9; 15:4–6; 88:81; 123:12–17

Study Help

"Share what you learn. As you do this, your thoughts will become clearer and your power of retention will increase" (*Teaching, No Greater Call* [1999], 17).

Notes

1. "Our Responsibility to Share the Gospel," *Ensign,* May 1985, 8.
2. In Conference Report, Apr. 1961, 112–13.
3. "Preparing Yourselves for Missionary Service," *Ensign,* May 1985, 37.
4. Thomas S. Monson, "God Be with You Till We Meet Again," *Ensign,* Nov. 1990, 87.
5. In Conference Report, Apr. 1970, 129.
6. "Life Is Eternal," *Ensign,* June 1971, 34.
7. *The Teachings of Ezra Taft Benson* (1988), 213.
8. In Conference Report, Apr. 1970, 128.
9. In Conference Report, Apr. 1961, 113.
10. *The Teachings of Ezra Taft Benson,* 188.
11. In Conference Report, Apr. 1955, 49.
12. *The Teachings of Ezra Taft Benson,* 110.
13. *God, Family, Country: Our Three Great Loyalties* (1974), 49–50.
14. In Conference Report, Oct. 1950, 147.

15. "Of the Most Worth," *New Era,* June 1989, 4.

16. "Of the Most Worth," 6.

17. "Our Responsibility to Share the Gospel," 8.

18. *The Teachings of Ezra Taft Benson,* 189.

19. "Our Responsibility to Share the Gospel," 7.

20. "To the 'Youth of the Noble Birthright,'" *Ensign,* May 1986, 45.

21. "To the Young Women of the Church," *Ensign,* Nov. 1986, 83.

22. "To the Elderly in the Church," *Ensign,* Nov. 1989, 5.

23. "A Sacred Responsibility," *Ensign,* May 1986, 78.

24. "Our Responsibility to Share the Gospel," 8.

25. *The Teachings of Ezra Taft Benson,* 208–9.

26. *The Teachings of Ezra Taft Benson,* 210.

27. "Of the Most Worth," 4–6.

28. *The Teachings of Ezra Taft Benson,* 211.

29. "Of the Most Worth," 6.

30. *The Teachings of Ezra Taft Benson,* 203–4.

31. *The Teachings of Ezra Taft Benson,* 204.

32. *Come unto Christ* (1983), 91–92.

33. Seminar for New Mission Presidents, Apr. 3, 1985.

34. *Come unto Christ,* 94.

35. "Principles for Performing Miracles in Missionary Work," seminar for new mission presidents, June 21, 1988.

36. *Come unto Christ,* 96.

37. "Our Responsibility to Share the Gospel," 8.

38. *Come unto Christ,* 96, 97.

39. In Conference Report, Oct. 1943, 21.

"Strengthen Thy Stakes"

"The stakes and districts of Zion are symbolic of the holy places spoken of by the Lord where His Saints are to gather in the last days as a refuge from the storm."

From the Life of Ezra Taft Benson

On January 13, 1935, members of the Boise Idaho Stake sustained 35-year-old Ezra Taft Benson as first counselor in their stake presidency. Under the direction of President Scott S. Brown, President Benson received many opportunities to serve, lead, and teach. For example, he was instrumental in helping a Melchizedek Priesthood holder return to activity in the Church,[1] and he helped lead the stake's efforts to implement the Church's welfare program.[2]

In 1938 the stake had grown to more than 8,000 members, so the First Presidency directed that it be divided into three stakes. President Benson said he was "shocked" when, on November 27, 1938, he was called to preside over one of those stakes. His wife, Flora, told their children that it was a blessing for their father to receive this call.[3]

President Benson's service as stake president was a blessing for the entire stake. He continued to teach principles of welfare, and he gave special attention to the youth. Before a session of one stake conference, he noticed a group of young men trying to sneak away from the meetinghouse. "They started slowly down the hall toward the back door, keeping their eyes on the foyer to be sure their exit wasn't being detected. About then [he] stepped out of his office, sized up the situation, and stretched his arms across the hall so that the boys fell right into them. 'I'm so glad to see you boys,' he said. 'Let's go to conference together.' He led them to the front bench, and later called upon them to bear their testimonies."[4]

One purpose of a stake is to "unify and perfect the members . . . by extending to them the Church programs, ordinances, and gospel instruction."

Less than two months after President Benson began serving as stake president, another surprise came to him. He was offered a job as executive secretary of the National Council of Farmer Cooperatives, which would require him to work in Washington, D.C. At first he declined the offer, but after consulting with Flora and the First Presidency, he decided to accept it.[5] When he was released as stake president on March 26, 1939, he wrote that it was "the most difficult day I have ever experienced. . . . In my remarks [to the members of the stake] I was greatly blessed of the Lord but had great difficulty controlling my feelings. There are no finer people in all the world [and] I love every one."[6]

The Bensons moved to Bethesda, Maryland, close to Washington, D.C. A little more than a year later, President Rudger Clawson, President of the Quorum of the Twelve Apostles, and Elder Albert E. Bowen, also of the Quorum of the Twelve, visited the area to organize a new stake. President Clawson met Ezra Taft Benson and said, "Brother Benson, the Lord wants you to be president of this stake. What have you got to say about that?" Again President Benson was surprised. He commented, "I don't know these people. I've scarcely lived here a year."[7] But he humbly accepted the call and presided over about 2,000 stake members in a geographically large stake. Flora commented on his service as stake president: "He loves it so. It isn't the title that counts with him but it's the joy of being able to help as many as possible see the truth of the gospel."[8]

Later, as an Apostle, President Benson visited stakes throughout the world. He commented: "I have sometimes said to my wife, as I returned from visiting in the stakes, that I do not know exactly what heaven is going to be like, but I could ask nothing finer over there than to have the pleasure and joy of associating with the type of men and women I meet in the leadership of the stakes and wards of Zion and the missions of the earth. Truly we are richly blessed."[9]

Teachings of Ezra Taft Benson

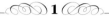

1

As members of the Church, we gather in the stakes of Zion.

Nonmembers sometimes inquire, "What is a stake?" Members likewise inquire, "What is the significance of a stake? What does it mean to us as members?"

To nonmembers, a stake is similar to a diocese in other churches. A stake is a geographical area comprising a number of wards (local congregations) and presided over by a presidency.

To members, the term *stake* is a symbolic expression. Picture in your mind a great tent held up by cords extended to many stakes that are firmly secured in the ground. The prophets likened latter-day Zion to a great tent encompassing the earth [see Isaiah 54:2; 3 Nephi 22:2]. That tent was supported by cords fastened to stakes. Those stakes, of course, are various geographical organizations spread out over the earth. Presently Israel is being gathered to the various stakes of Zion.[10]

A stake has at least four purposes:

1. Each stake, presided over by three high priests, and supported by twelve men known as a high council, becomes a miniature church to the Saints in a specific geographic area. The purpose is to unify and perfect the members who live in those boundaries by extending to them the Church programs, ordinances, and gospel instruction.

2. Members of stakes are to be models or standards of righteousness.

3. Stakes are to be a defense. The members do this as they unify under their local priesthood officers and consecrate themselves to do their duty and keep their covenants. Those covenants, if kept, become a protection from error, evil, or calamity.

We build temples only where we have stakes. The blessings and ordinances of the temple prepare one for exaltation. Of course, it is not possible for every stake to have a temple, but we are presently witnessing some remarkable, yes, miraculous developments, in the building of temples in different parts of the world. Such a program permits members of the Church to receive the full blessings of the Lord.

4. Stakes are a refuge from the storm to be poured out over the earth.[11]

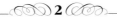

Stakes are organized to help parents teach the gospel and lead their children to the ordinances of salvation.

In the Doctrine and Covenants we read:

"Inasmuch as parents have children in Zion, or *in any of her stakes* which are organized, that teach them not to understand the doctrine of repentance, faith in Christ the Son of the living God, and of baptism and the gift of the Holy Ghost by the laying on of the hands, when eight years old, the sin be upon the heads of the parents. For this shall be a law unto the inhabitants of Zion, or *in any of her stakes which are organized*." (68:25–26; italics added.)

Here you see one of the major purposes of stakes. They are organized to help parents "who have children in Zion" to teach them the gospel of Jesus Christ and administer the ordinances of salvation. Stakes are formed to perfect the Saints, and that development begins in the home with effective gospel instruction.[12]

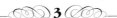

As stake members reflect the Lord's standard of holiness, the stake becomes a beautiful emblem for all the world to see.

The Lord states: "For Zion must increase in beauty, and in holiness; her borders must be enlarged; her stakes must be strengthened; yea, verily I say unto you, Zion must arise and put on her beautiful garments." (Doctrine and Covenants 82:14.)

Here the Lord declares another great purpose of a stake: to be a beautiful emblem for all the world to see. The phrase "put on her beautiful garments" refers, of course, to the inner sanctity that must be attained by every member who calls himself or herself a Saint. Zion is "the pure in heart." (Doctrine and Covenants 97:21.)

Stakes of Zion are strengthened and Zion's borders enlarged as members reflect the standard of holiness that the Lord expects of His chosen people.[13]

Each stake serves as a defense and a refuge from enemies seen and unseen.

Yet another revelation from the Lord gives this explanation of the purpose of stakes: "Verily I say unto you all: Arise and shine forth, that thy light may be a standard for the nations; and that the gathering together upon the land of Zion, and upon her stakes, may be for a defense, and for a refuge from the storm, and from wrath when it shall be poured out without mixture upon the whole earth." (Doctrine and Covenants 115:5–6.)

In this revelation is a command to let our light so shine that it becomes a standard for the nations. A standard is a rule of measure by which one determines exactness or perfection. The Saints are to be a standard of holiness for the world to see. That is the beauty of Zion.

The Lord then reveals that the stakes of Zion are to be "for a defense, and for a refuge from the storm, and from wrath when it shall be poured out without mixture upon the whole earth." Stakes are a defense for the Saints from enemies both seen and unseen. The defense is direction provided through priesthood channels that strengthens testimony and promotes family solidarity and individual righteousness.

In His preface to His revelations in the Doctrine and Covenants, the Lord warned: "The day speedily cometh; the hour is not yet, but is nigh at hand, when peace shall be taken from the earth, and the devil shall have power over his own dominion" [Doctrine and Covenants 1:35].

Today . . . we see the fulfillment of this prediction where Satan, in undiminished fury, is displaying power over "his own dominion"—the earth. Never has his influence been so great, and only those who have taken the Holy Spirit as their guide—and followed counsel from priesthood leaders—will be spared from the havoc of his evil influence.

*Gathering with fellow Saints, we see that a stake can "be for
a defense, and for a refuge from the storm" (D&C 115:6).*

The Lord also states in that prefatory revelation that He will have
power over His Saints, "and shall reign in their midst" [Doctrine
and Covenants 1:36]. He does this as He works through His chosen
servants and stake and ward authorities.[14]

As the Church grows, it is very important that we build solidly
and well, and that our prospective stakes have the basic ingredients that are necessary for success and that existing stakes work
tirelessly for full stakehood in the sense of spiritual achievement.
These stakes are to be the gathering spots for the Zion of today, and
they need to be spiritual sanctuaries and to be self-sufficient in as
many ways as is possible.[15]

The stakes and districts of Zion are symbolic of the holy places
spoken of by the Lord where His Saints are to gather in the last
days as a refuge from the storm. You and your children will gather
here to worship, to do sacred ordinances, to socialize, to learn, to
perform in music, dance, drama, athletics, and to generally improve
yourselves and one another. It is often thought significant that our
chapels have on them a steeple, with spires toward the heavens

symbolic of how our lives ought to be ever moving upward toward God.[16]

The Book of Mormon prophet Nephi foresaw the day when the Saints would be scattered in stakes all over the world. He saw the time when the Lord would extend His protection to them when menaced by storms of destruction that threatened their existence. Nephi prophesied: "And it came to pass that I, Nephi, beheld the power of the Lamb of God, that it descended upon the saints of the church of the Lamb, and upon the covenant people of the Lord, who were scattered upon all the face of the earth; and they were armed with righteousness and with the power of God in great glory." (Book of Mormon, 1 Nephi 14:14.)

Through revelation we know that there will be perils, calamities, and persecution in the latter days, but through righteousness the Saints may be spared. The promise of the Lord in the Book of Mormon is sure: "He will preserve the righteous by his power." (1 Nephi 22:17.)[17]

Suggestions for Study and Teaching

Questions

- After reading section 1, how would you respond to someone who asks why Church members are organized in stakes?

- President Benson reminded us that stakes help parents teach the gospel to their children and provide priesthood ordinances for them (see section 2). In what ways has your stake strengthened your efforts at home?

- When have you seen members of a stake come together to set an example "for all the world to see"? (See section 3.) How have you benefited from these activities?

- In what ways does a stake provide protection "from enemies both seen and unseen"? (See section 4.) What opportunities do we have to participate in our stake? What are some blessings we can receive as we do so?

Related Scriptures

Isaiah 25:3–5; Matthew 5:14–16; Moroni 10:31–33; D&C 101:17–21; 133:7–9

Teaching Help

"A skilled teacher doesn't think, 'What shall I do in class today?' but asks, 'What will my students do in class today?'; not, 'What will I teach today?' but rather, 'How will I help my students discover what they need to know?'" (Virginia H. Pearce, "The Ordinary Classroom—a Powerful Place for Steady and Continued Growth," *Ensign*, Nov. 1996, 12; quoting *Teaching the Gospel: A Handbook for CES Teachers and Leaders* [1994], 13).

Notes

1. See chapter 20 in this book.

2. See chapter 21 in this book.

3. See Sheri L. Dew, *Ezra Taft Benson: A Biography* (1987), 122; Francis M. Gibbons, *Ezra Taft Benson: Statesman, Patriot, Prophet of God* (1996), 104.

4. Sheri L. Dew, based on an account by Don Schlurf, in *Ezra Taft Benson: A Biography,* 122.

5. See chapter 1 in this book.

6. In *Ezra Taft Benson: A Biography,* 144.

7. In *Ezra Taft Benson: A Biography,* 156–57.

8. Flora Amussen Benson, quoted in *Ezra Taft Benson: A Biography,* 159.

9. In Conference Report, Oct. 1948, 98.

10. *Come unto Christ* (1983), 101.

11. *Come unto Christ,* 104–5.

12. *Come unto Christ,* 101–2.

13. *Come unto Christ,* 102.

14. *Come unto Christ,* 103–4.

15. *The Teachings of Ezra Taft Benson* (1988), 151.

16. *The Teachings of Ezra Taft Benson,* 151–52.

17. *Come unto Christ,* 104.

"Jesus saith . . . , I am the way, the truth, and the life: no man cometh unto the Father, but by me" (John 14:6).

A Christ-Centered Life

"The best measure of true greatness
is how Christlike we are."

From the Life of Ezra Taft Benson

President Ezra Taft Benson frequently quoted the Savior's counsel to the twelve Nephite disciples: "What manner of men ought ye to be? Verily I say unto you, even as I am" (3 Nephi 27:27).[1] This principle—the need to be more Christlike—was a recurring theme in President Benson's ministry, especially during his service as President of the Quorum of the Twelve Apostles and as President of the Church.

Having dedicated his life to serving the Lord, President Benson spoke with power and conviction when he shared the following words of testimony:

"I testify to you that there is no greater, more thrilling, and more soul-ennobling challenge than to try to learn of Christ and walk in His steps. Our model, Jesus Christ, walked this earth as 'the Exemplar.' He is our Advocate with the Father. He worked out the great atoning sacrifice so we could have a fullness of joy and be exalted in accordance with His grace and our repentance and righteousness. He did all things perfectly and commands that we be perfect even as He and His Father are perfect. (See 3 Ne. 12:48.)

" 'What would Jesus do?' or 'What would He have me do?' are the paramount personal questions of this life. Walking in His way is the greatest achievement of life. That man or woman is most truly successful whose life most closely parallels that of the Master."[2]

As President Benson exhorted the Saints to follow the Savior's perfect example, he reminded them that they could do so only with the Savior's help. He declared:

"I know the Lord lives. I know that He loves us. I know that apart from Him no one can succeed, but as a partner with Him no one can fail.

"I know that God can make a lot more out of our lives than we can.

"May we all have the moral courage from this moment forward to more fully strive each day to think on Christ, learn of Him, walk in His steps, and do what He would have us do."³

Teachings of Ezra Taft Benson

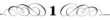 **1**

The example and teachings of Jesus Christ provide the great standard for all mankind.

Two thousand years ago a perfect man walked the earth: Jesus the Christ. He was the son of a heavenly father and an earthly mother. He is the God of this world, under the Father. He taught men truth, that they might be free. His example and precepts provide the great standard, the only sure way, for all mankind.⁴

No other single influence has had so great an impact on this earth as the life of Jesus the Christ. We cannot conceive of our lives without his teachings. Without him we would be lost in a mirage of beliefs and worships, born in fear and darkness where the sensual and materialistic hold sway. We are far short of the goal he set for us, but we must never lose sight of it; nor must we forget that our great climb toward the light, toward perfection, would not be possible except for his teachings, his life, his death, and his resurrection.

. . . We must learn and learn again that only through accepting and living the gospel of love as taught by the Master and only through doing his will can we break the bonds of ignorance and doubt that bind us. We must learn this simple, glorious truth so that we can experience the sweet joys of the spirit now and eternally. We must lose ourselves in doing his will. We must place him first in our lives.⁵

In the 14th chapter of John, Jesus is tenderly saying his farewell to his disciples after the last supper. He tells them that he goes to prepare a place for them in his Father's house; that where he is, they also may be. And Thomas says to him:

"Lord, we know not whither thou goest; and how can we know the way?

"Jesus saith unto him, I am the way, the truth, and the life: no man cometh unto the Father, but by me." (John 14:5–6.) The road lies before us. It is clearly marked.[6]

We come unto Christ as we look unto Him in every thought and emulate His attributes.

In Book of Mormon language, we need to "believe in Christ and deny him not." (2 Ne. 25:28.) We need to trust in Christ and not in the arm of flesh. (See 2 Ne. 4:34.) We need to "come unto Christ, and be perfected in him." (Moro. 10:32.) We need to come "with a broken heart and a contrite spirit" (3 Ne. 12:19), hungering and thirsting after righteousness (see 3 Ne. 12:6). We need to come "feasting upon the word of Christ" (2 Ne. 31:20), as we receive it through His scriptures, His anointed, and His Holy Spirit.

In short, we need to follow "the example of the Son of the living God" (2 Ne. 31:16).[7]

The Lord said, "Look unto me in every thought." (D&C 6:36.) Looking unto the Lord in every thought is the only possible way we can be the manner of men and women we ought to be.

The Lord asked the question of His disciples, "What manner of men ought ye to be?" He then answered His own question by saying, "Even as I am." (3 Ne. 27:27.) To become as He is, we must have Him on our mind—constantly in our thoughts. Every time we partake of the sacrament, we commit to "always remember him." (Moro. 4:3; 5:2; D&C 20:77, 79.)

If thoughts make us what we are, and we are to be like Christ, then we must think Christlike thoughts. Let me repeat that: If thoughts make us what we are, and we are to be like Christ, we must think Christlike thoughts.

. . . Our thoughts should be on the Lord. We should think on Christ.[8]

Let our personal lives, our homes, and our work performance reflect our Christlike character. So live that others will say about you, "There is a true Christian!"

Yes, we believe in Jesus Christ, but more—we look to Him, we trust Him and strive to emulate His attributes.[9]

Christ is our ideal. He is our exemplar. . . . The best measure of true greatness is how Christlike we are.[10]

To be like the Savior—what a challenge for any person! He is a member of the Godhead. He is the Savior and Redeemer. He was perfect in every aspect of His life. There was no flaw nor failing in Him. Is it possible for us . . . to be even as He is? The answer is yes. Not only *can* we, but that is our charge, our responsibility. He would not give us that commandment if He did not mean for us to do it [see Matthew 5:48; 3 Nephi 12:48].

The Apostle Peter spoke of the process by which a person can be made a partaker "of the divine nature" (2 Peter 1:4). This is important, for if we truly become partakers of the divine nature, we shall become like Him. Let us examine closely what Peter teaches us about this process. Here is what he said:

"And beside this, giving all diligence, add to your faith virtue; and to virtue knowledge;

"And to knowledge temperance; and to temperance patience; and to patience godliness;

"And to godliness brotherly kindness; and to brotherly kindness charity" (2 Peter 1:5–7).

The virtues outlined by Peter are part of the divine nature, or the Savior's character. These are the virtues we are to emulate if we would be more like Him. Let us discuss a few of these important traits.

The first characteristic, to which all the others are added, is *faith*. Faith is the foundation upon which a godlike character is built. . . .

Peter goes on to say that we must add to our faith *virtue*. . . . Virtuous behavior implies that [a person] has pure thoughts and clean actions. He will not lust in his heart, for to do so is to "deny

The Apostle Peter, here pictured with the resurrected Jesus Christ, taught about how we can emulate the Savior's character.

the faith" and to lose the Spirit (D&C 42:23)—and there is nothing more important in this work than the Spirit. . . .

Virtue is akin to holiness, an attribute of godliness. [We] should actively seek for that which is virtuous and lovely and not that which is debasing or sordid. Virtue will garnish [our] thoughts unceasingly (see D&C 121:45). How can any man indulge himself in the evils of pornography, profanity, or vulgarity and consider himself totally virtuous? . . .

The next step Peter describes in the growth process is to add *knowledge* to our faith and virtue. The Lord has told us that "it is impossible for a man to be saved in ignorance" (D&C 131:6). In another place God commanded, "Seek ye out of the best books words of wisdom; seek learning, even by study and also by faith" (D&C 88:118). . . . While any study of truth is of value, the truths of salvation are the most important truths any person can learn. The Lord's question, "For what is a man profited, if he shall gain the whole world, and lose his own soul?" (Matthew 16:26) can be applied to educational pursuits as well as the pursuit of worldly goods.

The Lord might also have asked, "For what is a man profited, if he shall learn everything in the world and not learn how to be saved?" . . .

Joining our spiritual education to our secular learning will help us keep focused on the things that matter most in this life. . . .

Another attribute described by Peter as being part of the divine nature is *temperance.* [A temperate person] is restrained in his emotions and verbal expressions. He does things in moderation and is not given to overindulgence. In a word, he has self-control. He is the master of his emotions, not the other way around. . . .

To our temperance we are to add *patience.* . . . Patience is another form of self-control. It is the ability to postpone gratification and to bridle one's passions. In his relationships with loved ones, a patient man does not engage in impetuous behavior that he will later regret. Patience is composure under stress. A patient man is understanding of others' faults.

A patient man also waits on the Lord. We sometimes read or hear of people who seek a blessing from the Lord, then grow impatient when it does not come swiftly. Part of the divine nature is to trust in the Lord enough to "be still and know that [he is] God" (D&C 101:16).

A [person] who is patient will be tolerant of the mistakes and failings of his loved ones. Because he loves them, he will not find fault nor criticize nor blame.

Another attribute mentioned by Peter is *kindness.* . . . One who is kind is sympathetic and gentle with others. He is considerate of others' feelings and courteous in his behavior. He has a helpful nature. Kindness pardons others' weaknesses and faults. Kindness is extended to all—to the aged and the young, to animals, to those low of station as well as the high.

These are the true attributes of the divine nature. Can you see how we become more Christlike as we are more virtuous, more kind, more patient, and more in control of our emotional feelings?

The Apostle Paul used some vivid expressions to illustrate that a member of the Church must be different from the world.

He commended us to "put on Christ" (Galatians 3:27), "put off . . . the old man," and "put on the new man" (Ephesians 4:22, 24).

The final and crowning virtue of the divine character is *charity,* or the pure love of Christ (see Moroni 7:47). If we would truly seek to be more like our Savior and Master, then learning to love as He loves should be our highest goal. Mormon called charity "the greatest of all" (Moroni 7:46).

The world today speaks a great deal about love, and it is sought for by many. But the pure love of Christ differs greatly from what the world thinks of love. Charity never seeks selfish gratification. The pure love of Christ seeks only the eternal growth and joy of others. . . .

The Savior declared that life eternal is to know the only true God and His Son Jesus Christ (see John 17:3). If this is true, and I bear you my solemn witness that it *is* true, then we must ask how we come to know God. The process of adding one godly attribute to another, as described by Peter, becomes the key to gaining this knowledge that leads to eternal life. Note Peter's promise, which immediately follows the process described:

"For if these things be in you, *and abound,* they make you that ye shall neither be barren nor unfruitful in the knowledge of our Lord Jesus Christ" (2 Peter 1:8; italics added).

. . . I pray that these qualities and attributes of the Savior may abound in us so that when we stand at the Judgment and He asks each one of us, "What manner of man are you?" we can raise our heads in gratitude and joy and answer, "Even as thou art." [11]

 **3**

The Savior will comfort us and lift us up in our efforts to stay on the path He has marked for us.

To the extent that we stray from the path marked out for us by the Man of Galilee, to that extent we are failing in our individual battles. . . . But we are not without his help. Again and again he told his disciples, and all of us, "Let not your heart be troubled. . . ."

"If ye shall ask any thing in my name, I will do it."

"I will not leave you comfortless. . . ."

"Peace I leave with you, my peace I give unto you. . . ." (John 14:1, 14, 18, 27.)[12]

Let us turn again to the Book of Mormon . . . to learn some principles about coming unto Christ, being committed to Him, centered in Him, and consumed in Him. We will quote but a few of the numerous passages on the matter.

First, we need to know that Christ invites us to come unto Him. "Behold, he sendeth an invitation unto all men, for the arms of mercy are extended towards them, . . . Yea, he saith: Come unto me and ye shall partake of the fruit of the tree of life" (Alma 5:33–34).

Come, for he stands "with open arms to receive you" (Mormon 6:17).

Come, for "he will console you in your afflictions, and he will plead your cause" (Jacob 3:1).

"Come unto him, and offer your whole souls as an offering unto him" (Omni 1:26).

As Moroni closed the record of the Jaredite civilization, he wrote, "I would commend you to seek this Jesus of whom the prophets and apostles have written" (Ether 12:41).

In Moroni's closing words written toward the end of the Nephite civilization, he said, "Yea, come unto Christ, and be perfected in him, . . . and if ye shall deny yourselves of all ungodliness, and love God with all your might, mind and strength, then is his grace sufficient for you" (Moroni 10:32).

Those who are committed to Christ "stand as witnesses of God at all times and in all things, and in all places" that they may be in "even until death" (Mosiah 18:9). They "retain the name" of Christ "written always" in their hearts (Mosiah 5:12). They take upon themselves "the name of Christ, having a determination to serve him to the end" (Moroni 6:3).

When we live a Christ-centered life, "we talk of Christ, we rejoice in Christ, we preach of Christ" (2 Nephi 25:26). We "receive the pleasing word of God, and feast upon his love" (Jacob 3:2). Even when Nephi's soul was grieved because of his iniquities, he said,

"I know in whom I have trusted. My God hath been my support" (2 Nephi 4:19–20).

We remember Alma's counsel: "Let all thy doings be unto the Lord, and whithersoever thou goest let it be in the Lord; yea, let all thy thoughts be directed unto the Lord; yea, let the affections of thy heart be placed upon the Lord forever. Counsel with the Lord in all thy doings" (Alma 37:36–37).

"Remember, remember," said Helaman, "that it is upon the rock of our Redeemer, who is Christ, . . . that ye must build your foundation; that when the devil shall send forth his mighty winds, . . . [they] shall have no power over you to drag you down to the gulf of misery" (Helaman 5:12).

Nephi said, the Lord "hath filled me with his love, even unto the consuming of my flesh" (2 Nephi 4:21). Those who are consumed in Christ "are made alive in Christ" (2 Nephi 25:25). They "suffer no manner of afflictions, save it were swallowed up in the joy of Christ" (Alma 31:38). They are "clasped in the arms of Jesus" (Mormon 5:11). Nephi said, "I glory in my Jesus, for he hath redeemed my soul" (2 Nephi 33:6). Lehi said, "I am encircled about eternally in the arms of his love" (2 Nephi 1:15). . . .

. . . That great soul Mormon [wrote a] letter to his beloved son, Moroni, with these words:

"My son, be faithful in Christ; and may not the things which I have written grieve thee, to weigh thee down unto death; but may Christ lift thee up, and may his sufferings and death, and the showing his body unto our fathers, and his mercy and long-suffering, and the hope of his glory and of eternal life, rest in your mind forever.

"And may the grace of God the Father, whose throne is high in the heavens, and our Lord Jesus Christ, who sitteth on the right hand of his power, until all things shall become subject unto him, be, and abide with you forever" (Moroni 9:25–26).

My prayer for each of us is that we too will follow that inspired counsel: "Be faithful in Christ." Then He will lift us up and His grace will be and abide with us forever.[13]

Suggestions for Study and Teaching

Questions

- President Benson declared, "No other single influence has had so great an impact on this earth as the life of Jesus Christ" (section 1). In what ways has the Savior's life had an impact on the earth? In what ways has His life influenced you?

- How do our lives change when we "think on Christ"? How are our thoughts connected to our attributes? As you study section 2, ponder what you can do to more fully develop the Christlike attributes mentioned there.

- How can the teachings in section 3 give us hope as we strive to be more like the Savior? How has the Savior helped you in your efforts to follow Him?

Related Scriptures

Mark 8:34; Philippians 4:13; 1 John 3:23–24; 2 Nephi 25:23, 26; Mosiah 3:19; Alma 7:11–13; Moroni 7:48

Study Help

"Plan study activities that will build your faith in the Savior" (*Preach My Gospel* [2004], 22). For instance, as you study you might ask yourself questions such as the following: "How might these teachings help me increase my understanding of the Atonement of Jesus Christ? How can these teachings help me become more like the Savior?"

Notes

1. See, for example, "Strengthen Thy Stakes," *Ensign,* Jan. 1991, 5; "Think on Christ," *Ensign,* Mar. 1989, 4; "In His Steps," *Ensign,* Sept. 1988, 4.
2. "Think on Christ," *Ensign,* Apr. 1984, 13.
3. "Think on Christ," *Ensign,* Apr. 1984, 13.
4. In Conference Report, Apr. 1967, 58.
5. "Life Is Eternal," *Ensign,* June 1971, 34.
6. In Conference Report, Apr. 1966, 128.
7. "Joy in Christ," *Ensign,* Mar. 1986, 5.
8. "Think on Christ," *Ensign,* Apr. 1984, 11, 13.
9. *The Teachings of Ezra Taft Benson* (1988), 328.
10. "A Sacred Responsibility," *Ensign,* May 1986, 78.
11. In Conference Report, Oct. 1986, 59, 60–62, 63; or *Ensign,* Nov. 1986, 45, 46–47, 48.
12. "Life Is Eternal," 34.
13. "Come unto Christ," *Ensign,* Nov. 1987, 84–85.

List of Visuals

Index

Less-active Church members, reaching out to, 253–60

Love
for God, 37–44
at home, 179, 181–82
in leadership, 246–47
for "lost sheep", 253–60
in missionary work, 277, 284

M

Marriage
covenant, 183–85
of Ezra and Flora Benson, 179, 181, 203
happiness in, 183–85
nurturing, 179, 181
See also Family; Home; Parents

Ministering to less-active Church members, 253–60

Missionary work
in all stages of life, 279–81
to all the world, 278–79
Ezra Taft Benson's enthusiasm for, 275, 277
humility and, 283
influence of the Holy Ghost in, 283
joy of, 277
love in, 277, 284
preparing youth for, 279–80
seniors and, 206–7, 280
success in, 283–84
tradition of, in Ezra Taft Benson's family, 275
using the Book of Mormon in, 127, 137–39, 142–44, 282
work in, 284
young men and, 279–80
young women and, 280

Modesty, 223

Mothers
counsel for, in spending time with children, 197–200

role of, ordained by God, 197
See also Fathers; Parents

O

Obedience
blessings through, 42–44, 78–79, 164–65
as the great test of life, 38, 44

Optimism, 71

P

Parents
honoring, 210–12
roles of, 194–200
should teach children about chastity, 225–26
should teach children about the temple, 174–76
unity between, 200–201
See also Family; Fathers; Home; Marriage; Mothers

Past, not living in, 86

Patriotism, 21–25

Plan of happiness, understanding of, leads to repentance, 78–79

Pornography, 221–22

Prayer
answers to, 53–56
of the Benson family, for Ezra Taft Benson, 48–49
constant, 49–50, 71
despite feeling unworthy, 84
in families, 50–52
improving our efforts in, 52–53
pattern of, taught by Jesus, 49–50
to receive the Holy Ghost, 161
to resist temptation, 222–23

President of the Church
blessings from following, 147–48, 152–54
is the most important prophet for us, 149–50